Marching to Captivity

The War Diaries of a
French Peasant, 1939–45

Marching to Captivity

The War Diaries of a
French Peasant, 1939–45

GUSTAVE FOLCHER

Translated by
CHRISTOPHER HILL

Edited by
RÉMY CAZALS and CHRISTOPHER HILL

BRASSEY'S
London • Washington

First English Edition 1996

UK editorial offices: Brassey's, 33 John Street, London WC1N 2AT
UK orders: Marston Book Services, PO Box 269, Abingdon, OX14 4SD

North American orders: Brassey's Inc., PO Box 960,
Herndon, VA 22070, USA

Library of Congress Cataloging in Publication Data
available

British Library Cataloguing in Publication Data
A catalogue record for this book is available from the British Library

ISBN 1 85753 166 3 Hardcover

Typeset by M Rules
Printed in Great Britain by Bookcraft (Bath) Ltd.

Contents

Contents

List of Illustrations

List of Plates

1. A poster, signed by the commanding general of the French 2nd Army, encouraging his soldiers in the fight against the invading Germans in May 1940.

2. The opening page of the third of the notebooks in which Folcher kept his diary, written whilst a prisoner of war.

3. Folcher in the uniform of the 12th Zouaves.

4. Three views of Schorstedt.

5. Folcher and fellow prisoners with a potato sorting machine.

6. Folcher watches his fellow prisoners playing cards.

7. The Christmas menu for 1942.

8. Folcher with some of his fellow prisoners.

9. and 10. Folcher's identity card as a 'working prisoner of war'.

11. and 12. A postcard sent to Folcher by his father, Augustin, in February 1944.

13. The section of Folcher's diary that describes the consequences of the Allied bombing of Stendal Station.

14. Folcher's demobilisation certificate.

15. The statue of a Zouave soldier on the Pont de l'Alma in Paris.

NORWAY

SWEDEN

North Sea

GREAT
BRITAIN

London •

• Hamburg
• Bremen
Hanover •
Berlin •

Magdeburg •

Warsaw •

Brussels •

GREATER
GERMANY

Sedan •
Paris •   Verdun •
Bar le Duc •
Dijon •

Frankfurt •

Luxembourg •
Nancy •
Strasbourg •

FRANCE

SWITZ.

Munich •

HUNGARY

Lyon •

ROMANIA

Nimes •
Marseilles •

ITALY

YUGOSLAVIA

SPAIN

BULGARIA

Mediterranean
Sea

ALBANIA

GREECE

| 0 | miles | 500 |
| 0 | kms | 500 |

Area of Gustave Folcher's
time as a POW in Germany,
1940-45

Zone of GF's manoeuvres with
the 12th Zouaves and capture,
Sept 1939 - June 1940

Departement du Gard,
GF's 'pays'

Folcher's Europe, 1939–45

Introduction

Gustave Folcher's war diaries were first brought to public attention by Rémy Cazals, now of the University of Toulouse-Le Mirail, who published them in French[1] in 1981. He in turn had been working with the support of the *Fédération Audoise des Oeuvres Laïques* (FAOL) on the oral history of the Great War, with special reference to the unpublished diaries of the soldiers of the Midi.[2] This had naturally led to an interest in the Second World War, and to one publication[3] by the time that M. Marius Averseng, the retired schoolteacher from the village of Aigues-Vives in the Département of Gard, 20 kilometres south-east of Nîmes, drew Cazals' attention to the records which the former Aigues-Vives postman, Gustave Folcher, had kept of his experiences during the Second World War.

Gustave Folcher was from a peasant family in Languedoc. Born on 25 August 1909, he had worked as a gardener for one of the wealthier families in Aigues-Vives, apart from a period of military service between 1930–31. His father worked on the same estate and had charge of a flock of sheep nearly 200 strong. 'He was busy with the flock', Gustave Folcher told Rémy Cazals, 'and I busied myself with the garden. I helped him as well, I did nearly all the work inside. He went to look after them outside and I did the cleaning of their quarters. As for us, we had a garden and a few small vines'.

Gustave Folcher left school at 13, and saw himself as someone who was barely literate. But his remaining schoolbooks show that he had a good hand and was accustomed, like all French schoolchildren of the time, to copying and reciting passages of classical literature. He also recalled how he used to get some of the best marks in the class for composition. Despite the fact, therefore, that he did not pick up a pen from leaving school until the age of 30, he was not wholly ill-equipped when the time came to commit his thoughts to paper.

The ten exercise books which Folcher subsequently filled with his experiences, first as a soldier during the 'Phoney War' and the subsequent catastrophic battle of France in May–June 1940, and then, for almost five more years as a prisoner of war, are a unique and remarkable record even for a war which has produced more books than any other. For the French edition, Rémy Cazals regularised the spelling and punctuation, which were too erratic to have made for comfortable reading. He also made some small cuts and divided the hitherto seamless text into chapters (the present translation follows his arrangement exactly). This was all done with the full agreement of Gustave Folcher. Cazals allowed M. Folcher's voice to speak for itself, with the occasional repetition and grammatical awkwardness wholly overshadowed by a natural simplicity and grace of style. This is the work of a man with considerable powers of observation, and with the ability to relate both the great dramas and the mind-numbing tedium of war in a way that holds the reader's sympathetic interest. If writing was the way in which Gustave Folcher coped with the often intolerable circumstances in which he found himself, he always retained sufficient clarity of mind and sheer interest in events to write in a direct and concrete fashion.

Over the centuries, millions of ordinary men have had little choice but to go to war in the service of their feudal lord, their religious leader, their state, their empire. Only in the 20th century, through a combination of improved education and awareness, the availability of writing materials, and the subsequent interest of historians, have their voices begun to be heard, albeit posthumously on too many occasions. The same is true, of course, for the countless civilian victims of war. This is why the testimony of people like Gustave Folcher is so precious. Whatever the justice of the particular cause – and the Allied cause between 1939–1945 was more just than most – the meaning of war for the average, powerless participant is easy to infer and almost impossible to know. Even the recollections of private soldiers soon become glossed by the passing of time, the creation of official mythologies and the natural emotions of pride and relief at having survived. Only records from the time have great value, and those created out of the normally inarticulate and low-ranking mass are rare indeed.

Accident helps to decide which testimonies of this kind survive. Gustave Folcher did not like playing cards. He was bored when his mates turned to *belote* to fill the endless hours of hanging around during the Phoney War. And so, as he recalled in the late 1970s, he turned to writing:

> In the Ardennes, I started there. I started to write at Vouziers, in a village near Vouziers. It was nearly this sort of time, before Christmas, Christmas

1939. We were up there, I remember, one afternoon, we were in a barn and, well, I don't know, the others were playing at cards, and I set myself down to write on this notebook, look the first. I sat down to write in pencil. I had that then (actually I also had an ink-pencil.[4] But it was even more useless than the pencil). Afterwards, once I was a prisoner, I got hold of a pen and a little bottle of ink . . .

Folcher kept some records in a little *carnet,* or notebook, which he kept on his person throughout the horrors of combat and captivity. But he did most of the writing-up of the 1939–40 experience once a prisoner on the labour farm north of Magdeburg where he spent the bulk of the war. Even then, he seems to have done most of the writing between 1943-45, when boredom and frustration became serious problems to be kept at bay. He was helped by the notes he had kept on itineraries, and by the maps which he managed to obtain everywhere, even in Saxony:

Everywhere I went, I managed to get myself a map, I liked to know where I was. And in Germany, you will not believe what I am going to tell you, although it was severely forbidden, under pain of death, I bought a map . . . from a guard! It was the guard who got it for me! And I still have it. It was very useful. It helped the whole *Kommando.*

The original diaries, which have been inspected by the English translator, are contained in ten exercise books, first of French manufacture, then of German. 'That one, three [*the number three*] my wife sent me in a parcel. You couldn't get as many as you wanted, do you understand. There, that's the name of my wife. Its her maiden name. We were married as soon as possible after the war . . . This exercise book (number ten) belonged to a German schoolgirl. We were next to the school, at the farm where I was. And it was the end, it was chaos. I went into the school, I opened a desk and I took the exercise book of a school-girl. Look, there's her name on it' (the name was Gisela Steindecker). The first exercise book is a later re-transcription of the 'illegible' pencil records of the first few months of the war, but there seems no reason to doubt its reliability. Perhaps some passages were reinforced by hindsight, but in general there is a strong sense of authenticity about the account.[5] It has subsequently been cited in a number of specialist works on the history of French prisoners of war in Germany.[6]

Even from the perspective of French historiography, however, the Folcher diaries can be seen as only a footnote, one small piece of the

jigsaw which historians are assembling in their search for a comprehensive understanding of the Second World War. On this view a
translation into English might seem unnecessary. But there are three
main reasons why this would be a misguided view.

First, is the captivating nature of Gustave Folcher's prose, already
referred to. This is one man's story, simply told, but of a compelling
series of events and written in an unpretentious, affecting style.
M. Folcher reveals himself, with his fears and his parochialisms, but
also with his open-hearted responses to the sufferings of others, and
his ever-surviving capacity for wonder, to be fully alive and human.
We can imagine ourselves in his position and we can identify with his
feelings, whatever our nationality or background. The very simplicity
and lucidity of the story-telling makes it universal. Moreover, the
reader can feel Gustave Folcher's moods and understand his reactions, exactly because the nature of his roots in Languedoc is so
firmly established. Some recent English accounts of life in the Midi,
better written by conventional standards, in fact seem thin and trivial
by comparison.

The second reason for bringing Gustave Folcher to an English-
reading audience is the relative lack of knowledge in the
Anglo-Saxon world of the Franco-German relationship, whether in
good times or bad, a relationship which has governed much of
modern European history and which continues to determine the
evolution of the region through its central role in the European
Union. There have, of course, been fine books written by scholars
such as Michael Howard or Alistair Horne on the war of 1870, or
Richard Cobb on the two World Wars, which have succeeded in
reaching out beyond the narrow world of academic scholarship.[7] But
these are exceptions. In general, even the reading public has little
sense of how important France and Germany have been to each
other over the last two centuries, (and how Britain, by implication,
has been more distant from both), let alone how extensively their
peoples have interacted, through the experiences of occupation
(three German, one French), transportation and (more recently and
benignly) twin-towning and other arrangements of cultural
exchange.[8] Gustave Folcher's diaries illuminate this dimension in
one particular way. The British, the Americans, the Russians and the
Italians all figure occasionally as part of the backcloth to Folcher's
war, but essentially his story is of a Frenchman's encounter with
Germany: with the irresistible power, efficiency and professionalism
of the 1940 *Blitzkrieg*. Once captured, Folcher watched the German
motorised columns sweep by, many soldiers taking photographs of

their defeated rivals – 'comfortably seated in deep armchairs, they made war almost as tourists'; with the confident, victorious population of the years 1940–43; with the strange ways of a German peasantry which did not drink with its meals and was not tempted to hunt much of the abundant local game; with the faltering, bomb-wracked population of 1944–45, anxious for help from their French prisoners against the oncoming Slav hordes, with their likely thirst for revenge; with the *Boche*[9] who bore responsibility for so many cruelties, even if it had been possible to feel affection for individuals, and who could not understand why their French captives should turn down the offer of freedom as French citizens inside the Reich, in return for renouncing their status as prisoners of war. The way in which Germany has deeply affected the lives of every French family, even obscure people from small villages in the far-off south, is brought home vividly by Folcher's tale, just as to a lesser degree we get a sense of the geo-political vulnerability of Germany, even at the height of its power, to the movement of peoples and armed forces from the west, once France manages to attract and to mobilise its allies. In 1941, Folcher's *Kommando* in the village of Schorstedt seems remote, another life away from the Midi or from the pocket of free France which remained *outre-Manche*. By late 1944, however, with news of the fall of Rome, of the Allied landings in Normandy and of Russian advances from the east, together with the tangible evidence of the relentless heavy bombing of railway junctions like that at nearby Stendal, we realise that in fact Schorstedt is only 70 miles from Berlin, 90 from Hamburg, and right in the path of the two arms of the Russian–Anglo-American pincer. Suddenly, Germany is no longer a continent entire unto itself, but the rapidly shrinking corn-stack in the middle of a harvested field, just like that we find in the course of Folcher's description of the 'great hare-beat'.

The third and last reason for translating the Folcher diaries into English is more general. We have already alluded to the way in which accounts like these represent what one French reviewer of the book referred to as 'these millions of anonymous Gustave Folchers . . . soldiers in the shadows, overlooked by glory but the foundations of that scrap of liberty which is left to us'.[10] These millions are the men and women who actually suffer the agonies which all wars inflict, and their perspective of war is all too often omitted from the histories of grand strategy, and even the detailed accounts of particular campaigns, which dominate the literature of war. This is not to say that the courage and suffering of the ordinary soldier is overlooked; reactions to the Great War ensured that 'the pity of war' has become a permanent part of our emotional vocabulary. Rather, it is to stress the continued comparative rareness with which the voice of the ordinary soldier himself is heard, let alone in the form of a continuous narrative over the period of an entire conflict. Even the great poetry and prose of 1914–1918 was usually the product of men who, although they might have served in the ranks (and officers like Siegfried Sassoon and Robert Graves were in just as much peril as any private), were accustomed to expressing their feelings through the written word.

In recent years the rise of interest in social history has led to a greater resourcefulness in the search for the diaries and letters of 'ordinary' people, and accounts like that of George Coppard[11] have had a considerable success, both popular and critical. But they are still few and far between even in the English language, while the work done by French scholars like Rémy Cazals and his colleagues has barely been noticed in Britain.[12] A translation of the Folcher diaries, which first appeared in France in 1981, is therefore an attempt to take one step towards bridging this gap, and towards making connections with the burgeoning field of oral history, itself partly a product of the school of historical scholarship inspired by the French writer Michel Foucault, which emphasises the importance of rediscovering those 'silenced' by the accounts of conventional history, with the latter's emphasis on those who 'made' great events. If the history of women, factory-workers, racial minorities, children and the dispossessed is now rightly to be written, then certainly that of the ordinary soldier, the cannon-fodder of centuries, should also be tackled, not least in his own words wherever that might be possible. This will have the additional advantage, in the translator's own field of International Relations, of helping to bring the study of war and society, which inevitably tends to deal in very broad brush-strokes, into a much closer and more human focus. At present there is a great deal of talk about the importance of redirecting International Relations away from the study of élites and governments and towards the people whose destinies they help to shape; but there are few signs of many practical things being done to advance that cause.[13] Gustave Folcher's notebooks, while only one story among the lost millions, do at least take us down this road, by conveying with great immediacy the worm's eye view of a Frenchman's war throughout the traumatic years from 1939 to 1945. He can stand as a symbol of the way in which even International Relations, that redoubt of high politics, is finally conceding something to the imperatives of social history and of sociology. The role of the (un)common man in war and peace is finally coming to the fore. Folcher was a man of his parish, his *pays*. Like millions of others he was catapulted onto the grand stage whether he liked it or not. Unlike most others, however, he found the resources to tell us what it felt like.

The Main Themes of the Diaries

Gustave Folcher's record has a strong narrative appeal, and following it through in the conventional way will reward a wide range of readers. But along the road there are many distinctive themes and sub-themes to learn from. There is a good deal to interest the student of the French Army, and later on the psychologist of captivity. We hear about the French prisoners' views of the Vichy government which administered their defeated homeland, and we get a good sense of what life was like for rural Germans under Nazism. The main themes, however, stand out because they represent Gustave Folcher's personal preoccupations as he tried to make sense of the often stressful and bewildering conditions to which he was subjected in six years of war and imprisonment.

The most obvious of these themes is perhaps better conveyed by the French word 'nostalgie' than by the English 'homesickness'. Gustave Folcher was a man who, like so many of his contemporaries, had not been used to travel. He had not been out of Languedoc before September 1939, let alone visited Paris or a foreign country. To be transplanted suddenly to the winters of north-east France, and worse, as Prisoner 90969 to the flat, dour country of Saxony, was therefore a shock and a deprivation of a high order. Gustave Folcher was of a sufficiently robust disposition to be able to survive the trauma, and indeed his natural curiosity about new places and ways of life meant in some ways that he was able to put the experience to some advantage – as, ultimately, the writing of the notebooks was to prove. But the yearning for home and for the south, with close local communities and its seasons marked by the cultivation of the vine, never left him.

From the time of his call-up, Gustave Folcher searched out men from Aigues-Vives, friends from nearby villages, or virtually anyone with some connection, whether by family or business, with the village. It was the same thing during the Phoney War and during the retreat. With the German tanks at their heels, a friend from Gallargues exchanged a few words with Gustave Folcher, then continued towards the rear while the Zouaves waited for the enemy. At the prison camp, he set himself up near the kitchens and stared at the thousands of men who were lining up to get their meals. At last, someone from Aigues-Vives! And with his friends, or the friends of friends, he made up a group where they could talk of home, and in their own language (Occitan, the language of the Languedoc region, has been in modern times mostly a spoken language). At Schorstedt, up there in a northern captivity with no known end, one thought dominated everything: to see home again. It came back, like a shooting pain, giving a rhythm to the hopes for each new year, in 1941, 1942, and three more yet to come. At the same time a kind of fear crept in: what would the village be like on his return? 'How am I going to find Aigues-Vives when I will not even recognise a quarter of the population?'

One product of Folcher's longing for home is that, paradoxically, we learn almost as much from the book about Languedoc – even though only a few days of home leave are actually set there – as we do about the northen zones of France and Germany where he spent the war. Nor is this mere romanticism, induced by separation. He writes realistically about the hard countryside of the 'garrigues', where the game is pitiful by comparison to that in Germany, and when he says that 'the tiny Razil', the rivulet that ran by his vines in Aigues-Vives, 'is much more beautiful than the Elbe', it is said with a laconic nod towards the indulgent subjectivity of the judgement – 'even though it's dry for half the year'. This is reminiscent of Joachim du Bellay's poem of 1558, which includes the lines (my translation):

> I'll take my Gallic Loire
> Over the Tiber in Rome
> My little place of birth
> Over Mount Palatine
> My gentle Angevins
> Over the ocean's far-flung wind.[14]

Food is one of the threads which holds the book together. It connects past and present; it is a way of thinking about home (quite tangibly, when food parcels finally started arriving in January 1941); and it is an ever-present physical issue, sometimes inducing real hunger through its absence, more often simply a relentless reminder of deprivation through its sheer mediocrity. Like all true *enfants de la patrie*, Folcher looked on a good menu as virtually a human right, and certainly one of the conditions of civilisation. The frequency with which concerns crop up over the next meal, or snack, during military service, and over the quality of German food during captivity, did not arise from the fear of starvation, real though that sometimes was. Folcher and his friends took a sensual pleasure in *un grand plat de salade* or *un bon bifsteck*, and they badly missed the simple, glorious routines of Mediterranean meals. Food for them was, in a way, France, and once some provisions started arriving at the *Kommando* via the Red Cross (not least the luxurious American supplies), their ingenuity ensured that on festival days at least, they could create some pretence of being at home. The menu they constructed for Christmas Eve 1943 contained no less than nine courses, from *saumon sauce provençale* to *pain d'épices*. And there was more than a hint of French cultural superiority in the discovery that the famous German beer was worse than that at home – in fact *la vraie pisse de vache* – and that the main way in which the German population embarked upon a culinary celebration was to eat large quantities of sickly cake. The real deprivation, however, was the lack of wine, a way of life in the Midi, not at all the means to inebriation alcohol so often represents in Northern Europe: 'most of the prisoners are lads from the south and being good southerners they adored their wine, something precious that we have seen nothing of for coming up four years'. Nothing could replace that beaker full of the warm south, in the phrase of the Englishman John Keats, and it is fitting that almost the first thing that Gustave Folcher does on Armistice Day 1945, as he stops in Belgium en route for Aigues-Vives, is to take his first glass of wine for five years: *il tombe bien bas*. His captivity ends symbolically there in Namur, back in French life, if not yet on French territory.

Another theme that binds the diaries together is that of Folcher's observations as a countryman. Until he went to war, Folcher's life was that of a peasant (although in English the word is never quite as resonant – or as neutral – as *paysan* in French, given the eradication of an English peasantry more than 200 years ago). Throughout his journey to the front he notes with interest the changes in landscape and farming techniques, from the villages in Lorraine with their piles of manure, to the fine livestock of the Almshouses in Metz and the grape-harvest of the same zone, not half as good as those at home. Even in combat, while the artillery, *Stukas* and machine-guns are firing relentlessly, Gustave Folcher discovers wounded horses, cows which moo desperately because no one has milked them, abandoned foals, a flock of geese crossing the battlefield. Back in a railway truck, he takes in Germany, its forests and fields, and the vines in the Rhineland. While his friends bang down the cards at *belote*, Gustave Folcher observes and diagnoses: those vines need copper sulphate! (were those at Aigues-Vives suffering too?)

Once arrived at Stalag XI-A at Altengrabow, Gustave Folcher soon decided that he would be best off by volunteering to work on a farm, and indeed he turned out to be far less discomforted by his physical circumstances during the next five years than some of his office-worker colleagues. There were even things to interest him, with the work and the seasonal rhythms of his village near the Elbe. He planted endless hectares of potatoes and beetroot, took part in the annual shoot of hares at harvest time, and made a speciality of collecting salads and mushrooms under the eyes of the incredulous locals. Clearly the continuity of his work on the land helped Folcher to survive the uncertainties and tedium of his captivity as well as he did, even if there was no pretending that, as he thought grimly while trying to take his leave of the old farmer's wife who had come to depend on him, 'her village meant much to us . . . all my thoughts were down there, on the shores of the Mediterranean'.

This is where the theme of war can no longer be kept from centre stage. Although Gustave Folcher was in engaged in combat for little more than a month out of over 68 months away from home, this is indelibly a story of war. Without the war he would probably never have left the Gard, and certainly never have written this minor classic of life in the ranks. And without Gustave Folcher's keen eye, we should not have such a rich sense of the meaning of war for those who live it, in a number of different respects.

First is the terribly poignant encounters with the past. The 'last war', is present everywhere, in the cemeteries that the soldiers go to visit, on the Meuse or the Moselle, and in the commandant's pep talk, citing the example of their fathers to them. They wander through the same regions in the same mud: 'Truly, and forgive me if I keep on about it' writes Folcher, 'but it is only in these areas of the east that you can see it like this. I have heard people tell, especially those from the 1914 campaign, stories of the bogs, but really you have to see it to believe it'. In headlong retreat, in 1940, after some hard fighting, the 12th Zouaves pass by Verdun and scan it for traces of their fathers' war, the trenches, the dug-outs, while an officer, 'who was in the last one', tells them about Douaumont and Fort-de-Vaux.[15] Gustave Folcher notes with typical understatement after a visit to the acres of white crosses in the American cemetery at Thiaucourt that this kind of experience, *ce n'est pas encourageant pour nous.*

Almost as dispiriting was the evident disorganisation and sense-lessness of much of the French war effort. Given the futile marches and counter-marches to which the 12th Zouaves were subjected, the poor state of their training and equipment, the lack of decent leadership and the almost total absence of air cover when the German attack finally came, the outcome was not at all Marc Bloch's 'strange defeat', but a predictable (albeit only predicted by the enemy) shambles in which the ordinary soldier was cast completely adrift. The plain, unheroic description of the ever-more hopeless and abandoned condition of GF's regiment in June 1940 is a fine piece of writing which conveys fear and courage in equal measure. The contrast between the ordinary soldiers' steadfastness and the reliability of officialdom is deftly sketched in: 'while with my own eyes I could see the tanks coming down to Sedan, the Paris radio was announcing that the enemy had been largely contained in Belgium, beyond our frontiers'.

Gustave Folcher is no strident political animal, but there is a touch of bitterness in his invitation to the enthusiasts of military parades to see what war is really like, in his description of an officer berating tired troops for marching too slowly, after the officer himself had arrived in a car, and in his final description of Avignon on the journey back, where some officers had commandeered a carriage while some men could not get on the train.

This critical faculty produces at times a near pacifist tone in Folcher's account. Certainly he possessed the generosity of spirit to feel for the German civilians as they suffered in their turn, under the terrible bombing of 1944–45. In his acknowledgement that the columns of frightened refugees were the mirror image of those he had seen in eastern France back in 1940, Folcher hints at the ultimate futility of war while not letting go of his conviction that this particular war was being fought against evil. His descriptions of the nightmarish destruction of the railway station at Stendal, and of the crash of a Flying Fortress near Schorstedt, are remarkably evenhanded, both suffused with a sense of sadness and horror. The scream of Allied bombs falling on Germany brought back the fear that Folcher felt during the battle for France, but once again he displayed the instincts of a natural war correspondent, and his picture of life in a disintegrating Germany is all the more valuable for coming from a foreigner who was not so hostile to his individual captors as to see everything through a triumphalist lens.

It is only towards the end of the diaries that the theme of Nazi Germany, observed in neutral language for most of the story, finally emerges into the open. Once again the stranger's eye gives a cutting edge to the judgements, curiously reinforced by the small scale of the savagery in comparison to what we now know about the organised murder of millions. Folcher notes how the Germans discriminate between their prisoners, with the French treated best and the Poles the worst. His account of the arbitrary hanging of a Pole for a crime he had not committed, and of the way in which his friends were forced to watch (and even in the case of one hysterical 15-year-old boy, to cut the body down), is the more shocking in its contrast to the tedious but relatively secure nature of life as a French prisoner.

Gustave Folcher is struck by the indoctrination of children into Nazism from an early age, with a fanaticism that he could not imagine occurring in inefficient, argumentative France, and by the adoration of Hitler, their 'famous painter', who is responsible for so much. He notes the lies of official propaganda, and how ordinary Germans suffered, whether through losing their sons on the Russian Front or losing their homes before the Allied advance. But his steady tone does not sentimentalise their plight. In his view the Nazi mentality has trickled down to everyday life, with the local population accustomed to playing the master, enjoying their power over the prisoners, meting out kicks and blows to the Slavs, and rejoicing in the power of the German military machine.

How much more shocking, then, was it for Gustave Folcher's warders when the reality of imminent defeat began to dawn. One of the most striking sections of the whole diary is the account of how the confidence of the local Germans gradually began to turn into fear, and how they implored the French to provide protection against the tide of Poles, Russians and Ukrainians aching for revenge. And indeed, the advancing American forces did place the French – still living in their prison hut – in charge of enforcing order in the local community until proper infantry support could arrive. As usual, Folcher accepted his responsibilities in a matter of fact and even-handed way, helping to ensure the round-up of pockets of remaining SS troops as well as preventing the worst excesses of vengeance. Still, he was not, after five years as a captive, about to pass up the pleasures of relieving an arrogant German officer of his bottle of French rum, or of reclothing himself from the shops broken open by looters. In general, the picture Folcher paints of the gradual disintegration of Nazism, under relentless military pressure from advancing armies on both sides, is dramatic, revealing and historically valuable precisely because it is so down to earth and personal.[16]

Finally the longed-for return home begins, and little more than a week after saying an unsentimental goodbye to his overlords in Schorstedt, Gustave Folcher steps down from a lorry in the centre of Aigues-Vives, at one o'clock in the morning, more than five years since he last set eyes on the village during the home leave of Easter 1940. And there he ends his story, with a natural sense of timing, leaving the reader wanting to know more about how he found his beloved Languedoc after such an absence.

There are only a few details we can fill in. Gustave Folcher could not go back to his old job as a gardener; he became a postman, and after 25 more years retired to cultivate his vines and his vegetables. He married Gilette Boudet, who had waited for him and sent him parcels, soon after coming home, and their son André was born in 1946. He had lost his mother in the spring of 1939, and his father, who had written to him through the long captivity, died in 1949. M. André Folcher and his family still live in Aigues-Vives, in the family house that Gustave knew before the war. Gustave's retirement was transformed by the interest taken by Rémy Cazals in his diaries, which had been passed around among his friends for some years, and their publication in 1981 led to many congratulatory reviews and letters from ex-*combattants*, many of whom felt their own experiences to have been articulated in them. Gustave Folcher never returned to the scene of the battles of 1940, nor even visited Paris, despite invitations from old comrades. He could not, of course, return to Schorstedt which had fallen into Russian hands and soon became part of East Germany. It might be thought that he would have had no wish to do so, but both his son and Rémy Cazals recalled that he had regretted the impossibility, and would have been curious to see again the place which had taken five years of his life.

Gustave Folcher died in August 1993, a month after learning of the plan for this translation. He is buried in the family tomb in the cemetery just outside Aigues-Vives, where a more famous Frenchman, Gaston Doumergue, former President of the French Republic (1924–31) and Prime Minister in (1913–14 and 1934), is also buried. Both served their country, both are sons of their *pays*. To Doumergue fell the highest official honours, but Gustave Folcher perhaps holds the greater distinction: against all the odds, he was able to speak for the millions of ordinary soldiers, and to leave a lasting sense of a Frenchman's experience of the war on the ground.

Rémy Cazals and Christopher Hill

Translator's Note

This book belongs first to Gustave Folcher and second to Rémy Cazals. My work has been limited to providing a translation from the French, as faithful to the plain style of the original as possible, and to making the text accessible to English readers. To this end I have provided extra footnotes where something might have seemed puzzling to an English eye, and have written an Introduction which incorporates much of Rémy Cazals' original version but doubles its length. I have also provided new maps and photographs, the maps by courtesy of the highly professional skills of Jane Pugh of the LSE's Drawing Office, thr photographs through the kindness of the Folcher family.

In these tasks I have been greatly aided by a number of people. In England, Professors Douglas Johnson and Philip Bell gave me important advice and encouragement at an early stage. The library of the National Army Museum has helped with technical queries. Jenny Shaw at Brassey's has been a most sympathetic publisher, and Carole Parsonage drafted a significant section of the translation at a critical stage. Elaine Childs, Judy Weedon and Martina Langer have patiently endured the problems of dictated drafts and transcriptions. Maria McKay read and corrected the whole text and has helped me throughout. I am most grateful to them all, as to the International Studies Division of the LSE's Research Fund, which has supported my work financially.

Outside Britain, I owe a great debt to M. André Folcher and his family in Aigues-Vives, who have encouraged me from the beginning and who have welcomed me generously into their home. For his part, Rémy Cazals has been more than collegial with his time and expertise, and I am immensely grateful to him. My greatest single debt, however, is to Colette Kleemann of the European University Institute in Florence. She has devoted days of her time in the midst of her other heavy commitments to reading and correcting the text of my translation, and her skills have saved me from many blunders. Her friendship, together with the hospitality of the whole Kleemann family and of Annalisa and Mario Poli, has been fundamental to the completion of the project. Yet if in many respects this has been a collective effort, I alone bear the responsibility for any mistakes which might remain.

Christopher Hill, January 1996

I

THE PHONEY WAR

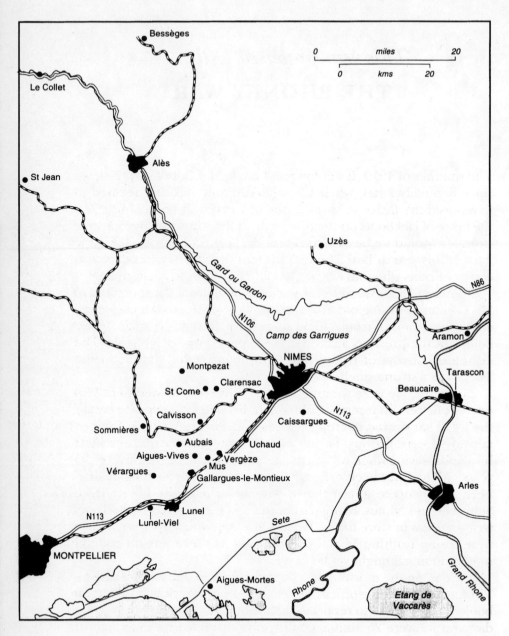

Aigues-Vives and its Neighbours

'This year promised well . . .'

The summer of 1939. It was long and warm and full of surprises, for since September last, when Chamberlain and Daladier seemed to have saved the peace at Munich, the talk had only been of war, and the noise of jackboots on the other side of the Rhine was getting ever stronger. Would we be able to get such a beautiful, wonderful grape harvest this year as last? The year promised well and we had faith in our politicians who, once again, would know how to avoid disaster.

20 August 1939. We were carting away dung from the sheepfold to Les Coulondres using old man Durand's lorry, and from there we saw endless columns of troops filing past on the Route Nationale. Never before in the previous alerts had it happened on such a scale. The ceaseless convoys of troops and equipment rolled past at speed. There was a strong smell of war.

25 August. We were washing the vats when they started to call up one by one certain reservists, older than us, who made up one part of the list. That started to create jealousies in Aigues-Vives. In fact certain wives were furious, having one or more children, to see their husbands leaving when we, for the most part bachelors of 25, 30 or 35 years old, had not been called. Even the old men, touching 50, had been called up to guard the bridges or to lead the horses from Sommières to Nîmes. Being part of the first reserve, I knew perfectly well what was in store for us. We would leave some days later, but we were losing nothing by waiting. So long as there was no general mobilisation, all might yet be saved.

But alas, on the morning of 3 September 1939, the walls of Aigues-Vives were covered by official notices. All those carrying mobilisation book number 7 had to report to their mobilisation centre during the day, and we were 25 annual contingents at the least – to all intents and purposes a general mobilisation. There were a good 30 of us departing on the last train in the evening for Nîmes, the majority having gone during the day. A train crammed, chock-a-block. There were still some of us from Aigues-Vives and we stayed together as

3

long as possible, for once separated it would certainly be for many months, perhaps even years. There were there Rousset, Toulouse, Morgues and an inconsolable Salençon, whose daughter had just been born some days before. Some got off at Nîmes; mostly the artillerymen. But at Tarascon there was a new separation, one half of the group going towards Marseille and Nice, the other towards Avignon and Lyon.

We take more than two hours to go from Tarascon to Avignon. I am the only one to get off at Avignon where there is an almighty bottleneck. No light, no one to give me information. I join up with a bloke from Marseille who, like me, has no instructions other than to report to the mobilisation centre number 155. But where is it? We stroll round the town, and down a glass or two as it is pretty hot. Numerous groups promenade up and down in total darkness, and it seems, in total disorder. At last, towards one o'clock in the morning, after having been turned away from the engineers' barracks, we arrive outside the Chabran barracks of the Algerian riflemen. I'm happy to recognise the guardsman at the entrance who is driving everyone away. It is a young lad from Clarensac whom I know very well, since he got married in Aigues-Vives only a short time ago. As a favour, he allows me in, me and my mate from Marseille, leading us into a huge room where we can each find a bed.

What a surprise on waking up to find myself lying only two or three beds away from another Aigues-Vivois, Galdi, who had been there for some days, being part of the mobilising staff. Together we leave to find Boissier again (the guard from Clarensac) and we celebrate our reunion with a good breakfast in the town. From these two I got all the information I needed and I go to enrol myself as present back at the mobilisation centre 155 which is based in the Renault garage, near the station. The garage, despite its size, is already nearly full. I wait my turn patiently. I show my service papers and to my great surprise I am attached to the 12th regiment of the Zouaves.[1] I who was counting on leaving in a regiment of alpine riflemen, having done my service period in the 141st infantry at Marseille! What a surprise! Alright, into the Zouaves. 12th Zouaves, under Colonel Tissanet. Immediately assigned to the 1st battalion, commanded by Catherino, and to the 3rd company commanded by the reserve captain Massip, a primary school teacher at Saint-Jean-du-Gard.[2]

A loudspeaker is already calling the roll. 3rd company, this way, and a good 30 of us are embarked in a bus which starts off at once. Where are they taking us? No-one knows anything. The bus leaves the town. We roll on through gardens on the outskirts of Avignon. A big estate and we stop. Here the 3rd company of the 1st battalion is forming. This is the chateau of La Verdière, owned by a religious order and halfway between Morières and Montfavet (Vaucluse).

Straight after arriving, a new sorting out. The captain, in front of a makeshift desk, made of a few crates, distributes the new arrivals. I am part of the 3rd section of the company, commanded by Lieutenant Levrat, a green officer who had only left the military school of Saint-Maixent two days before – and he was the only regular officer in the battalion, all the others being reservists, many teachers or priests. Only one regular, and I have to end up in his section! There are four or five of us down for the 3rd section and we are taken straight to the section's quarters, which is a bivouac in a nearby farm. In the courtyard about 15 lads who had arrived before us are clustered round a young officer who is haranguing them. He comes up to us, shakes our hands, tells us that henceforth we are making up, together with the comrades already arrived and those yet to come, a new family to stick together in the good and bad days which lie ahead. For the moment, it is time for a meal, straight after which you will be dressed and equipped, and so it goes.

Some bad news: the rule that is set out on the mobilisation order, which no-one had noticed but which is strictly enforced, states that all those called-up must bring with them enough provisions for three or four days. That starts off some moaning in the farm's loft. In the barracks, there are canteens, but in these isolated farmhouses, far from anywhere, in unknown territory . . . besides, it is forbidden to wander off. Luckily there is a solution. Because of the mobilisation there are no trucks available for civilians, and in the courtyard of the farm there are mounds of melons and baskets of grapes which are in the process of rotting given that there is no way of transporting them. The bailiff would love to be able to sell them, but realising that there is nothing much to be got out of us he leaves us free to take advantage, and we stuff ourselves to death with the melons, grapes and some pears.

Two o'clock. First call. The lieutenant arrives. Another, and this time the last, distribution to sections. He puts me, for the moment says he, as rifleman in the 9th section of Sergeant Vernhet, a decent Catalan chap who, so as to ensure peace in his group, will do more than his share of the fatigues. It's normal, we are at war and the sergeants are no longer stuck-up mess types in fancy dress. For the moment, NCOs and other ranks, we are all equal.

One-two, one-two, one, towards the company's headquarters at La Verdière. We present ourselves in groups of three or four before a

major who asks us if we have anything to report. Those who complain
are taken aside for a more thorough inspection. As for the others
they are passed ready for departure. Directed into a vast hangar
where our comrade Galdi is in the midst of emptying a lorry of equipment and effects, we draw our military clothing in a pretty hit and
miss fashion, and then we exchange amongst us trousers, boots,
greatcoats, immediately pulling on all the new kit. They hurry us. We
get mess cans, beakers, flasks and then immediately it's the time for
arms, gas masks, haversacks, munition bags, ammunition for the guns
and for the rifles, magazines full of bullets for the machine gunner of
the group that we all have to supply on demand and according to his
needs, plus a pile of things – mostly odds and ends – that don't seem
to be of any obvious use. The soldiers from Marseille start to say:
don't put any more down, we've got too much. There's a touch of
frenzy about the whole bazaar.

Our civilian effects are taken away and it's as men of war that we
return to our billet. It is not yet 24 hours since I left home and
already the company is on a war footing. We let the lieutenant know
that we have had nothing to eat.

'The company can only draw provisions for you in three days, it's the
rule, you ought to know it.'
'What we couldn't know was that we would be sent out into farmhouses
far from anywhere: we assumed we would be staying in the town or at
least in a barracks where there were canteens,' we say.
'Strictly speaking it's forbidden to go outside the camp. Sort yourselves
out, I don't want to see you.'

A quarter of an hour afterwards groups of friends have already
formed and we clear off leaving the loft where we were supposed to
be bedding down. Some go towards Morières. As for us, that's to say
me and two blokes from Bessèges, we set off towards Montfavet, a
pretty little town where we have an excellent supper. We treat ourselves to a bottle of sparkling wine to celebrate the comradeship of
the good and bad days which lie ahead.

At six o'clock, reveille; it's the lieutenant himself who comes to get
us up from our straw beds. In an hour, we must be in the courtyard to
fall in. Some big mouth says to the lieutenant: 'Without any coffee,
without any breakfast?' He replies: 'Did you really expect to have
café au lait and croissants at reveille?', then he softens, telling us that
from tomorrow he will do the necessary to make sure that we eat. A
roll call in columns, then our first drill; we lack fitness, but that will

come, he tells us. Two days go by in preparation. Somehow or other
we set up our packs, and assemble our weapons. We go to Morières to
try our gas masks, in a barn hermetically sealed, transformed into a
gas chamber, where we are shut in company by company.

8 September 1939. At reveille, the lieutenant tells us to hold ourselves ready, the order for departure could arrive at any moment. We
eat at midday. The rumour is that departure is on for today. The
afternoon passes from one shadow to another for it is very warm,
stormy even. We discuss it all in our groups. Where might we really be
going? Nobody knows . . . into the Alps, to the North, to the East?
Nothing comes out and when we question the lieutenant he doesn't
seem any better informed than us.

Five o'clock, meal time, where the captain in a little speech lets us
know that departure will be at six o'clock. We are going to board a
train at Avignon station which must be at least 10–12 kilometres away.
The sun has not yet gone down, it is warm, indeed very warm, wearing a greatcoat in high summer, we who were accustomed scarcely
three or four days ago to be in shirtsleeves and sandals. The new military boots are heavy on the feet. After some kilometres, three or four
perhaps, we are covered in sweat. We are not used to carting around
such a clutter, for the whole load, arms and ammunition, must be
close to 40 kilos. The column breaks up, several men lie down on the
embankment by the road, not being able to do any more, and it is in
a really sorry state that the column drags on. Our section holds well
enough together. By contrast other sections are completely dispersed.
The inhabitants of the suburb of Avignon are very kind bringing us
full buckets of cold water to drink. Some of them distribute full baskets of grapes and fruit. Night falls when we cross Avignon. We are
stretched out down the boulevards, along the ramparts, in a truly pitiful state. Nearly half the battalion has left the column and labours far
behind. We march through the middle of a crowd of sad civilians
calm and silent who, I believe, understand better than us where we
are being taken. We arrive at the station, my section embarks in the
middle of the train. In a corner of a wagon, a pile of boxes of tinned
food, mostly bully beef, sardines, tuna and chocolate, a little cheese
and a full bag of ration loaves, which lead a Parisian to point out that
we must be going far to have been given such reserves. Our arms are
piled up in a corner of the wagon, and the section, jammed together
like the aforesaid sardines, stretches itself out, legs over each other,
on the hard floor of the cattle truck. We stay there long hours. It
takes a long time for the stragglers to turn up and it must be not far
from midnight when gently, very gently, the train begins to move.

France Seen From a Goods Train

After leaving we cross the Rhone and arrive at Pont-d'Avignon, in the Gard Département. That still feels like home, but not for long, as we go up the right bank of the Rhone via Bagnols and Pont-Saint-Esprit. In the wagon, no-one sleeps. A group plays cards by the glow of a candle. And there, squashed together, the section makes its final introductions. There are 35 of us there, from almost everywhere. First there is the quarter master sergeant, the lieutenant's second in command, who takes over when the lieutenant is not there, as is the case now. The officers travel in the passenger-coaches at the head of the train and leave the troops in the charge of their deputies for the journey. Ours, sat in a corner, says absolutely nothing, starting no conversations and taking part in none. I never knew from where he came, as I never even addressed a word to him. He seems an enemy already, and will be sent to Coventry by the section. Then three sergeants, one for each group. Roure, from Aubenas in the Ardèche, is the head of the 7th section, a decent chap who takes his new job seriously and has a laugh with us. Denjean, an excellent mate who is a hairdresser in Carcassonne and takes everything as a joke, will be one of my best friends in the field. He is the leader of the 8th section. And lastly there is Vernhet, a Catalan from the Perpignan area, who almost always speaks Catalan with two or three other people from the same part of the world. He is the leader of my section, the 9th, and he passes around a flask full of good wine that he has brought from his native Catalonia. He looks like a good lad, as ready to do a fatigue as to order it. I think that we will get on well. The first corporal and three ordinary corporals make up the hierarchy of the section and it seems that apart from our quartermaster sergeant everybody, even the lieutenant, seems to want to be mates.

As for the men, that's to say the privates, there are lads from everywhere. The biggest group, seven or eight of them, are from the Basses-Pyrénées. There are some from the Gard who talk dialect with the two or three from Hérault, while two from the Ardèche and three from Lozère chip in. There are two or three from the Aube and Vaucluse, plus the inseparable contingent from Marseille, and a group of four from Troyes in the Aube. All the four are hosiers and speak a French which we find pretty difficult. Two Parisians complete the contingent. With my friend Antérieu, the miner from Bessèges, Sugier René, who will remain my best friend for a good part of the campaign, and Sergeant Denjean from Carcassonne, we make up one of the best teams of the section, and boasting aside we will prove one of the most resourceful when it comes to sliding something through or getting something out of the lieutenant.

And meanwhile the train rolls gently along, for it is heavily loaded, with around 1,200 men, plus equipment, horses, a field kitchen and a general service wagon for the whole battalion. We have just gone through the station at Teil, and the eternal question starts again: where can we really be going? Alas! we know only too well, but sometimes one can be mistaken . . . still, first light appears and some men begin to complain they are hungry. Groups form and without more ado we attack the victuals piled up in the wagon. Some eat sardines, others tuna, but most fall on the bully beef (which is pretty good), with a bit of cheese and a mug of wine (for our canteens are full, and my word that will do). Then straightaway I manage to find a place in the door of the wagon, my feet hanging over the steps.

For the moment the weather is bad, impenetrable mist covering the valley of the Rhone. You can't see beyond the railway. Inside the wagon, some of us lie down again, if that's the right word for being stretched out on the boards with the clickety-click of the rails drumming through our backs. It's more bearable sitting up, it seems to me. A game of *belote*[3] is once again under way. For myself, I stay, despite the thick fog, in the door of the truck, my legs dangling, for I feel that if I go my place will be immediately taken. There's space for no more than four or five on each side. The fog lightens a little, and the train, which is already crawling along, slows right down. We are entering the station at Givors where we can only see the smoke from chimneys and a few factories. A long enough stop and then we slide quietly off again. The sun pierces the fog occasionally and soon will burst out triumphant over the morning mist. We arrive in the outskirts of Lyon, and from the train we can soon see the town, the city and its huge extent. The hill of Fourvières rises up in the distance. After a rather long stop that we happily use to fill up our already empty canteens, spreading out on the platforms and buying the morning papers, at the head of the train the bugle sounds the depart and everyone leaps quickly back into their wagons. We start off again on the Paris line,

but after a few kilometres we leave the main route and are taken off
to the left on a little single track. Where can they really be taking us,
on a route which seems to be heading for the centre of France?

Now the sun has triumphed and shines over a lovely countryside.
Some very pretty views. It's superb. We go along the side of a mountain, which dominates huge valleys that go for several kilometres, a
real feast for the eyes. It is magnificent, and I wouldn't give up my
place for any money. Sometimes the valley narrows, and one can see
a river down below, little houses which look like nests, then it is the
hill in front that we can see with the fields on its slopes, with little
vines seemingly hooked onto the walls. We wind around these hills.
Sometimes the train makes a semi-circle, and you can see the two
wheezing engines at the same time as the queuing wagons in the
long train. There are flowers everywhere, meadows and always alongside the track pretty herds of cows that one can't help but admire. For
me, who's never been outside Bas-Gard I can't settle down, for these
are not at all the same views as at home, where at this time of year we
only see vines and the fields are roasted by the sun. But where are we
and what is this area that I like so much? Nice villages, sometimes on
the slopes sometimes on the bottom of the valley follow one after
another, but the names tell us nothing that might help us get our
bearings. As it seems to us, we are heading towards the centre of
France and we suppose we are in the Nivernais.

Midday approaches and we see a small town emerging that seems
just like Lunel, as much through its setting as through the station
itself. This is Paray-le-Monial. The train stops and soon enough there
is a rush for the street, canteen in hand, heading for the buffet, the
bar and all the other shops. The policing of the train is completely
overrun. Several other troop trains have also stopped; there is a great
crush trying to get served. Luckily nurses from the Red Cross and
other organisations hand out cold drinks. That does us a lot of good
since it was beginning to get very warm in the wagons. We eat on the
station platform, always the same cold meal. Bully beef is in pride of
place and luckily there is no shortage of it.

A brawl breaks out in the station. Some refugee trains coming
from the Alsatian frontier have stopped here. These poor people
among whom there are a good many very young children, have put
out their bedclothes to dry on the wagon doors. Most of the cover-
ings have rosettes of swastikas in the corners, with a large swastika at
the centre. It's because of this swastika that we are having to go to the
war. Seeing it, the soldiers grab the sheets and drag them away but
the civilians hang on to them even though they are being dragged

along the track, and kicks and punches rain down from everywhere. The officers rush up but cannot stop the scuffle. They do the only thing possible: the bugle sounds and the train starts, while the swastika refugees are still grappling with other troops.[4]

We start out again in lovely countryside. But is it heat, or tiredness which starts to make itself felt, especially after eating? We pay less attention to the beauty of our surroundings. Then, in the station at Paray-le-Monial, we have seen the refugee trains, the trains of artillerymen with their guns, tanks and other engines of war, and all that reminds us that we are not going on holiday. The old question returns: where are we going, what will tomorrow bring? Rumour has it however that we might simply be going for training to the camp at Montargis for a few days. Anyway we will see. We doze in the wagon and some of us even snore, for dinner and the warmth of the midday have knocked us out. Going round the hill we see the river, which is the Loire slowly winding past. Towards the middle of the afternoon we reach Nevers. The station is crammed full of troop trains and refugees, for the most part coming from Strasbourg.

The young ones tell us of their problems, while the old content themselves with watching, for most of them do not speak French. The women and above all the kids beg us for something to eat for they are not too well provided for having left in great haste. We hand out some of our bread and abundant supplies of tinned food to them, which seems to make them very happy. And then we go off again following the valley of the Loire, which we can see occasionally, and where we see fishermen and bathers on little beaches. The evening falls as we cross over the Loire which is magnificent in the setting sun.

Towards midnight we have a prolonged stop. We open the doors a little, it's almost like being in an oven it is so dark, not one light. The train has halted in total blackness. Far away there are some fairy lights or night-lights. That leads to a debate. From one wagon to another, the rumours circulate that we have arrived at Montargis, the first destination on our journey. Are we going to disembark? Some people begin to get their equipment together. We light some candles. But suddenly the train jerks into motion and the discussion starts all over again. According to the Parisians who are there, we must be on the Paris line, which makes me well pleased. If we could go to Paris, I wouldn't mind spending several days there.

We go on, and suddenly we realise that we are turning our back on the capital, in a north-easterly direction. We are at present in the Département of the Aube and there the train stops. It is Romilly-sur-Seine where a lot of hosiery is made. Two comrades from the section are very happy to find themselves back home. One of them can even see his wife who is lodging nearby. Alas it is not long after that the bugle sounds again and big Pop, the grenadier of the section, only just manages to catch the train, which has already started, on the run. Next stop Troyes that we reach towards the middle of the morning, seeming to me to be an attractive enough town so far as one can tell from the spot we are in. A brief stop and after some time continuing through the mist, we arrive towards midday at Mailly camp.

On the disembarking platforms there is a mad dash, not for a drink but to wet our heads and have a basic wash in the cold water which fills the huge containers put there to water the passing horses. That does us a lot of good and relaxes us a little. Is this our destination as rumour has it? Yes? No, no order for disembarkation is given. Our lieutenant comes to visit us, he tells us that he doesn't know any more than us as to our destination; by way of compensation he takes two of us and gets us to draw rations for a meal, as well as coffee, wine and cigarettes. We give him an ovation, which makes him smile. We eat slowly on the platform. The sun has finally defeated the fog and it's almost pleasant sitting on the benches which litter the platforms.

Two o'clock. The bugle sounds at the other end of the train while quite a few, and I'm among them, were asleep. On we get and start off again quietly. We cross the barren military camp then a huge stony plain. Not a tree, no vegetation at all, it tires our eyes. Very different views from those of the day before. Towards midday fatigue weighs heavily on us. It's now Sunday afternoon and we have been in this wagon since Friday evening, which is now quite a long time. We are still on this arid plain where we cross several major roads. At last, here we are, a river, that's better, villages, well-cultivated fields and finally a town. Our new stop is Bar-le-Duc. Troop trains of all kinds, artillery, engineers, infantry, always trains of soldiers. The Red Cross trains and the hospital trains are there, waiting on events. The orders become stricter, no getting down from the wagons. We stay there a good while and then start off again. Towards Metz.

From now on, we understood. It is useless to keep up the illusions; it is down there in front of us and every turn of the wheel brings us nearer, where the great drama is played out, and that's where we're headed. As we go on, we see a huge cemetery with the crosses laid out in lines, left over from the war of 1914 which doesn't do much to cheer us up. We are on a strategic route: four tracks abreast, two lines climbing up, two going down. We go alongside a train of engineers coming from Versailles and we are able to chat with the Parisians who are abreast of us. The afternoon draws on, we have crossed the

Department of the Meuse, then into Meurthe-et-Moselle, and we continue through. The clickety-click of the rails ends up by irritating the strongest of us, even the most fanatical card schools have given up. The countryside hardly interests us any more, our minds are full of future events. At last here we are in the Department of the Moselle and soon we see the river itself with its long shady stretches flowing quietly like a big canal. Through Pagny-sur-Moselle, that's where there was the old Franco-German frontier from the war of 1870. Novéant-sur-Moselle. The train slows down and settles alongside a platform on a siding. Are we going to get off here at last? We wait for a moment. The orders come with the lieutenant in his uniform: 'Get yourselves kitted out!'

Disembarkation. For us this is all done quickly enough; it's not the same thing for the horses and the mobile kitchens, the gun carts and the transport company. While waiting for the end of disembarkation we take a break on the very banks of the Moselle, under the big trees which make a superb promenade. The countryside is magnificent. We make short work of the stock of tinned food which from now on we have no need to hoard, but then night falls and with it comes the fatigue of 50 hours of very uncomfortable travelling. The lieutenant smiles, this is war and there are many more of them to come. For the moment we only want one thing: to be able to relax in some barn and to sleep, to sleep ourselves out.

Night Marches: Discovering the
Villages of Lorraine

Here we are again, the order arrives, and we leave, packs on backs, and this time on foot. We are probably going to make camp in the village which is on the other side of the river, for the first company has already started on to the bridge. We in our turn get over the river. We pass through the village where, to our great surprise, they don't seem to want us to stay the night. There's no doubt that we shall have to camp in the woods or in the fields near at hand. On the right the balloon corps has pitched camp, with their huge sausages fastened to the earth.

Now night has completely fallen, but we keep on marching. We can't believe that after 50 hours in the train they are going to make us march right through the night. Halt! At last we must have arrived, but no, it's simply a pause, we have been marching for an hour. It's not possible, people begin to murmur; frankly, as far as I am concerned, I can do no more. Ten minutes rest and down there at the other end, the Commandant's[5] whistle pipes up again. Forward! We remount our packs, trail our rifles and face down the kilometres. On questioning the lieutenant tells us that he doesn't think that we will have to go very far, but in the meantime we have to follow on. The second halt arrives. This time everyone is at the end of their tether, the straps on the new packs have cut into our shoulders. Feet, unused to new boots, are blistered; the greatcoat really is too much and we arrive at the third halt soaked in sweat. This time the grumbling is not contained and the officers are strongly challenged, something to which they respond by starting us off again.

The lieutenant, being a professional soldier, has been broken into marching. However he is very kind and doesn't reply to those who coarsely get at him but takes the bag of cartridges from one, a rifle from another, a light machine-gun into the bargain; finally he is the one most weighed down. Many straggle at the rear, unable to do more. Despite my great fatigue I hold on and earn the credit for carrying all my own kit. Finally, in the dark, a village can be made out, our stopping place. It's with relief that I find a nice spot in an attic under the roofs where I stretch out and half bury myself in the hay. I still have the strength to change my shirt being literally soaked through to the bones. I am suffering horribly with my feet which are cut on all sides. No matter, I fall asleep well enough in the hay and do not even hear the first shells of the anti-aircraft defences fired at passing aircraft a few moments after our arrival.

Monday morning 12 September. A late reveille. I get down from my loft. My pal Sugier and I go to have a bit of a wash in the village square where there is a fountain. There the inhabitants tell us that we are in Fleury (Moselle), a very pretty name that doesn't describe the village very well for, in the few streets which make up the settlement, we see only enormous piles of cow dung producing evil-smelling liquid manure which then forms puddles in front of doors and windows right in the centre of the village. Well washed, we look for lunch. The civilians are very kind and the farmer's wife who is lodging the section offers us big bowls of milk, and *café au lait*, with bread and plenty of sugar for a small sum. We can get our provisions at the village grocery where we buy, among other things, the small plums called *mirabelles*, at 10 sous[6] a kilo. They are very good and we eat ourselves to death for we quickly notice that around the village along the riverbanks, or the walls of the farms, in all the gardens, the trees are bent down under hundreds of kilos of plums of all types.

Midday. Before parade the incidents of the night before are talked over, above all in my section which contains several big mouths, as Lieutenant Labernadier says, and which rebelled strongly against the 22 kilometres that they made us do after more than 50 hours in the train. A good enough stew for dinner. In the afternoon there is a general treatment for our feet, which we dip, group by group, in the big cooking pots, perhaps the same ones in which they made the soup, half full of a medicine with a blue methylene base, so as to heal and harden our feet. Then, no chance of idleness, trench manoeuvres. We get our trenches behind the village. What a godsend! In a big garden full of plum trees groaning with fruit. Mirabelles and other types are just ready, we get sick eating them, in fact a little too much to the point that in the next night it's constant coming and going through the attic window and the shaky ladder that serves us as a staircase to get up into the attic. A good number have bad diarrhoea, which isn't such a bad thing, since the constant diet of bully beef all through the journey had made us very constipated. We have to stay there some days, so they say. Well that's not too bad. There are two pleasant cafés for us to drink in, and everything is new for me who always likes to find out about the life of the part of the country that I am in. I talk a lot with the peasants who get me to visit their cowsheds and beautiful cows. One morning, I visit the model farm attached to the almshouse of the city of Metz, where there are some very fine cattle. There are more than fifty milking cows, very well looked after and with the most modern equipment. The first days do not seem too long for me, for whenever I have a moment I go into the farms, give a hand to some-one or other of them, thus earning myself some good bowls of milk. The life of the peasant is so different from in our part of France that it really interests me a great deal. In the evening in the bistro we wait for the roll call and there are always a few singers to organise a small concert. We go to sleep in our hay, and there we sleep well.

But, alas, everything comes to an end and after four or five days – clearly on the basis that the holidays have lasted long enough – they abruptly give the order for departure. To cap our unhappiness it rains, not heavily, but a fine rain that never stops falling and which hardly gladdens my heart. The Lieutenant calls me. What can he really want of me? A trained observer, he has already judged his men and remodelled his section according to his observations. 'The machine-gunner in your group is sick, and he is not going anywhere. He has to be hospitalised. You will take the place of your friend Sugier, while he goes to be the gunner. You will be his assistant as a loader.' The Lieutenant is clear-sighted and likes to put in charge of his three machine guns teams of friends who understand each other pretty well. This doesn't amuse me too much because, although on the one hand I give up my heavy Lebel for an ordinary light rifle, I also have to give up my bag where my personal effects are. For this bag is very precious, containing as it does my change of clothes such as shirts, handkerchiefs, socks, jerseys, that you always have to hand; it has some provisions as well, a sausage, a block of chocolate, a little cheese, all that's there ready for the moment when you need it; while the loaders and firers of the light machine-guns leave their bags in the company's lorry, and you never know where this lorry stops, espe-cially since it follows at a distance, leaving when we arrive or rather arriving when we leave. Yet I have to accept the proposal, above all because I will get to be all the time with my friend Sugier, which makes me very happy.

By the time they give us the order to depart it is the depths of night. I fill my new bag, with 10 cartridge clips, each one with 25 machine-gun bullets, plus 100 rifle bullets; all this is much heavier than the individual bag I used to have, and it's on we go! Immediately after departure we leave the road and it's by small footpaths, at one time across fields, at another through large woods, that we trek in indian file and in total darkness. We can scarcely make out the Zouave who is in front of us. Happily the aluminium mess tins which are attached to the back of the bags shine up and act as a kind of red light for those following blindly on. The first few kilometres are alright, despite the enormous weight that pulls your shoulders down. The first halt comes and goes, then the second, but when the third and then even the fourth arrive, the legs don't want to take any more. At the blast on the whistle marking the halt one flops, or rather collapses, it doesn't matter how, it doesn't matter where, in the water or in the mud. Sweat runs everywhere and we lie down on the road; the cold overcomes us but nobody moves. We are so exhausted that we would willingly give in and just die there on the spot. Ten minutes are soon gone and in the distance the Commandant's whistle beckons, but no one makes as if to move. The Lieutenant is there, he shakes and scolds us one after the other. Without him we would not get up and go again. It's hard to start out again, it's very burdensome, we drag our feet along the soil, our knees don't want to bend. We drag our boots, then things warm up again and off we go. Our shoulders are cleft apart by the straps.

Towards two or three o'clock in the morning, being able to do no more, I am asleep on my feet, when suddenly going through a wood I stumble on a root and roll into a hollow for five or six metres. In the fall I lost my helmet and my rifle and despite being woken up by all this I search for them in the dark night in the completely opposite direction from the hollow. In the end an officer arrives and very kindly lends me his electric lamp and I find all my equipment in the water. We pass through a fair number of villages. When coming into the village we always believe that that is going to be the end of the stage, but no, we leave by the other side and everything continues. The Lieutenant encourages his men, relieving their loads by turn. He tells us that a certain number of kilometres still remain, which in the night always seem longer.

At last about four or five o'clock in the morning we arrive. It's still night, we have been marching for eight or nine hours, it's never stopped raining, although we're soaked as much with sweat as with rain. For a billet, they have given us a kind of corridor in a barn with two openings to the north and to the south but no door. A stream of air blows inside to the point that we can't light the lantern. We have to make the best of it. What can we do in the black night, in a land which is totally foreign to us? I unfold my blanket and, completely soaked, I sleep on top of it, on the mud floor.

A cockerel which starts scratching wakes me up by touching my feet. It is broad daylight, all the section sleeps higgledy-piggledy, jumbled up one on the other in the long corridor. My Lieutenant, who I hadn't seen during the night, sleeps near me. I put my blanket over him. I am cold, in fact very cold. I put on my boots, completely stiff from the water that they have taken in and go to make a tour round the courtyard of the farm. I discover the kitchen. I knock to ask for a bowl of milk or a warm drink, offering to pay, of course. The family, which is in the middle of eating, doesn't give me too kind a welcome. To my great astonishment they do not seem to understand what I'm asking from them. I have to insist, mostly by gestures, to get a bowl of warm milk in the end which does me a great deal of good. I would happily have warmed myself and even dried myself a little in front of the huge fire that burns, but I see that they would prefer me to make my exit. I do not push myself and I go out into the courtyard, where I see in an old kitchen a big wood fire on which is cooking an enormous pot of potatoes for the pigs, that's a stroke of luck, and I take the chance to get myself in front of the fire, on a crate which is hanging about, not so much to warm as to dry myself. But then an old charlady arrives to put wood on the fire. She speaks for a long time in a language of which I do not understand a word. For my part, I explain to her that I will take care of the fire, but without success. At least she seems friendly, and since she doesn't tell me to leave that's all that matters. I go to get my friend Sugier who's still sleeping and both of us dry ourselves after a fashion, while warming ourselves up as well.

We leave on the village's only road, and what a road! I can't describe what we see. I am quite incapable of finding the words to describe such a spectacle. There is mud half way up my leg, if not more. There is dung all along the road with manure high in the ditch to such a point that we give up taking the letters that we have just written to the battalion's office at the other end of the village. No one wants to risk himself in such a treacle to go to eat and it needs all the Lieutenant's authority to get us to the parade ground.

On parade, we are told that at nightfall we will be leaving again for a new stage which will take us up near to the front line. After the 35 kilometres of the last night in driving rain, to be forced to have another dose is not something that is going to make us laugh. When night comes, after bolting down a tin of rice and drinking coffee, the pack goes back and off we go! We leave Ancerville, which is the name of the village from where we carry away a pretty bad memory, Ancerville-the-Disgusting as the section's smart alecs have already dubbed it. And on we go! This time we march on a main road, on the tarmac; which is much better, and getting even better now the rain has stopped. Today I feel myself to be in good shape despite the little sleep from the night before and the hard march of the previous night. Training is beginning to bear its fruit. The first dozen kilometres almost go well, but towards midnight once again it starts to rain. A good number of the Zouaves are at the end of their strength and quit the column, lying down no matter where, in the stables, a ruined barn, a hut which they find at the side of the road. Towards the third break, my friend has a serious fainting attack and cannot go on any more. Although for quite a while I have only been able to carry my own bag with great difficulty along this endlessly climbing road, I take his for some distance. The Lieutenant, good chap as he is, is often the heaviest burdened although he doesn't have to carry anything, and he holds on well, soothing by turns those who struggle the most and seem to want to give up, carrying the rifle of one or the bag of another, if not to say all at the same time.

The last kilometres are very hard and I am completely drained when I arrive in the village after a march of about 30 kilometres. At our billet we have a good barn full of hay, and it's enjoyable to sleep on top of it, completely soaked still in boots and equipment, our bayonets and cartridge belts still on us. Some people even sleep with their packs on their backs, not being able to unbuckle them they were so exhausted. It's often only at reveille like today, that most people, if not all of us, realise that we have slept in full kit, including the pack, without taking off either boots full of water or streaming greatcoat, without even having the strength to stretch out their blanket. That is the state which one is in at the end of these long marches.

When I wake up it is broad daylight and I am agreeably surprised to be in a huge barn full of fragrant hay. What a great bed we are going to prepare for tomorrow night in this hay, assuming we are still here! I get up still soaked from the night before; my first deed is to cast an eye over the village, to see where we might be able to get a bit of a wash. We are right in the centre of the hamlet. A street sign tells me that we are at Haute-Vigneulles, very near to the frontier on a level with the Maginot line which lies there before us. I have a little wash at the fountain, then like the day before I look for somewhere to have a drink of milk. There are very few civilians, the village being evacuated. The few that I see neither speak nor understand French. They speak a patois from their area which probably draws on German. We have to spend several days here. I profit from them by washing my few dirty clothes that I stretch out in the loft, for outside the weather is poor, raining at times. We start to dig some shelter trenches. In the afternoon in the gardens around we eat plums and particularly the beautiful apples with which the gardens are over-flowing. At parade time come our orders and they are tough. It is forbidden to light a fire or to make a light, everything must be done in complete darkness, for we are, it seems, on the edge of a combat zone. We make a good bed in the hay since we must stay here. Well wrapped up in the covers, night has not arrived before the whole section is snoring in competition.

Just as we were all sleeping a deep sleep after the hard fatigues of the nights before, at about two or three in the morning a loud 'get up inside there and be quick about it!' boomed out. The lieutenant, his electric light in his hand, made his tour of all the nooks and crannies of the farm, for there were Zouaves sleeping almost everywhere. He kept on shouting 'Get ready, all on the road, we're leaving in fifteen minutes'. To wake us up like that just when we were sleeping so well! For the one time that we had a good billet! But there it is, that's the sad reality. We have to get ready, which is not easy in complete dark-ness with our bags completely unpacked, one boot here, the other covered up in the hay. Everybody jibs at this, and the lieutenant has to hurry us. To get together all the clothes and equipment which make up the pack of a campaign soldier, and the whole thing com-pletely laid out since we were supposed to be staying a few days! As for us, the assistants to the machine-gunner, we have two packs to pre-pare, the one with personal belongings for the lorry and the other one that we have to carry. All that has to be done without lights. This does not take place without several tellings-off and hard exchanges of words with the sergeants, the section leaders who want to make things happen. The soldiers like me who regret not having been able to fin-ish this night's sleep are in a very bad mood. At last, by some means or another, we finish equipping ourselves and go out on to the road where, in the pitch dark, is the bustle of the battalion's departure. However, the minutes pass and we are still there, stamping our feet in the mud. To soothe the waiting, we get to drink a bowl of scorching milk that a neighbouring farmer distributes before the move off. The lieutenant turns up and in chorus we all pose the same question: 'Where are we going?' He smiles and doesn't reply. And we still wait. We could have slept an hour more, for certain companies with horses and heavy material take much longer than us to get themselves ready.

Suddenly we hear the crackling of a machine gun over there, not very far in front of us. It's the first time that we have heard that outside the shooting ranges. Are we supposed to go over there? There must have been something serious to make them give us this unforeseen order in the middle of the night. Finally the order for departure arrives and ahead we hear the commandant's whistle. The day rises up as we leave, a grey dawn in the mist, but at least it doesn't rain, it simply drizzles a little. After leaving we question the lieutenant: 'Are we going to the line? Do we go any further?' Meanwhile we can hear the persistent noise of machine-guns firing not far away, there on our right in the trenches which are in front of the works of the Maginot line. In the end the lieutenant decides to tell us. We are going about 15 kilometres to the rear to do manoeuvres. That goes down better with the section. This noise of the machine-guns, this advance taste of the trenches, doesn't bode well for us.

We go through several little villages and towards nine o'clock we reach the banks of the Nied, a small tributary of the Sarre, that flows quietly towards Germany. There we halt, waiting for orders, and lie down on the road, for although the march was short we are still drained from the efforts of the preceding days. For my part, I couldn't have gone any further. My feet are complaining, bleeding everywhere, and I believe this is the same for everybody, to judge by my friends alone. Finally, we cross the river and enter into the village of Raville that another battalion has just exited, leaving the place free for us. After crossing the bridge we see on the first barn the number of our section. It's there that we are going to be billeted. Once we go in we are disagreeably surprised. The barn is ruined, full of rubble fallen from the roof which is half collapsed, leaving gaping holes to the sky. There is no hay and no straw, we have to sleep on the rubble or on the earth, unless we go to pinch straw or hay from the neighbouring farms, in the places that the other sections are billeted. Some people even go to scrounge the ration of hay that the artillerymen we see there are giving to their horses tethered all along the roads and the river. The village is like most of those in the Moselle, dull and dirty, with huge piles of manure outside the doors giving onto the half-ruined streets.

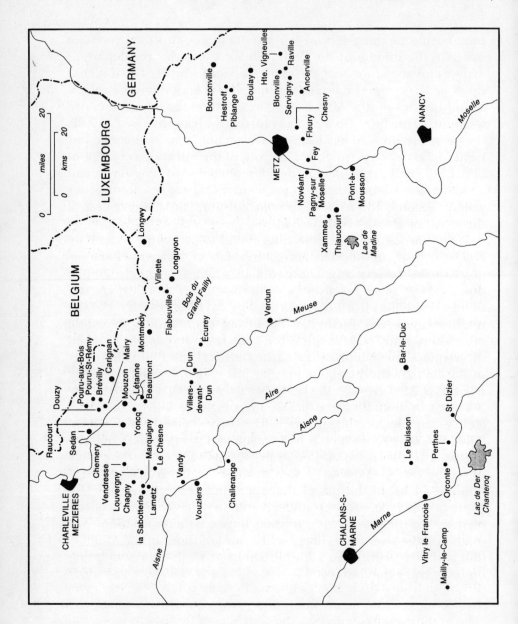

Folcher's War, September 1939 – June 1940

Mother Pelican

The next day, Sunday, there is an opportunity for everybody to go to the religious services which take place thanks to the chaplains of the battalion, in the church, small but pretty, situated on the hill on the outskirts of the village, and surrounded by a cemetery as in all the villages through which we have passed. That must be the custom here, for everywhere you can see the cemetery around the church, even where that might be in the main square of the village. We leave to carry out our exercises in the neighbouring woods where among other things you see a great deal of game, and hares in particular. We spend several days there. It's very pleasant weather during the day, a warm sun, but in the night it is very cold, for even though we are in mid-September heavy white frosts come down every night. We make trenches right on the edge of the Nied. During a battalion manoeuvre when we all go forward line abreast, a group of hares jumps up and runs in every direction. Five of them are killed with blows from shovels, but many succeed in getting through our net! The hunters from our part of the world would be happy to see so much game. In the evening we meet up in the area's two bad bistros. But they are not very well supplied, and we have to go to the neighbouring village, that is Bionville, where there are several groceries and good bars, well-supplied.

The days drift away despite our bad billet where, one night when it started to rain, we were obliged to put up our tents inside the barn to save us from a drenching. The tiredness has passed; our feet being looked after, we are really well again. We found a nice farmer's wife who in the evenings boils up a big cooking pot for us with more than 10 litres of milk. The tin of sugar is on the table and we can drink milk as and when we want. For our part, we pay her generously and the farm becomes the rendezvous for all the section, which unanimously baptises the lady farmer, who is large and with a large swelling in the middle of her neck that never seems to finish, Mother Pelican. Mother Pelican becomes popular in the section and we boast of her

23

merits to our lieutenant who jokes about it, but who does not want to come with us to her place. Furthermore, she builds up her little business for, by dint of working on her, we succeed in making her prepare a large plate of salad and chips for us, as well as a good steak with the meat that we bring her.

We have several outings near the village of Servigny-lès-Raville. We still gorge on plums, pears and lovely apples for all the paths and all the banks of the streams are lined by trees weighed down with the fruit. As for the artillerymen, they bury their horses one after the other. The poor beasts that have just been requisitioned are not used to sleeping out, to the cold, to the rain, or to the change in diet, which in effect hardly consists of more than a few oats eaten in the mud. The trees on the side of the river or the road no longer have bark on them, they have been completely gnawed away by the horses.

One evening, as night comes down, a column of artillery crosses the village. These are the batteries formed in Nîmes. The column is interminable and, as I do not know anybody, I leave the edge of the road, all too soon however, for somebody from Aigues-Vives is passing through and asks around if there is any one here from his neck of the woods. This is Maurice Angevin who bumps right into one of my friends from Saint-Cormes. He is told that there is indeed a person from Aigues-Vives in the company, but they cannot find me, since I had at that moment just left for Mother Pelican's. There are many formations in the area: the 14th Zouaves, which I know contains people from Aigues-Vives, has one of its battalions in the village right near us.

In the end, on a beautiful afternoon, while we are in the middle of a manoeuvre in a wood, the order arrives to stop, and to return to the village to make preparations for departure that very evening at nightfall. One thing that we will not miss is our billet, for really we were very badly placed. But in the end we started to get used to it, once we were acquainted with people, and above all with our Mother Pelican who won't, of course, be following the column. We shall miss her a great deal. It is now 30 September, and the column moves off towards eight o'clock in the evening, still with our full load. We are the last to leave the village, since my section has to form the battalion's rearguard.

The Maginot Line

It was good weather, with a moon shining like broad daylight, and so we managed easily to eat up the kilometres. We arrive in a pretty little town called Boulay. The town is on the edge of the Maginot line and as a result completely evacuated. Despite the darkness, with the help of the moon we can see from the edge of the town numerous camps, barracks and military huts, all new. This is the fortified part of the line, at its greatest strength. Furthermore one can see, still on our right, the countless tracks from Décauville which go towards the fortifications. Going out of the town we keep hugging the Maginot line, and continue to pass new camps. In the end, without getting too tired, and towards midnight or one o'clock in the morning, and after eating a snack we had been issued with, we reach our destination, 25 kilometres on. We have reached Piblange. It's a decent billet, and we lie down happily to sleep on the hay.

The following morning we start work; it's a matter of digging an empty tank trench in the valley between the two hills, each one of which acts as a fortress. We are put to work, with our poor farming tools, and often in water. But after three or four days we give this up, to be replaced by Algerian riflemen from the same division. We go back on exercises, me being part of the company's 'Z' team, that's to say in the group which has to deal with the gas weapons, and I have to follow a course twice a week in the village school so as to learn how to look after the victims of gas, as well as to be able to detect the nature of the gas used in an attack.

We are billeted with a small farmer, retired from the railway, who doesn't know what to do, whether to go or to stay. The village is almost completely evacuated but that makes it a sadness for him to abandon his house, which is understandable, for immediately somebody leaves everything is pillaged. That's the way of war, despite the numerous notices, stuck on the doors, threatening every pillager caught in the act with death. He, or rather his wife, is very kind and prepares and kills for us a little pig weighing 15-18 kilos, that we buy for 30 francs each from the peasants who are leaving and cannot take them away. For a few sous each we eat like this for a few days. Nicely prepared with cabbage or new potatoes, this is a real feast, top marks to our railwayman.

We leave this farm at the end of a few days so as to give up the place to the artillerymen who arrive with their motorised 75s. All of us in the section are lodged near to the station in a brand new barn full of hay. This is the place to sleep really well!

One regiment comes down from the line, or rather it simply abandons its positions; these are the 'merry men',[7] a regiment that has been formed with old lags from prison, emptying at a stroke all the central prisons and remand homes. These hooligans have been punished with long prison stretches and they do not want to stay in the front line. They wander around at random, stealing and looting everything in their way. The officers cannot make them obey, it seems they have hung their colonel! We see them go by in complete confusion, in groups of four or five, dragging all the little Alsatian carts containing the most unimaginable objects, trinkets, clothes, food of every description, poultry and pigs. Everything is looted, everything is stolen. Any village evacuated is sacked just like the rest. The odd café still open favours these wasters; a machine-gun is put over the counter and they take everything. They go through like this for three days, many of them having abandoned their equipment or changed their military clothes for civilians', probably thinking that a nice overcoat is a lot better than a soldier's greatcoat. They even push their cheek as far as stopping officers' cars and interrogating them roughly, asking nearly all of them for tobacco. Some fights take place with people from our regiment, which these characters rob as much as possible as they pass. They make a clean sweep of the stocks in the company's field kitchen. Whipping out knives and bayonets, they even scrounge from the table on which we are eating, and we, rather than fight, give in.

The good weather continues, a lovely sun, and we continue to eat masses of all kinds of fruits, together with really excellent nuts that we find in abundance. You know, it won't be too bad if this goes on.

One afternoon, while on exercise in the woods, we come across the entrance of a fortified work with a huge concrete shell. We even visit an emplacement which is right in the midst of construction, of putting in place the firing-protection covers.[8] It is impressive to see this, where the cement is gushing forth, floated on top of a dome of steel which, to judge by its dimensions, must weigh several thousand kilos. But then, that's it, tourism is over, and they tell us that it is nearly our turn to join the dance; we have to relieve the outposts one night in the very near future. This will not mean going very far, for the most forward lines are only about 15 kilometres in front of us and you can hear the ceaseless fire of machine-guns as well as, at intervals, a few shells coming down, though without doing much damage to either side.

Meanwhile a pretty little village is evacuated there on our right; they evacuate the equipment, because the inhabitants have already been gone four weeks. There are the lorries from the army service corps which carry things endlessly from the town to the village station, for that is the last military post, the engineers having blown up the rails further on and up to the frontier. Every day there are convoys of the most diverse kinds of material. Bedding, furniture, clothes, household utensils or other varied tools, everything is emptied out on the platform of the little station, in the greatest disorder. Thus it is that I can see a tipper truck, full of boxes of all kinds of shoes, coming from a shop in the town, empty all the contents of the container onto the platform as if it had been full of stones or sand. And the best thing is that they stayed there for several days, all higgledy-piggledy in the mud, the boxes burst open under the rain, for at that time it rained every day. And how many other objects were lost there, without benefiting anyone! A completely new stove which was rusting, a mattress, eiderdowns, blankets of all kinds, curtains, ready to wear clothes, all brand new coming from the shops in the town, were there getting soaked. Platform after platform was filled with all kinds of material as if in a public dump . . . One day the men from the Service Corps who were emptying a sweet shop brought us a big oats-sack full of sugared almonds; there were more than 80 kilos. The whole section ate them for days on end, filling the pockets of their greatcoats. Some people made up parcels to send to their children, but the commanding officer prevented them being sent off. Bouzonville was the small town that was emptied in this way.

One night we are leaving on patrol, taking us very close to the front line which seems calm tonight. It's a black night and a fine drizzle envelopes you, you can't see your colleague in front of you, walking across fields, stumbling over the beetroot or the cabbage or getting down into a stream, where you flounder in the water up to your knees, all in total silence. We come back towards the middle of the night soaked through to the bones. For a first reconnaissance mission it was quite a lot, especially as two comrades were missing at roll-call, getting lost crossing a small wood, which happened easily enough since we were forbidden to utter a single word. Both of them returned at daybreak, covered in mud and streaming water from everywhere. A battery of motorised 75s comes to take up a position near the village, which very soon attracts reconnaissance aircraft. We think that things could soon get worse. And well, well, all the officers leave to spy out the company positions. The NCOs as section leaders go in their turn to recce for their respective sections the positions that we are going to take up at the outposts during the night to come. The gaiety has subsided, everyone ponders silently, sucking a sugar almond, on what lies ahead. What will be our first engagement, our true baptism of fire? The CO, on parade, makes a little speech, in which he declares that our fathers in the Great War, (probably this one will soon be called the Small War), went up to the trenches singing, which leads one Zouave to reply that the few who returned came back crying.

This time, it is planned for tomorrow night, everything is ready, packs, arms and ammunition, and we take a siesta one last time on the hay – which we shall soon be missing – before entering the realm of mud and blood. The Commanding Officer himself goes on reconnaissance at night-fall but comes back half-dead, a shell having half-buried him, though it caused more fear than actual harm. And we await the order to depart, the minutes being long in the waiting. Our positions, according to the NCOs, will be beyond the barbed wire lines opposite Sarrelouis. Any retreat is impossible, it seems, as behind us is the barrier of an immense network of barbed wire.

At last, towards 10 o'clock in the evening, the order comes: 'into uniform, with equipment, pack on back', and here we are again silently on the road, but without our mobile support, the kitchens and light vehicles[9] not following the column.

However from the sections that have gone before us the rumour comes back that orders have changed, that we are not going to act as a relief in the way foreseen. Is it really possible after all these preparations? We follow the main road, then, not very far from Thionville, we turn to the left, turning our back completely on the front line. Can it be true that we are not going up the line? I ask the Lieutenant who smiles, which makes me think that he's giving me a little tip, for there were no smiles from him this afternoon. In the end, at our first pause, the news breaks. The Lieutenant explains to us that we have just been replaced by a regiment of Moroccans which is taking our place in the Fifth Division, and in consequence is going up into the line. We are taking their place in the Third Division, which since it has been in the line from the beginning, is now coming back for a rest. Being part of this division, we do as they do; although we haven't earned it, our fate lies elsewhere.

Quick March!

We keep marching and at regular intervals we see the searchlights turning their beams on the frontier, we think probably to find aeroplanes. Now and then flares punch through the darkness on the horizon, but for the moment we turn our back on all that, and that brings a little joy once again back to the battalion. On this particular night is it the joy of not having to go up into the line or maybe the decent weather, for by chance it's not raining, which makes the battalion march along well, despite the heavy packs pulling on our shoulders? It is Tuesday 9 October.

At about four o'clock in the morning I lie down with a pair of my friends under a threshing machine in a barn and, in the straw, lose no time in falling asleep. But there it is, there was hardly more than two hours sleep before a team of men arrived to thresh the wheat, despite our recriminations, which are reasonable since to be woken up like that is no joke after marching more than 30 kilometres loaded down like donkeys. The farmer doesn't mess around any more, and despite our cries starts up his machine, and its clanking noise forces us to clear off.

They are bringing in the grape harvest in the area. I go to see it, as it interests me: just think, the harvests at home, marking the time of the year, that we couldn't make this year.[10] I spend the afternoon with the team of harvesters, in a poor vineyard where little bunches of grapes are hanging hardly bigger than *jacquez*.[11] Then the farmer takes me to see his cellar where a man is stirring up by foot, with his clogs, this meagre harvest, which the chap boasts about, telling me that he is the biggest producer in the area: about 10 hectolitres of a wine that he gets me to taste, which isn't wonderful. All the same I praise his produce to him.

The night comes with the rain, it rains in torrents, it is only just five o'clock in the afternoon when our packs go back on our backs and we start off under the downpour, which redoubles while we get on the road. The road resembles a river, so hard is it raining. We go through

29

some small villages, and after the first break, we are in the suburbs of Metz. We go into the town, at the moment it's still raining buckets; the first small bars, cafés, or even shops still open are taken by storm, everyone wanting to avoid the worst of the rain, despite the protestations of the officers who want to keep us in a column. In the end they are the ones left alone on the road. We are soaked through to our shirts, we drink a glass while huddling together around the stove, for soaked with sweat and with rain we are beginning to feel cold. Outside the officers shout after their sections which are completely dispersed, scattered everywhere in whatever shelter they can find. They proclaim the worst threats against us, but nothing works and it is with difficulty that they manage to get us grouped on the boulevard. Many are still missing. Up front, the Commandant fulminates, he shouts himself hoarse and the departure whistle blasts out, but a good number of the Zouaves stay indoors here, there and everywhere. We start up again, and it continues to rain but less strongly. In the darkness the sections have been dispersed, the companies are mixed and it is like that that we cross the city of Metz where, I must say, whether through the darkness or the rain, I don't see very much. We go into long tunnels under the station. The opportunity is too good, and the battalion, or what's left of it, collapses on the pavements that line the route under the tunnel, despite the Commandant who up front continues to cry himself hoarse with dire warnings, but who, willingly or not, is forced to order a new halt. Ten minutes soon pass and the whistle sounds out at the head of the column; it echoes under the vault, no one budges. The men are at their limit. It is around 10 o'clock in the evening; during the five hours of marching it has not stopped raining, a violent rain, accompanied by a strong wind that freezes your face while at the same time sweat is streaming down from everywhere, for under our wet clothes our pack is even heavier. I shall have a sad memory of this crossing of Metz where the roads and boulevards were transformed into rivers. The officers regroup their sections, but many are still missing at roll-call. My section is scarcely at half strength and we still have 20 kilometres left before arriving at our rest point. However we start off again slowly dragging our legs; it rains less violently, but it is hard, very hard, to have to march. At last after several pauses and much suffering we arrive at our destination. It's in the village of Fey which is two or three kilometres from the first village where we had been billeted on our arrival in the Moselle region, that is Fleury.[12] The pain is too great and we do not even search out the section's billet. We lie down in full kit, completely soaked, in the first barn we come upon, without even taking off either my equipment or my boots which are engorged with water, the water that they have been soaking right through the night. I am completely exhausted after these 40 kilometres of marching where, many times along the route, I thought that it would be better to die immediately than to suffer so much.

I wake up, it is midday; I am cold, I am frozen, I am completely astonished to have on me my cartridge belt, my bayonet. I had not even taken off my gas mask bag, I had thrown my rifle down to one side, my pack on to another and I have lain down at the entrance of the barn on the bare earth. I have never felt so low and so tired. The kitchen is there near at hand, and I can warm myself up a little, while drinking coffee, for the cook is a colleague, a man from Moussac in the Gard.[13] My completely-soaked greatcoat steams from everywhere. However the officers put us on parade, and in the middle of the square, against the normal routine, is the Commandant. He is furious, and exceptional measures will be taken against the laggards. More than half of the battalion has not yet re-joined from the night's march, those who are collapsed in the road along the route are all but threatened with court martial.

The parade is pitiful; we are told of a new departure at nightfall with 40 kilometres to do. The battalion will leave towards five o'clock; the 3rd section will make up the advance guard which will be composed of the 9th section which will take up guard duties at the headquarters of the battalion at the arrival at our next stop. This blow takes the biscuit, my section to be the advance guard and to go on guard on arrival! For the moment, it is two o'clock in the afternoon, in an hour the advance guard has to leave and there are only five of us, the other five who make up the section have not yet re-joined after last night's stage. They continue to arrive in groups of four or five, dragging their legs, incapable of more. The Commandant is furious; he puts a doctor permanently on duty and, after a hasty visit all those fit to leave the same evening, that is soon, are identified one by one. Our colleagues from the platoon turn up as we are about to leave, hobbling along since they can do no more and the news 'it's useless to get out of your equipment, we are leaving again immediately for another forty kilometres and with guard duties on arrival' completely kills them and they drop down in the middle of the road. However they give us a very good meal with coffee and rum, and we start up again. Here we are once more on the road, 10 men and Sergeant Vernhet. All the same, someone has had pity on us, or is it really that the Commandant was afraid of arriving alone on his horse at the first halt, which would surely be the outcome? But he sees clearly, this

Mickey (this is the nickname that the battalion has given him), for he gets us to take off our packs which will be carried on the lorries. We feel the effects of the lighter burden, for we have no more than the African pack made up of a blanket rolled in tent cloth, with a little bit of personal linen, the whole thing rolled up on our shoulders, and like that we can march more easily, just carrying our rifle.

For the moment we are going down a decent road; it's not good weather but at least it's not raining. It drizzles a little on and off, but that is nothing in comparison to the day before. It is still broad daylight, and we knock off the first kilometres quickly enough. At the end of the valley we can see the Moselle and its big trees. And we arrive at the village of Novéant-sur-Moselle where, on 11 September, we were disembarking from the train which had brought us, one month to the very day, for it is now Thursday 11 October. During this month we have eaten up the kilometres around the Department of the Moselle, so as to come back to our departure point. We pass the river, but in the other direction from our arrival, we turn to the left and follow the river along the main railway track that brought us. We pass the boundary stone which marks both the limit of the Department of Meurthe-et-Moselle and the old Franco-German frontier of 1870. We come into the village of Pagny-sur-Moselle as night falls and go into the first café, as much to get something to drink as to get directions on the route, for our group of 10 soldiers has only one sergeant, who knows no more than us; without a map they have started us off like that without any indication other than some vague names of villages. Two decent chaps who are drinking near us, being from the area, but cannot even agree themselves on the route to follow, finally advise us to go via Pont-à-Mousson, which according to them would give us still 45 kilometres to arrive at the next stop. This news struck us all of a heap, for after the 12 or 15 kilometres that we had already done, we were counting on having covered more than half the march. The news defeated us, and it's with great difficulty that we start off again. In the village square, the captain was giving the orders to his battery which was pitching camp there. We go forward to ask him our best route. He is very kind, spreads out his ordnance survey map and explains to us by the light of his torch our approximate route, taking us through Thiaucourt and not through Pont-à-Mousson, which brings the total down to 22 kilometres still to cover.

Immediately after leaving the village, the road climbs steeply, badly, full of ruts, of water and of heavy mud sticking to the shoes, the march slows down, we arrive at a crossing and do not know which route to take. There is a farm there, and by good luck the farmer had not yet gone to bed. A very decent man, he puts us back on the right road, accompanies us for a little while and makes us take a short cut. This time we flounder in the mud half way up our calves, the ends of our coats drag in the mud. Several regiments and convoys of artillery having passed ahead of us, it is in a veritable bog that we advance. In all my life I could never have imagined such mud. Our puttees are covered with it, it trickles from everywhere. Truly, and forgive me if I keep on about it, but it's only in these areas of the east that one can see it like this. I have heard people tell, especially those of the 1914 campaign, stories of the bogs, but really they have to be seen to be believed. We keep on marching and get back on the road which is only a bad track in an even more pitiful state than the short cut. For the fair amount of time that we were floundering without ever coming across a village it became heartbreaking, above all as fatigue reappeared, and it is with great difficulty that we continue. Our legs want to do no more, and what's more we are dropping with sleep. It might be midnight or one o'clock, when a battalion of Moroccan riflemen of the 14th regulars passes us with such an ease of marching style that we are completely crushed. We try to stick closely behind but it is impossible and we soon have to give up, not being able to keep up an equal rhythm. Moreover one comrade from the section can go no further and collapses in the water-filled ditch. We lift him up, encouraging him a little, and go on slowly.

In the darkness, on the right, we make out a farm. I go into the courtyard, where to my great joy I can see a light in the kitchen. Two girls, about 20 years old, open the door to me. They are in the company of three soldiers who, in distress like us, have settled there, and after having drunk a little coffee have decided to sleep in the barns. My colleagues and I would do as much with the greatest pleasure, but we can't even think of it, since on arrival we have to be the guard. In the end we have a nice cup of coffee, well-laced with rum, served to us by these kind young women, and we get back on the road.

On our left at the top of a high hill, a light pierces the black night with its pulsing beams. The sick comrade goes forward with difficulty. He keeps himself upright by a superhuman effort, suffering terribly from a hernia. At last, right at the end of the valley some night-lights tell us that the station is near. This is Thiaucourt. We go into the sleeping little town, where only two or three guards are watching and they gladly lead us to a first aid post where we leave our comrade, completely drained and unable to do the 6 kilometres which are left to us. We stretch ourselves out for a moment on the pavement from where it is absolutely impossible to start up again. Our legs are completely stiff and refuse all movement. On my life, I would not have believed that we could have marched in such a way. For the three nights that we have been marching we must have done more than 120 kilometres, this stage being by far the longest of the three. When you think of that, at a time when, on the main roads of France, we see everywhere filing past ceaselessly, lorries, vans, cars, without counting the trains, while we, always onward, are loaded like donkeys with all that is necessary to march on foot, it is frankly out-rageous. Finally, dragging ourselves rather than marching, we leave the town, in the process of which we take two or three wrong turnings which cost us a few extra kilometres. Some gendarmes put us on the right route and towards five o'clock in the morning we arrive in the village of Xammes, the end of the stage. It is nearly 15 hours that we have been marching, drained, completely at the end of our tether, incapable of more. The battalion adjutant waits for us anxiously at the entrance to the village. He finds that we have really taken our time, since he says that he has been there more than two hours, but he forgets to tell us that he came in a car, which is somewhat less tir-ing. The battalion adjutant pours each one of us a good half-quart of rum, to pick ourselves up, but is unlucky enough to let us see the reserve of rum that we have to guard in the Police Station, two big milk churns of 30 litres each, which has the effect of making the group forget a little of its fatigue, particularly the two of us who are rag and bone men by trade and soaks by preference. After changing my shirt and allowing a little air to my wholly bruised and bloody feet, I have to put back on my boots and full uniform so as to do my hour's guard duty in front of the police post. One hour after us, the battalion turns up, strung out and in a pitiful state, having also lost half of its total strength on the road. Once my hour on guard has passed I stretch out on a mattress which is there in an apartment at the guard post, and I need no lulling to fall right asleep in the next five minutes.

Friday 12 October. I wake up, or rather a comrade wakes me because my hour of guard duty has come back round again. I have slept seven hours without a break and that has done me the greatest good. It's naturally broad daylight, it's nearly midday. Outside the weather is horrible, the violent wind driving a fine rain that falls without relief. The day goes well enough, but we are still on guard the following night. The relief is only supposed to be arriving on Saturday morning, which makes us moan a great deal, for after having marched for three consecutive nights, with more than 100 kilometres in our legs, and still having to pass the fourth night on guard – that is a bit rich.

The relief arrives on the morning of Saturday 13 October, we rejoin our section which is well enough billeted in a barn full of hay; it's there that we are going to be able to sleep well. But for the moment it's not a question of sleeping. Our colleagues are right in the middle of cleaning, or rather I should say polishing, preparing for a review of the troops at 11 o'clock that the General commanding our new division, the Third North African Division, is going to make. It is not without protesting that we also get ourselves ready, for coming off guard duty we have the right to rest, and because of that we refused to attend the review. But the lieutenant turns a deaf ear and whether we like it or not we have to carry out the order. We understand that our lieutenant, who is proud of his platoon, cannot present himself less one section of his platoon on perhaps the first occasion when as an officer he is presenting his men on parade. It's in haste that we prepare ourselves because our comrades are already ready. The lieutenant himself gives a hand to quickly polish our gear.

We spend all the afternoon and the following night in sleeping 18 hours at a single go in a good bed of hay wrapped up in our blankets. This really is a refreshing sleep, I feel fit and really in good form again.

On Sunday after having eaten our meal we decide, with my mate Sugier, to go and visit the American cemetery which, according to the friends who went on that visit yesterday evening or this morning is worth the trouble to see it. We are here right in the middle of the area where the victorious American offensive took place in 1918 which decided the Allied victory. We leave despite uncertain weather, with at times a fine rain falling. But that doesn't make us draw back, we have gone through so many torrents that one more or less makes no difference. We march a couple of kilometres on a decent road and suddenly in the middle of big trees we are in front of a huge monumental façade all in freestone. We go inside through a massive doorway which is in the middle, and in front of us, on a vast lawn stretched out as far as the eye can see, are lines of crosses, all in white marble, which like a young vine back in my part of the world, keep an impeccable symmetry. Whichever direction you look in they are always in a straight line, not one sticking out beyond another even by a millimetre. It is admirably kept. We are fascinated by this green sward, so well cut that it is really a vast carpet extending right to the horizon, the soft green is truly moving. We go down the central pathway where

the crosses from time to time become stars, also in marble, perhaps
to mark the tombs of officers or probably a question of religion.[14]
Whatever it might be, the stars are cut and placed in the same symmetry as the crosses, with which they are as one. To the right, to the
left, on the transverse pathways, at each central point and at the end
of each path are monuments which recall the facts of individual or
collective feats of arms in the American offensives. And always the
crosses and the marble stars, more than a metre high, follow each
other on the green carpet. It is at the bottom of the central pathway
that is the most beautiful monument. They built a superb chapel
which one gets to up several marble steps. At the end of the chapel –
the whole thing in white marble – is a vast marble map encrusted with
gold which shows the critical points and the different battlefields of
the American offensive in the region Pont-à-Mousson-Thiaucourt,
on the ground of which has been built this superb cemetery which
holds the remains of those who took part in the glorious American
offensive in 1918 and who lost their lives there.

Our visit is finished and it is in silence that we leave this immense
field of rest thinking of the thousands of men who sleep there, so far
from their families, of their sad fate and of that which awaits us, for
it is not encouraging in the situation in which we find ourselves, to
see almost everywhere these vast cemeteries of white or black crosses.
We get back to the village as night falls. On our arrival we learn that
departure has been officially announced for tonight at midnight.
We eat our supper, draw some rations for the journey, and after a couple of hours spent in one of the village bistros, we prepare our
kitbags, on which we doze while waiting for departure. At midnight,
the column moves off and the eternal question returns: where are we
going? What is certain, is that we are going to get on a train at
Thiaucourt station, where we swiftly arrive after a short and problem-
free march. On the unlit platforms, with the least noise possible, we
find our 'couchette' wagon (horses in lengthways: 8, men: 30). We
embark, bags under our heads, against the partition wall of the
coach, packed like sardines. Each one stretches out as best he can,
the boots of one on the stomach of the other; somehow or other we
are all bedded down. We fall asleep all the same, for the train stays a
long time at the platform. In the end it starts softly enough and the
clickety-click of the rails lulls us to sleep.

In the Manger

When day comes, we realise that we are coming down into Bar-le-Duc, which we reach towards eight or nine o'clock. This is quite a long stop that we take advantage of to have a snack on the platform. Lots of troop trains are halted in the station and the talking point is always the same: where can they really be taking us? Some people claim that we are going to Marseille to embark for North Africa. Others set loose the notion that we are going up north, into the Pas de Calais. The Parisians, more observant, rightly point out that we haven't been given rations for the trip, apart from a mean snack, and therefore we can't be going that far. Their reasoning is generally thought to be the nearest to the mark, but to be truthful nobody knows anything. The bugle sounds and we gently move off. Almost immediately we head in the direction of Reims. The plains are covered again with water, the streams are transformed into torrents and the rivers overflow everywhere into the fields. All you can see is vast expanses of water, produced by the downpours of the last few days. At the moment we are travelling through Champagne, in the middle of chalk hills where, on the very side of the railway embankment, can be seen the shelters and dugouts, still propped up, that our fathers dug on the Champagne front during the war of 1914.

Towards 11 o'clock there's a stop, at the village of Challerange, not far from Grandpré. The train stops at a platform and the order to get off is given. The companies group themselves not far from the station, in the middle of huge fields. The weather is superb, a real sun that warms us up and which is an invitation to stretch out on the green grass, even though it is by now 15 October. We have a long break, during which the heavy equipment and the horses are unloaded. At midday we have our meal at this spot and we eat it with a good appetite after we have been to fetch the food that the cooks have prepared on the truck where their evil-looking tame crow sits, gorging himself on the waste produced by the field kitchen.

Towards two o'clock the battalion is called back into order and we

start off again – but on foot. Once out of the village, we cross a vast
airfield laid out there for the war on the huge meadows and fallow
lands. There are English fighter squadrons here; the pilots and
mechanics rush up to the edges of the road as we pass. These are the
first Englishmen that we have seen since the whole merry-go-round
started. They really like seeing the Zouaves marching past and distribute a large number of cigarettes which are gratefully received.[15]
We can see their small fighters, ready for take-off, arranged in groups
of four or five and camouflaged under clumps of trees.

We pass enormous fields where they are tearing up the sugar beet
which is piled in great mountains on the side of the road. We go
through nice villages which all have a much more pleasant air than
the villages of the Moselle. The inhabitants are very kind to the
troops, they bring us drinks on the side of the road and make generous distributions of good, big apples that we devour. Although it is
very tiring, the day's march is much more interesting than the long
night marches across the Moselle. While marching we can always
admire the landscape, which in this hilly countryside changes ceaselessly. We cross the river Aisne and down its agreeable valley we reach
the next stop somewhat late into the night, after 30 kilometres of
marching. We are in the village of Vandy where, despite the late
hour, the villagers are still up. We are really tired, and with good reason: we have had nothing to eat. The kitchen, who knows why,
couldn't follow the column. We are given a tin of sardines to share
between five, without bread, and this causes an outbreak of great
discontent in the section, which feels that after such a hard march, we
were entitled to a rather heartier meal than that. With my partner I
go round the village and in a big farm we are given as much hot milk,
well-sugared, as we want. We even get some bread which we dunk in
it, which does us a lot more good than the sardines. The meal over,
we drink a small glass of liqueur and stretch out with pleasure on the
straw in the barn where my section is lodged.

The next day reveille is pretty late and after drinking coffee in the
field kitchen which finally showed up in the night, and washing in the
fountain, we tour the village that is a bit too nice for us to have any
chance of staying long. In fact, at roll-call we learn the next destination; departure at midday after the meal, without our packs, which
will be carried on the lorries, which makes us predict a really long
march. The 40 kilometres in prospect do not make us rejoice.

However we go on across charming countryside climbing some
pretty high hills on slopes which are often steep, and coming back
down almost perpendicularly on the other side, which is extremely

tiring. We cross the hills of the Ardennes, which are virtually mountains. In the valleys, well-cultivated fields alternate with grasslands. On the slopes are many fruit-trees among which apples predominate, beautiful apples that are to be seen along the whole route. We eat ourselves to death on them, red, white, all types. We keep going through villages which seem to have an easy enough life in this region where there is also a lot of livestock, cows and above all colts, in the fields.

After having gone up and down I don't know how many times, we were crossing some large woods of oak and hornbeam which stretch as far as the eye can see. From the top of these hills you cannot see the end of them. Night falls, and we stop in the village of Lametz, a prolonged stop, but not our destination, that village being still a few kilometres further on. Although being able to do no more we have to put ourselves to it, and through a vast wood we arrive towards 10 o'clock in the evening at Marquigny (Ardennes). I am really tired, to such an extent that, as on the day before, I don't look for anything to eat. Moreover, for my part I have eaten several kilos of apples on the journey, which means that I am not hungry.

The platoon is scarcely at half-strength, the other half having come to a standstill, whether in the farms of the preceding villages or in the cowsheds encountered in the course of the march. We are badly billeted, the platoon having to share a cow manger where there are five very badly-kept cows, covered in dung. We spread ourselves out all the same and sleep there next to the cows which chew and give us funny looks.

The next day means a visit to the village, which being pretty small, hardly captures our hearts. Built at the bottom of a valley, surrounded by many high hills covered with thick woods, the village is dirty. Many of the houses are in ruins or virtually so. However, in the square appears a beautiful large house – almost new compared to the others – that is dubbed 'the chateau'. It is there that the Colonel with his staff install themselves. It is 16 October and we learn that we are to stay there for some weeks. It is really bad luck to be in such a hole, where nearly all the platoons are badly billeted. The walls of the lofts and the barns, no less than the roofs, are all draughty. So we settle down the best we can in the manger of the cows, which we have to keep clean so as not to be stunk out, and we even have to feed them so as to sleep quietly. The farmer is an old soak who thinks only of drink instead of working, and no longer does anything now that his workers have been called up, not even to groom his horses and colts, which are very beautiful.

The days pass. We exercise by scouring the surrounding woods in every direction. The shelter trenches are dug not far from the camps. Then, and we are now in November, the major works begin, which the companies take part in two days a week by turn. We go some 20 kilometres away to work on the embankment of a railway being built for the transportation of equipment used to construct a second fortified line, of the Maginot-type with blockhouses. Then we are put on wood-cutting to clear the way for where the anti-tank lines have to pass and to give fields of fire for the blockhouses being constructed. All that takes us quite far into the forest, 15, 18, 20 kilometres, and as many to come back, always on foot, and when we come back from these days we are completely exhausted, not by the work but by the march, for really this is overdoing it. It means that we do not do a great deal of work, everybody thinking on arrival about resting on the site so as to gain strength for the march back. Often in this month of November, we return soaked in the evening, as a result of rain that hasn't stopped during the day, while we march in the mud, for the tracks under the trees are so trodden down that they are no more than huge quagmires. As for cutting through the woods, they are so thick that it's not even worth thinking about it. We go forward in this mud, and often our legs sink in up to halfway for at least 10 kilometres which is very tiring.

The Phoney War

In the village we get organised as well as we can. The farmer makes us clear out of his stable so as to bring in his heifers and we are currently in the open granary with the rain coming in in a good many places. We plug the holes in the mud walls with straw. Just now the nights are long. After eating our meal we go for a stroll to the only café in the village, but it is small and the tiny room is packed out. Two poor old boys are in despair with so many people. A village of 150 inhabitants which is suddenly invaded by 1500 men, that changes their habits a little, so that the poor old man re-stocks his café in vain when he is cleaned out the same evening, and then has to wait for one or two weeks without anything. But we are beginning to know the surroundings and we make several trips around and about. It's the village of Chagny, three kilometres away, which is our first choice. There are no troops there and three café restaurants where you can get good enough meals well-washed down, which means that you get back to your straw bed in a happy enough mood. There is also La Sabotterie and Louvergny, but although they might be better than where we are based, they have troops and this means that we are not very well received. The small town of Le Chesne is not far, since we are halfway between Mézières-Charleville and Vouziers, where the bolder spirits, despite the fact that it is forbidden, venture a visit on Sunday.

December. The days are cold and the nights stretch out, also very cold in our awful lodgings. In the village square they have just installed a fireplace, a kind of soup kitchen made of wood, where we can get warm drinks and even sample some bottles of chateau-bottled wine. Up until nine o'clock in the evening you can play various games at the centre or at least read the various books held in the library. There we can do our letter writing, warm enough and in some real comfort.

Often in the evening we go to the farms where, while drinking a bowl of warm milk, we listen to the information coming over the

41

radio. The farm of old Legros is one of the main places frequented, for a veritable den is starting up there, where, apart from milk, are sold a good many litres of rum and eau-de-vie of all kinds. What's more a dance is put on where the female partners are provided by the daughters of a baker who comes on her round every evening to sell bread and cakes, to which she adds a real trade in writing paper, ink, pencils and all sorts of knick-knacks, even selling a few fancy gifts to the keenest. One day when I was buying a *brioche* and speaking in dialect, this good woman replied to me in the same idiom and I learned that she was a native of Saint-Jean-du-Gard, married after the other war to a man from the Ardennes who was a refugee in the Gard, who she had followed back to his area after the war, where he had the occupation of a baker. She was very happy to meet some people from her home area. She brought with her her two daughters who were nearly 20 and who were sometimes accompanied, particularly on Sunday evenings, by some of their girlfriends. That made for quite a good gathering where some of the men with more courage than the others made it possible for the group to spend several happy hours. These evenings went right on into the night even though the order for lights out had been given long before.

For some days now, passes for leave have been arriving. The first people begin to go home, Christmas approaches and the cold redoubles. Manoeuvres take place, with the division's tanks participating, during a violently cold snap. One afternoon when the weather was good enough the raising of the colours took place on the platform at the exit from the village, near Louvergny. The regiment is present in full strength and is drawn up company by company in a square formation on a vast field of wasteland. The Colonel arrives mounted on a superb horse and cuts through to the centre of the square, just as the shout 'present arms' is heard, while the music of 'La Marseillaise' sounds from all the trumpets of the unit. The horse shies and dislodges the Colonel by rearing dangerously, but he is a good horseman and manages to master the beast. However, he dismounts to make his speech for the presenting of the colours by an honour guard, gloved in white, in the middle of the huge open space. Then there is the review and march past on the main road towards Charleville to the sound of the Algerian military band.

Here we are at Christmas, which we must spend in our sad village. They give us what we need for a midnight supper together and a pass for the night out. With some comrades we go to Midnight Mass. The little church is full to bursting and a well-organised choir sings various Christmas carols. The stronger singers among us don't take much persuading to help them out. After Mass, we have our feast in the loft and that goes on so late that at six o'clock in the morning, when the band comes along with a full complement of drums and bugles to sound the reveille in the farm, we have still not gone to bed.

Towards 10 o'clock I go up to the church which is on the top of a hill looking down on the village. It is magnificent from up there. There is a heavy frost and the sun, which comes through at this very moment, makes its magnificent crystals sparkle brilliantly. After Mass they serve up an excellent meal where we have a piece of the traditional turkey well washed down with two or three different kinds of wine. In the afternoon my friends all go out into the various places round and about. As for me, I prepare my pack and all my equipment for, unless the unforeseen happens, I am to be one of those allowed to go on leave this evening.

Towards eight o'clock in the evening, I get my pass, and it is in a happy state of mind that I go to the chateau to wait for the departure of the battalion's small lorry, which is due to take us to the little town of Le Chesne. It is extremely cold, but so what now that we are going. Towards 10 o'clock, we are at Le Chesne from where some excellent buses deliver us to Vouziers where we arrive towards midnight. The town is very quiet. Most people have celebrated Christmas the night before, and have turned in early. It is not at all the same at the station where, in the huts on planks which serve as waiting rooms, there is a great hullabaloo. There are soldiers from all the branches of the army, waiting like me for the leave train, and some of them, after suitably celebrating Christmas, make more noise than is necessary, which starts a row with those who want to sleep and it needs the intervention of some of the officers to get everything calm again. It is horribly cold in these huts even though two stoves are red right up to their stove-pipes.

Six o'clock. We go down on to the platforms after drinking a horrible mug of coffee handed out by the soldiers. At last an awful train with old wagons arrives from Verdun, and a general scrum takes place. Day breaks in a thick mist which is really more like frost for the telephone wires along the railway are as thick as cables. Slowly, towards nine o'clock, we arrive at Reims. After the obligatory formalities at the station where they check our passes, we are directed into a lodging centre which has been installed in the old covered-market, or rather a huge exhibition hall. On the way, all the roads going across us and all the squares are guarded by armed men to hinder any escape from the column by soldiers who, like me, would very much like to see the town and in particular the Cathedral. At last, on

the corner of a road, I succeed in slipping away, followed by a colleague. We stroll down several roads and boulevards, but it is not a
very cheerful walk because the freezing fog is ever thicker and you
can't see more than 20 paces in front of you. At last we are before the
Cathedral. To be at Reims and not to be able to see this monument,
of which we have heard so much, that would really be too hard. We
do a tour round it without being able to see very much because to
some degree the fog, and to some degree the sandbags piled up
against the most beautiful parts of the building, hide it all from view.
You can scarcely see the huge towers which spring up towards the sky.
We were getting ready to go back inside when an MP patrol traps us
in the passage and takes us back to the lodging centre, which is well-
enough appointed. The ladies of the Red Cross offer us something to
eat and drink but at a pretty dear price. Inside someone is screaming
down the mike, giving out as soon as they are available the numbers,
destinations and departure details of the trains. Between fifteen and
eighteen thousand men are there which makes for a tremendous
din. Between the announcements, some of the men take part in a
sing-song and the hours pass quickly enough.

13.30. Train number six, destinations Dijon, Lyon, Narbonne, at
last this is the one which is going to take us home, a terrific express,
which take it from me is better than the cattle trucks. We leave Reims.
The sun bursts through the mist and we don't miss the chance to
look at the city disappearing into the distance, with its superb towers
shining in the sun, their dimensions, in comparison, make the houses
seem quite small. Vitry-le-François, Saint-Dizier, Chaumont, where we
begin to see quite a lot of snow, which astonishes us given that we
have not seen any at all in the Ardennes. Then it's Langres with its
elevated town perched on the top of the plateau which carries its
name. Spending part of the journey standing at the door of the carriage I look out all the time at the canals which follow one after the
other with their lock-gates and their big barges. Everything interests
me. Night falls and despite myself I have to leave the doorway. Now
we are going down the valley of the Rhône on the right bank. We go
through the Département of Ardèche, then into Gard and at the
doorway I breathe in happily a light mistral which is not blowing too
cold. It's quite a few days since I breathed the mistral. We used to
curse it often but nonetheless I find it good this morning. It is so
different from the climate of the Moselle or the Ardennes.

Six o'clock, Nîmes, at last. However I stay on the train and get
down at Lunel, and at half past seven I am at home where I am happy
to return after such a trip. After parents, friends and familiar routines

it's above all my bed which gives me pleasure, the big bed that is so good after having slept, half dead with fatigue, no matter where, in barns on straw, on the earth, in a ditch or in a wood. I spend my leave at home where I put myself back to work.

But that's it; 10 or 12 days are quickly passed, and I have to go off again. I leave on 7 January, a Sunday evening, and I make the return journey in a much less cheerful state than when setting out. I get off at Fismes, not far from Reims, which is the official station for people returning, where I meet up with some friends who, like me, are returning from leave. Together we wait for the train which has to take us up to the front. A heavy frost falls which freezes us, for there are so many soldiers that the small waiting-rooms cannot contain all the flood of them; the cafés nearby are full to bursting and we stamp up and down the frozen pavements. At last we leave and towards 11 o'clock in the evening we arrive at Vouziers. It's horribly cold in the vans and in the small lorry which takes us to the billet. In a black mood I go back to my miserable attic where it is freezing hard. My section does justice to the couple of bottles that I have brought with me, and I notice that works are still continuing. We have changed sectors, abandoning the wood of Louvergny and Vendresse and it's in the wood of La Cassine which is a bit farther, but on the road, the one thing compensating for the other. It's horribly cold. The whole month of January it freezes hard, the thermometer often going down to between −20 and −30, even going as far as −35. We have to saw the bread in slices that then have to be grilled to be unfrozen. The wine is taken to the wood in canteens from which nothing will flow. In the farm we suffer a great deal from the cold. We have, it is true, installed a stove, made from a nasty petrol can, which is endlessly stuffed with wood, but there are so many draughts that the warmth given out vanishes immediately. At the end of January a heavy covering of snow falls. One morning at reveille our blankets are all white, the snow as much inside as outside.

One Sunday evening, the platoon in which a friend from Calvisson is serving, accidentally sets fire to its farm. The fire makes rapid progress despite the prompt help given, and the whole farm burns, including the equipment, which the platoon has not had the time to get out. The bags of cartridges and of grenades explode in the middle of the fire. Through the whole night, in two-hour shifts, we have to operate the fire pump by hand, even though the fire may be out, for everything has burned up, and just in case the fire returns, it has to be kept going; if the pump has been stopped only for five minutes the pipes freeze up. I am doing my guard duty between midnight and two o'clock and I catch one of those flus which really hit you, and I go into the infirmary on 1 February with quite a fever. Three days later I am on my feet after a series of cuppings.[16] It is still snowing and we continue working just the same, but the company is reduced in numbers. Despite its nominal strength of 160 men, there are often only 20 or 30 men who can march, the others being more or less knocked out by the wave of influenza. On several occasions there is a rumour that we are about to depart, and we even make a couple of false starts.

In mid-February the weather eases a little. Towards the 20th, the snow starts to melt, and we go to the station of Vendresse to unload wagons of rails, scrap iron, barbed wire and all the other material for the building of the fortified line. Since no soldier wants to march nearly 40 kilometres there and back, the staff decide to place the lorries of the engineering corps at the disposal of the companies, which is a lot better and the work advances quickly. The end of February is beautiful and on 2 March we leave the billet of Marquigny. We march as the rearguard of the battalion and, via Louvergny and La Cassine, we arrive at midday at our halt at Chémery-sur-Bar. Although tired by the kilometres and our packs, we go around the village which is very pretty, situated on the main road to Raucouart and Sedan. We stop off in some of the bistros of the town then we go to bed early in the garrets of the town hall where we are billeted, for tomorrow we have to go off again.

Sunday morning at four o'clock we are back on the main road. A light cold wind is blowing. It makes for good marching, and we also knock off the kilometres. We go through several small villages, then we are at Raucouart, with all its factories, where we go through marching in step since the Colonel is on the village square watching the battalion march past. We climb and descend endlessly. At the summit of one of these hills we see the valley of the Meuse which stretches out before us to the horizon. On the left, Sedan with its clock tower which helps us to identify the town. We go down towards the river, and towards 10 o'clock in the morning we go through Remilly where several formations from our division are stopped and watching, with the civilians, the Zouaves marching through the streets.

We pass near to Sedan, leaving it a little on the left. We cross the Meuse, and several canals, on bridges which are all mined, ready to go off, guarded by the engineers. After the Meuse, a huge plain between that and the Chiers which flows into the Meuse. This plain, the Lieutenant explains to us, was supposed to have become one of the finest aerodromes in France. And indeed we see on the sides of the road unfinished works. They dug a vast lake for seaplanes at the cost of billions, over several years, without any benefit, for after several governments had come and gone the project was abandoned and the billions swallowed up. We are following the Chiers at the moment. On the left, a smart little place, Douzy, one of the last villages before Belgium. We turn to the right, still following the outline of the airfield and we arrive after an hour at our stop in the village of Mairy, perched halfway up a little hill from where the view stretches to the left over the plain of the Meuse which, at two kilometres from the village, flaunts its silver ribbon. In front of us there is the Chiers one kilometre away. We are in the groin that the two rivers form. The billet is in the stable of an old farmer who has no more stock. It's good enough, although there isn't really too much straw, the little which does cover the bare earth having served as the bedding all winter for our predecessors. We settle in well enough, and despite tiredness I take myself off to visit the village which is pretty big. The main road as usual is full of large piles of manure which flows right up to the doorsteps of the houses. Many animals, cows and brood mares in large numbers. Two nice cafés are already full of Zouaves. I go up to the end of the village where the church is, small but very fine, and as in all these places surrounded by the cemetery. The monument to the dead of the 1914–18 war, civilians and soldiers, then, to finish, a little military camp serving as barracks for the troops of the fortress and of the engineers who are there. A big mess hut and a sports field, a decent set up of shower baths which we are entitled to use, complete this little barracks.

Monday morning 4 March, on waking, they explain to us that we haven't come here to enjoy ourselves but really to toil. The defences are nearby, surrounding the village, and immediately we begin. Each platoon studies its combat positions opposite the Chiers, on the Belgian frontier, one kilometre from Douzy for my platoon, and for my section right in the village square, where I have to set up my machine-gunner. Each section under the orders of the Sergeant and under the direction of Lieutenant Levrat, fits out its own position. Other platoons and companies do the same, facing the Chiers or the Meuse. The defences progress rapidly for we are on the spot. On some days we leave them so as to help the engineers to dig the foundations of the casemates all along the river. Then after the carpenter-joiners have made huge frames, we pour in the concrete. Once started, the pouring continues ceaselessly day and night by the glow of an electrical plant. For 80, 100 or 120 hours the concrete gushes forth whatever the weather, despite the rain and storms. By teams of 120 or 150 men, who are relieved every eight hours, the defences progress very quickly for all the villages are veritable anthills of soldiers of all kinds. The endless lines of lorries carry gravel, cement and scrap iron, and the casemates arise from the earth from everywhere. The work is very well directed by the officers of the engineering corps who put every man in his right place, not hindering his neighbour. Everyone works, for it's a matter of holding our ground with the machines, each one of which pours out 15 barrel loads of gravel and three sacks of cement every five minutes of work. The defences hurry on, we even work on Sunday morning from six until ten and when the concrete is flowing, all day.

Sunday 10 March, I go with some friends to see the area round and about, just to pass the afternoon. We go to Brévilly where there is the Second Battalion of the Regiment. Then after a stop at various drinking haunts – which make a pile, for there are a lot of troops everywhere – we cross the Chiers and visit the village of Pouru-Saint-Rémy which really seems more like a small town and owes its importance to several big smelting works which are on the river. We go on as far as a small village, Pouru-aux-Bois, on the Belgian frontier, from where one is looking over all the valley of the Chiers and over the Meuse, the view stretching into the distance as far as the town of Carignan.

On 13 March, I go away again for my second leave. After the evening meal I go with some colleagues to take the train. Going alongside the Meuse we arrive at Mouzon, a pleasant village on the Sedan road and, through Reims and the usual journey, I arrive at home on the morning of the 15th, and spend the Easter holidays there. I leave again on the evening of the 26th, and at Lunel I meet again one of my colleagues from Gallargues, a regular solider who is also in the 12th Zouaves, but not in the same battalion. We are heading for the same place and that makes things a lot better. I return to the billet on the night of the 27th, where nothing has changed. The defences are much further forward and are worked more intensively than ever, interrupted from time to time by guard duty, whether at the posts or in the various important munition depots set down all over the place.

The month of April is really beautiful and the defences improve all the time. On 21 April I go with some colleagues to visit the surrounding hills. Everywhere are casemates, trenches, telephone wires. Further behind, the artillerymen have also worked, digging in their 75's, and even the 155's are half-buried, camouflaged as best we can from the view of aeroplanes. We come back along the banks of the Meuse on which float a large number of barges full of material for the construction of the defensive line. It's nice weather and in the fields we gather not flowers but the leaflets dropped by German aeroplanes in the last few days, of all types and sizes.[17] At the end of April work stops suddenly. Everyone to combat positions, leave cancelled. It's only a false alert which lasts for four or five days and then work starts up again. However, now we are seeing every day some aerial combat. The machine-guns crackle and we all go outside to see the planes which are manoeuvring high up, leaving behind them the smoke trails of their movements, climbing or diving. This last week in April, the artillery of the air defence corps fires repeatedly. I no longer work and I am permanently on air defence with a mate. In the middle of a field, near to the section that is working, we have installed our two twin light machine-guns on a special anti-aircraft firing apparatus, and every day, lying down in the cool grass, we wait for events, binoculars in hand. We look more at the people passing by on the main road for Sedan than at the aeroplanes which go over only rarely, and outside our range of view. The beginning of May passes like this. The platoon is at the moment putting down the long lines of barbed wire which surround our positions and are going to join up with the big network of barbed wire which is more than 10 metres wide. In the evening the boules matches are in full swing. A big fête is being organised for Whitsun, with a boules tournament, singing, dancing and several other games, not forgetting the *belote* competition. The regiment's band is supposed to lend a hand, because it's the day of the village fête. Everyone goes at it cheerfully to celebrate for they have planned two days without work to reward us for the hard labour we have just done.

II

A ONE-SIDED BATTLE

The German Air Attack

Suddenly, without warning, as dawn was starting to break on the morning of Friday 10 May , the bugle sounded reveille. It might have been between 3.30 and 4, two hours earlier than usual. But already the orders arrive, with our half-dressed lieutenant. 'In uniform, pack on back, leave nothing here, in five minutes everyone outside in position, each one in his combat post'. What an avalanche of orders! At last we are up and somehow or other get prepared, with bag, ammunition, weapons, everything is taken to the positions which isn't more than about 100 metres away for me, for I take my place in a shelter that we have made in the main square of the village, a shelter built with stones and surrounded with sandbags. From there my view and my field of fire stretch on to a straight sloping road which goes for a kilometre up to the Chiers, where, immediately over the bridge is the village of Douzy, and beyond that the Belgian frontier.

The whole battalion is ready in position when the sun rises. At this moment I receive the order to leave my position and to go as on every other day to set up my twin machine guns in their usual place for air defence, in the fields at the end of the village, between two forts, 300 metres from the river. We begin to think that this doesn't look like a manoeuvre. The newspapers don't arrive as they usually do every morning, when they are distributed to us in profusion after reveille. The day looks beautiful and the sun climbs in a cloudless sky. Seven o'clock. Nobody, not even the engineers, seems to be starting on the defences. That worries us and seems a bit suspicious. Rumours circulate but no formal news. Somebody brings me a written order, which says that we have to be on full alert, enemy aircraft being reported flying low and machine-gunning all the troops in Belgium. Five minutes after this, the news breaks: Belgium and Holland have been attacked at daybreak. The consequence is not long delayed for suddenly, towards 7.30 and in a frightening din, four planes emerge from the hill behind us shaving the roofs and the trees. They rain a veritable hail of bullets down on us raking the positions and guard rooms.

That lasted scarcely more than a few seconds, but as a start it took us very much by surprise, not seeing them come behind the hills, plunging nose-down into the valley and machine-gunning everything they went by, without even having the time to make any gesture to protect ourselves. The lieutenant commanding the company gets us to make a report of each pass made, and also of our firing back. But so many attacks follow one on the other that it is useless to make reports. Suddenly about 40 aeroplanes emerge, all from behind, and with a frightful throbbing of engines plunge down on our positions, dropping bombs in strings and machine-gunning nearly at point-blank range. One of them passes me in a flash at barely 30 metres from the range of my guns. Although it passed so quickly I still had the time to make out the machine-gunner, his weapon in his hand, which was spitting out its bullets in every direction. It's so quick and so powerful that despite oneself one instinctively makes a gesture of protection and just when you are thinking again of firing, the bird is already far away. That doesn't matter, but in the middle of this field without shelter, hearing the bullets whistling everywhere around me, I was afraid.

During a lull, towards eight o'clock, the town crier, his horn in his hand, tells the civilians by order of the battalion staff that they must bring all their grazing stock back into the village. Poor people, who only yesterday were in the middle of working in their fields! They are incapable of any movement, all more or less – and with good reason – dead with fear. They carry out the order all the same and bring back the cows, mares and chickens which are in large numbers in the fields surrounding the village. They hurry between two bursts of gunfire, for time presses. In an hour, the paths left free in the network of barbed wire will all be irremediably closed. Some of the people abandon their beasts rather than risk their lives. Poor things, seized with panic, they let out terrible howls and don't want to move on.

Towards ten o'clock, after a lull of at least an hour, the dance begins again. Some planes, at meteoric speed, spray us copiously with bombs and bullets. It's frightening to see these machines diving while spitting from everywhere and making a howl produced, we think, by the bombs which are falling down. In any case the noise is terrible and despite ourselves we are not too reassured. With my firing partner, we have rapidly dug a hole and made a parapet all around with stones and earth. Inside there, you feel all the same more secure than on open ground. It makes us even braver, and at each overflight we empty our magazines, that is 50 rounds, on these meteors which seem to be laughing at our poor guns. In this limited area we have nearly 50 machine-guns or twin light machine-guns, firing at the same time, but that doesn't intimidate these planes which become more and more daring, shaving our positions ever closer. We fire too quickly, not being able to take the plane at the desired angle of shot, which is anyway virtually impossible given their high speed and above all their very low altitude, despite the refined aiming mechanism which our gunners have been supplied with.

At midday a new lull. Mealtime passed, nobody was hungry. What's more the mobile kitchens left the village immediately after the early hours of the morning and have been set up in the wood eight or ten kilometres behind us. In fact we are thirsty for the horrors of the first hour made us feverish and it's with relief that we drink some wine diluted with really cold water. Towards two o'clock the battle starts up even more impressively, but it seems that the planes are flying less over our positions. They always come from behind the hills, swoop down on the small town of Mouzon and follow the Meuse in the direction of the river as far as Sedan where we lose sight of them. It would seem that the main railway line is their only target this afternoon. The line which links Paris to Belgium via Charleville-Mézières and Sedan seems to interest them, to judge by the number of bombs which are falling now on the left side of the river, toward the railway side, and now on the right side, where there is the main road from Belgium to Sedan. Several of them continue to pass over the village while machine-gunning us, but they do not drop bombs. However, on our right, on the side of the Chiers, several fires have broken out, the great sawmill of Brévilly in flames. Several of the farms and houses burn also at Pouru-Saint-Rémy. There are even some at Carignan that one can see on the Chiers, at the extreme right of our viewpoint.

The town crier passes by again and, from my position, I hear him very well warning the population to hold themselves ready for any eventuality, the village being ready for evacuation from one minute to another. I am relieved, and I go to take my post in the position on the square of the village, where I learn from colleagues that the 3rd Battalion is leaving to go forward to Belgium, towards Arlon and Luxembourg. For the moment, this does not apply to the 1st Battalion which stays in its positions on the frontier in the outposts. Towards four o'clock, a new series of bombardments begins, on the road which runs along the side of the Chiers, on the Brévilly side. A plane, crossing all the unfinished aerodrome, lets drop a whole string of bombs, and goes on to crash in a huge explosion of noise on the other side of the river. Immediately a black column of smoke rises from the point of the crash. That's one which will not come over us again, we think. But it has wreaked havoc, a bomb fell directly on a car coming from the 2nd Battalion for refuelling. The soldier-driver was killed and horribly mutilated, several others coming behind with cars were wounded, four horses lie dead on the field and what is more, and this is the most terrible thing, a little boy of about 12, who had been in the car for who-knows-what reason, was also killed. From my position, with field-glasses, I can make out very clearly the sequence of this sad spectacle. One hour later, I learnt that the soldier who had been killed was actually someone from the Gard with three children, being from around Nîmes, and whom I had often chatted to when refuelling.

However, one fact surprises us a good deal, something which in the panic of the morning we had not thought about, and which is now on every tongue all the time: what are the French and English aeroplanes doing? Where are they, given that there is not a single one of them hunting down all this formidable deployment of air power? But no, not one makes itself seen. You can't even hear the noise of our engines, so very different from that of the others. Now evening descends and that brings on redoubled violence. An observer from the Battalion has his thigh shot through by a bullet. However one plane is hit by the firing of our machine-guns and crashes behind the village of Douzy, immediately over the Chiers.

Night falls and with it calm returns. Those off duty profit from it by going to the rear to fetch a meal. The town crier comes by for a third time and announces to the poor civilians their new fate, to have to hold themselves ready to evacuate the village during the night. We eat the meal on the grass, right on the edge of the trench of the first group from the section. Apart from three or four men on guard in their respective positions, all the section come together there to eat. When we have got really settled and the stew, good enough that evening, was going down well, for despite everything we'd begun to be hungry, at that precise moment when one of us was handing round the wine, two aeroplanes burst in without us even having heard them come. We all throw ourselves pell-mell into the trench. It is just in time, for at the same moment a rain of bullets hurtles into the ground on the edge of the trench. After they have passed over, we get ourselves back out of the trench and our first concern is for the plates and bowls which are nearly all turned over on the grass. Quite a few of the mugs have had the same fate. But nobody is hit, that's the essential thing, although a miss was overdue. We find several marks of bullets in the fruit trees around the trench.

The civilians put together their meagre bundles, for they are leaving the village at one o'clock in the morning, the village having to be completely evacuated by daybreak. It is sad and that tears me apart. Poor people! To abandon like that their house, cattle, poultry and everything which yesterday seemed to be really prospering, and gave them their pleasure in life. Some women cry in the crowd on the square, the children look wide-eyed, not yet understanding everything that is happening. I shake the hand of some of the farmers with whom I have been in the habit of chatting in the evenings. The poor chaps are overwhelmed, most of them having been in the other war, four years without even seeing their family, who then were living in occupied territory, having to abandon everything now right in the middle of May, when the harvest, which took so much trouble to get underway, promises to be beautiful. Several of these men force themselves to reassure their families, in which task I help them, although I think at least the same as they do, I keep telling them that the measure is only temporary, and that in a few days they will get back their homes. Almost the whole village is amassed on the square, the spectacle is poignant, and the chaplains from the battalions try to reassure these poor people. At last the column moves off, which is not too soon, for the scene is very sad, the majority leaving on foot carrying a small bundle, others on bikes, large families with their wagons drawn by two mares who leave behind their foals of one, two or three months old. The old people and the children get into the cars. The village returns to calm, troubled only by the cries from the cows in the fields, abandoned to their fate.

Day breaks, very beautiful like the day before, and towards six o'clock the dance starts up again like before, bombs and bursts of machine-gun fire follow one after the other nearly without interruption in a dreadful throbbing. A bit of bad news for the section arrives: our lieutenant, one of the best that the battalion possesses, even though he is very young, is leaving us to go to the regiment's general staff. This is really bad luck, with the captain going off sick, now our lieutenant, the only capable one in the company, also has to go away.

The day passes like its predecessor. We stay cowering, everyone like a bird in its nest. As for me, on the insistence of my colleagues, I abandon the middle of the square, where the position seems not to provide all the desired guarantees; I set up my machine-gun in the dormer window of a cellar under a private house and all the group takes its place in the cellar. From there I can fire, half stretched out on the footpath, with my field of fire on the road being wider even than in the middle of the square. From there I see the road straight ahead for nearly a kilometre, the bridge over the Chiers, and even the first houses in Douzy.

The refugees pour along the road coming from Belgium, Luxembourg or some of the French frontier villages. Some young women or fiancées come to see and to kiss their husband or fiancé one last time for many of the soldiers in the barracks are from the neighbouring villages. And there are heartbreaking scenes to see. Some of them won't go except through the intervention of the officers. Sedan is being evacuated and with my binoculars I see on the road that crosses the valley of the Meuse interminable convoys of refugees, frightened by the passing of the air monsters which continue to pound our positions. The day draws to an end and all the time the refugees pass by in every kind of transport. I see poor old women coming from Luxembourg and Belgium, dragging with great difficulty, the poor things, little wagons, children's prams and some of them even wheelbarrows, often with a baby of only a few months old sitting on top. And the endless file-past continues.

At nightfall I go to pick up our meal; we follow the Meuse on the main road toward the woods of Mouzon where the field kitchens are based. After much grovelling in the ditches to let the aeroplanes go over, we arrive at the kitchens which are in a great state of alert for they have been hunted the whole day by the planes. Any indication of smoke coming from the woods, any clearing where there might be evidence of horses, lorries, army re-supply trucks, is irreparably sprayed with bombs. The cooks are far from having a hideaway, several of them have even been badly injured, for they are loading the wounded into an ambulance. It seems there must have been some deaths. For the time being, our company's kitchen is intact and we go back with the day's meal and wine and stocks of tinned food for the next day's ration.

The new night is calm. The foals whinny, not having had their feed and some of them being abandoned by their mothers. It's a dismal night. In the stables the calves, not having had their milk either, let out cries which move you, they are so unbearable. I open several stables and the beasts go free, it doesn't matter where. However on the Belgian frontier in the direction of Luxembourg, we see flashes of light and hear clearly the heavy noise of canons that never stop firing. It would seem that it is coming from the direction of Arlon in Belgium. The more the night goes on, the more the noise gets nearer, it all being nonetheless still quite a long way off.

And now it's Whit Sunday which dawns, another lovely day, the Sunday that we had looked forward to, with all kinds of merry-making and the local festivities. Yes, it is really going to be a lot of fun! The planes pass over as on the other days but seem to have moved away a little from us in favour of the frontier that they pound ceaselessly. Towards the middle of the day, soldiers in the greatest confusion appear on the road from Belgium. These are the soldiers of different formations among which are the Zouaves of the Third Battalion who had advanced towards Luxembourg. They tell us the most unbelievable things; and the Third Battalion has been hit hard for it is reduced by more than half. That doesn't seem too funny to us since it has all the appearance of being a retreat, and we, who in the morning were thinking that we'd hardly been informed of events, by not having any more newspapers or letters, start to be strangely and officially informed.

At the beginning of the afternoon, a message is sent around all positions to redouble our awareness, the motorised enemy advance guard having been observed almost at the Belgian frontier. And always there are soldiers from all branches of the army who arrive and move on behind us. At half past three the first light tanks and armoured automatic machine-guns are reported on the side which goes down from Belgium to Pouru-aux-Bois. Immediately our artillery goes into action and the first shells from our 155's pass over our heads with their swishing sound to go on and explode beyond our line of vision. Towards four o'clock, although we were waiting until the last minute, because French soldiers were always coming over it, the bridge on the Chiers goes up in a frightening explosion, cutting the road from Douzy. Thereafter no one comes across and from the other side of the river I see through my binoculars, French soldiers continually turning up.

The aeroplanes leave us almost quiet on this Whitsun afternoon, and three of us keep lookout. The remainder of the section takes advantage to sleep a little. Two have even drunk more than they should for in the cellar where we are, there are some good bottles, champagne and fine wine, beer and cider, and also some bottles of aperitifs. Several bottles of the cherry and the plum are opened despite the sergeant and some amongst us who, knowing two of our mates in particular, would not want to see them blind drunk at such a moment. As for me, I drink some cider alternating with some glasses of Suze.[1] Towards four o'clock, everything being calm in the vicinity, I climb up with a mate into the attic of the house. From up there the view stretches right over the whole valley of the Chiers, and we can see and count 84 planes which bomb and machine-gun in rotation the frontier to our left, maybe on the troops who are resisting while withdrawing onto Sedan.

Suddenly our 75's come into action and from our skylight we can see that they are firing on the tanks and armoured automatic guns which are coming down the hillside. We go down again into the house. In going through the living room, I mechanically spin the dial of the radio and I am completely astonished to see that the current hasn't yet been cut. I get a station from Paris which is giving news, and what news! Although with my own eyes, I see the tanks coming down on to Sedan, the Parisian radio for its part, announces that the enemy is largely contained in Belgium beyond our frontier. I start to understand. With that I am put in the picture, you can always trust the radio!

I go to my post. The heavy gun fires on the bridge at Douzy which the explosion has not properly destroyed. Various houses collapse in an unbelievable din. Finally the third shell makes a direct hit on the bridge and it crashes straight down into the river. Night falls and we can still make out very well the tanks which are coming forward down the road, on the other side of the river. Our guns of all sizes at present keep up a barrage of firing in front of Douzy on the road coming from Belgium. The forts stay quiet, the enemy being outside the range of their guns, the only forts which could be able to fire being either unfinished or not yet armed. A liaison officer brings an order: 'Hold yourself ready, probable relief tonight'. No, it's not possible, we don't believe it. When, for the two months that we have been there, where each automatic weapon, each man with his gun has a clearly defined role, each one his own field of fire, properly marked out, when for two months, every day, they make every machine-gunner study and learn his own fire plan, we should be relieved at the precise moment when the attack on our positions is going to be unleashed at any minute! But yes, it's like that, and another order confirms the first, saying that the changeover will be done towards midnight, in complete silence.

However the night has descended and we hear all the time from across the river the ever-stronger noise of tanks and automatic guns, and of other motorised units, punctuated at regular enough intervals by the bursting of shells from our big mobile guns which fire endlessly. I go to take guard on the road itself, with my machine-gun. Another man comes with us, we take a full sack of cartridge clips. We go forward up to the unfinished forts scarcely 300 metres from the bridge which has just fallen. We camouflage ourselves in the ditch, setting up our firing position on the side of the road, for the order is to fire on no matter who and no matter what presents itself, and without warning. The big guns are firing at present into the square of the village of Douzy, and from time to time in a terrible fracas, houses collapse. They give us an order: 'Look out, do not fire, the corps of irregulars which went on patrol along the river is going to come back along the Douzy road'. In effect, three-quarters of an hour afterwards, we make out the patrol which arrives hugging the ditches. They have noticed that the enemy, despite the firing of our guns, are arriving in greater and greater numbers. Nothing abnormal on this side of the river. In its first dangerous sortie the commando section has lost a man, who must be supposed to have fallen into the hands of the enemy. Towards eleven o'clock the commandant himself, accompanied by a captain, comes to make a round. At that moment five or six bullets fired from I-don't-know-where whistle round our ears and make us duck. I was scanning in vain through the darkness, just like my colleague, our fingers on the trigger ready to fire, but we see nothing. However we have the impression of having been fired on from quite close. The commandant and the captain who had been lying in the ditch go back on all fours. Half an hour later I am relieved. It is none too soon for our guns are firing at shorter and shorter range and some shells are not clearing the river, or fall into the water, which starts to alarm me. By crawling more than walking, we get back up to the village where, in the cellar, I meet up again with the remainder of the section who are awaiting the relief.

Midnight has passed and nobody has yet arrived. Only the shells, with their irritating rustle, shoot by regularly. I stay in the square, and it's an hour and a half before the relief turns up. And what a relief! For the most part they are old men, and a very small number of them, one platoon having to replace our company. Is this possible, at barely two paces from the enemy? They don't have much ammunition. I leave them some of my cartridge clips, partly to please them, but above all to unburden myself, for I sense that there is going to be trouble on the road ahead. In two, three hours more it is going to be daybreak, and we will need to have made progress before the aeroplanes give us some help. The newcomers are very happy to find that they can drink at will for they have marched a long way to come up to us. For that they are happy to take over the cellar and its contents. But they are less pleased when we tell them to pay attention and above all not to smoke, for the slightest imprudence could cost them their life, the enemy being only a few hundred metres from the village; at that moment we strongly suspected that some patrols have crossed over the river and were prowling around the village. That surprises them a great deal for nobody has told them that they are going into battle, and suddenly to find themselves two steps from the enemy without being warned, is really upsetting.

Knocking Down the Miles

We load up our packs and rifles and come on to the square where the company is assembling. We hang around for a long time, for there is always some section which is missing at roll-call. At last we have a full complement and we start off immediately. It wasn't a moment too soon, for if the enemy had realised we were gathering they would have been able to make our ears burn. We take the road which follows the Meuse and head towards Mouzon. We march quickly for it will soon be daylight and then it could go badly with the planes about. We get past Mouzon at daybreak. We cross the Meuse and go through the evacuated town, where some houses have really caught it in the last few days. A big building, half demolished, makes a lamentable sight. The church, which is classed as a historic monument, has not yet suffered too badly. We leave the town and by a small road climb the hills where we can see several batteries of 155s being installed, protected as well as they can be from the view of aircraft among the copses and hedges. The sun rises through a mist which intermittently hides it. If this mist could only thicken up, we think to ourselves, for without doubt in a few minutes the whole crazy dance is going to start and I haven't a clue about what is going to happen. By good fortune the mist does thicken and comes right down to the ground, we can't any longer see for very far. What luck! If that could only last! We march for some time across the hills, always following the paths in the fields rather than the roads, where we see vehicles from time to time. Supply wagons, artillery trucks, vans which have copped bombs are there, collapsed on the road. Some disembowelled horses here and there, some of them badly hit, are not yet dead, and they let out plaintive groans as we pass. The mist clears and the sun shines again, chasing away the last wisps of the haze. We are once more on the banks of the Meuse, on a little path following its meandering route, which in this place seems to flow into a huge basin. High wooded hills surround it on all sides and the valley, narrowed at this point, forms a great arena, a very pleasant countryside

62

to look upon. The engineers are in the process of finishing huge works which consist of a large wooden bridge veering from the path on which we are walking, by making a big semi-circle over the river itself and coming to rejoin the same path. This makes me think that it must be to avoid some minor and very short twists of the path which follows the river half way up the slope and which the big tractor-drawn artillery probably won't be able to take. Suddenly what we have been dreading for a long time inevitably happens. The air attacks, with their formidable throbbing, make their appearance and the passes follow one after the other as in the days before. We camouflage ourselves under the big trees or in the copses on the riverbanks, only going forward by bounds between two overflights, which completely dislocates the battalion, each company taking different paths and the sections leaving long intervals between themselves so as to make sure the men are not in large groups. At the top of one hill, the pioneers take stones from a quarry that lorries cart away so as to finish the approaches of the bridge, a man with a loud hailer warning them of each air attack, where everyone hurries to camouflage themselves the best they can. Now we go down. On the right, a downed aircraft is burning itself out. Another, a little further away, is stuck right in the middle of a potato field, but is not burning. At the end of the valley is the village of Létanne where we stop to have a drink. I take advantage of this to get myself a little bread from the troops who are there. Some of the inhabitants are still there, running after their panicking cattle that they want to take away with them. As soon as we are out of the village the planes call us to account again. It's impossible to go further on without getting ourselves massacred. Not another tree, not the slightest stream or fold in the ground. Scarcely halfway up the hill, the planes rake us with machine-gun bullets or strings of bomblets. Everyone protects himself as best he can, whether by throwing himself on to the ground or taking to the fields so as to space ourselves out as much as possible. But the attack continues, the planes follow one after the other almost without end. We can't go on any further, it's useless to try. Between two attacks the majority of us, and I am among them, set off for a wood across the fields at a run, as quickly as possible. We hide ourselves in the thickets. It is high time for now the bombardment redoubles. The whole battalion withdraws into the wood, but many are missing at roll-call. The machine-gun company has been hit worst for a little later they tell us that they have had sixteen killed by a bomb and a good number wounded. The commandant's orderly with his two horses is also left on the road. The driver and the orderly of the

colonel, who while waiting for him as he verified the positions of the
advance guard at Mairy, rested for a moment on the first floor of a
cottage, were killed by a plane which crashed down on the house, a
sad act of fate for those who believed themselves to be safer than us.

We stay there a good while without budging; we rest half asleep,
while at irregular intervals the bombs rain down. Meanwhile, from
here and from there, some of the Zouaves come out of the thickets.
We start getting hungry, no orders arrive and we decide to go and see
what is happening in the village. Four men from the section go down
through the thickets as far as the road. At last, at the end of an hour,
after having very often wriggled along flat on their stomachs, they
return. Nonetheless they bring the meal with them, having found the
kitchen camouflaged at the entrance to the village. We eat with
appetite, but we are falling down with fatigue. No orders arrive, and
with my loader we make a nice nest in the middle of a little thicket,
but we sleep very badly. It's the bombs, then the nightmares which
wake us when we have scarcely gone off to sleep. Night falls while a
lieutenant brings us back together to a clearing in the wood. 'We're
going to spend the night here' he says, 'get down nearer to the road
and settle down to sleep.' The whole company settles down by the
same hedge in a tight circle. A big unexploded aerial torpedo is
there. Everyone makes his nest with leaves and dry grass; and we do
not waste time in getting off to sleep.

It could be about 10 o'clock, the lieutenant shakes us, going from
one group to another, telling us to stand up quietly, and we leave. Not
even a whole night of sleep. It takes the lieutenant's return, who on
this occasion makes no joke of it, to persuade us to get up. We are
dead with fatigue after two or three hours of sleep, while it would
have needed a complete night to put us nearly back in shape. It's useless to gib at it. Already I hear my own name, nominated to go and
find some provisions in the village for the platoon. We get ourselves
ready as best we can and leave the thicket. The full moon shines
clearly on the path which goes down to the village. I go with two colleagues to draw some boxes of tinned food, bread and wine, and
when we go back we find the company on the road, ready for departure. We start off soon enough, for some companies, quicker than us
to get ready, have drawn ahead.

Soon we are crossing what seems like a pretty big town. This is
Beaumont, I don't really know if it is Beaumont-en-Argonne. In the
main square, several roads converge and naturally, our short-sighted
lieutenant takes the wrong one and then makes us force the pace to
catch up with the battalion. After many kilometres, we encounter a

battery of artillery going in the opposite direction. They haven't seen the battalion and it's then that our officers realise that they have made a mistake on their maps. About turn, which leads to grousing and the lieutenant hears certain none too flattering words said about him. We have to go back as far as Beaumont where a liaison officer puts us on the right road. It's necessary to make up for the lost time and to force the pace. At last we catch up with the battalion which is having a break. We set off without any break for us, and frankly we are at the end of our tether. After two or three halts, we leave the road to take a pretty stony path. We pass in front of a farm, and soon are stopped by a small village at the end of the valley, surrounded by high hills with woods along the top.

The Defence of Yoncq

We stay there long enough; the officers, who have gone off, we
assume to prepare the billets, do not return quickly. Most of us, lying
down on the road, start to fall off to sleep. For myself, I get up, for
after having sweated so much I feel the morning cold grab hold of
me. Day is breaking, it might be half past three, perhaps four o'clock.
I rejoin the platoon next to us which is discussing our situation and
where I find my friend from Sommières. Where are we going? Some
hold that we have been consistently marching towards the rear and
that we must be far from the banks of the Meuse. For my part, in the
pitch darkness, I have not been fully aware of what's going on, in an
area we do not know. An order finally arrives and our NCOs make us
go on as far as the village square. Ten minutes later, the officers who
are returning from a kind of council held by the headquarters staff
rejoin their companies. But what's happened? They are completely
stunned and don't even venture to speak. What's going on? Rumours
circulate from one group to another and soon the mystery is
unveiled. The enemy is there, right in front of us, and is going to fall
on us at any minute. It even seems that there are none of our troops
in front of us. As a surprise, this is a surprise. We all had a sense of
the danger, but to be so near to combat, so suddenly, when we had
believed ourselves to be marching towards the rear throughout the
night! Day breaks; however no precise order is given, we stay waiting
at the foot of the clock tower. What? No one knows anything. Our
lieutenant, commanding the company, is of all of us the one for
whom the blow has been hardest. He is completely incapable of giving any order, he turns from one section to another stammering
and without getting out a proper word. At last, we take the initiative
on our own part, for the sun, which is beginning to shine down on
the summit of the hills, reminds us that in a few minutes this hole of
a village could become our tomb. My platoon, with staff sergeant
Vernhet who commands it decides to leave the village. The other
companies, well commanded by quite good captains, are already

setting themselves up halfway up the hill, which incidentally, is rather steep, to the south of the village. At last we meet an officer from the headquarters staff who, plan in hand, gives us our combat position. Opposite the village square, we scale the hill through a garden and a sloping meadow and we all set ourselves up, hiding ourselves as much as possible along the row of big trees. The whole battalion is soon enough camouflaged and at five o'clock you can no longer see any man in the open. Everyone has hidden himself as best he can, his eyes riveted on this road to the north of the village, which, along the ridge of the hill, comes out of some pretty thick woods and then goes down 600–800 metres to the village through almost arid fields, without a tree or any vegetation whatsoever.

The first hours of the morning pass like this, planes go over in quite tight little groups, plunging down the valley, shaving the trees, but not machine-gunning us. Nobody fires. A true silence of the grave hovers over the hills. At intervals the clock tower rings out clearly the quarter and the half hours, a ringing which in our ears seems more like a death knell. Further off we can hear the cows bellowing madly, for having been abandoned for some days now without being milked, they are suffering and do not know what's happening to them. Poor beasts! We watch them wander from one field to another in herds, at one time to the watering place, at another going on as far as the village square. From time to time, a cuckoo lands in the neighbouring hedge, chirps its song and realising quickly enough that it is not alone takes offence and flies off. Meanwhile the day goes on and nobody budges, their eyes always fixed on this road. Waiting is tiring, we are anxious, we would like to know and yet we would wish at the same time not to hear the very news which, as we guess, can only be cruel.

Midday. It's pretty hot, I am thirsty and there is nothing in my canteen. The fatigue is cruel, our eyes close despite ourselves, but only for a second, for nerves dominate over sleep and we continue to stare at the road; but, I don't know if it's the sun, the tiredness or by force of concentrating on this road where the midday sun is dancing, I have visions, a mirage. It seems to me that I am all the time looking at vast hangars and buildings, while in fact there is nothing except this road winding across the hill.

To escape this obsession, I leave the hedge and walk a little under the apple trees, but what is it that I see there in front of me, to the east? Yes, I am not mistaken, down there right on the horizon, between two hills, the flowing Meuse and after it the road from Mairy to Mouzon with its double line of trees. I tell one of my colleagues, I think Riquet, and the two of us can't help but agree. It's pretty good, to have marched all night and a bit of Whit morning, plus the night of Tuesday, to find oneself nearly opposite our departure point on the opposite bank of the Meuse! We learn then that we are at the village of Yoncq. Behind the hill that we are constantly watching and from where the road descends is Raucourt and, a little further on, Sedan.

The afternoon passes, still nothing. Various groups move, some sections take up other positions. Suddenly, from the summit of the hill emerge three tanks, and just as soon an order: 'Don't fire, they're French.' Indeed the machines go down as far as the little stream which goes along the bottom of the valley, at the entrance to the village, turn, climb up again and disappear into the woods from where they had come out. We are told at this moment that the German army has succeeded in crossing the Meuse, near Sedan, which at this moment is all on fire, for we can see on the horizon plumes of smoke climbing into the sky. The order arrives to redouble surveillance for the time is coming near for us. To go into combat in such conditions against tanks, without a trench, without any protection, when for nearly four months we had modernised, refined (if we may say so), our trenches which wound between blockhouses and fortified positions, with reserve provisions, telephones, first aid, camp-beds, nothing was lacking there, sheltered against planes partly by concrete walls. To have abandoned all that to engage in combat in the open fields, without trenches, without shelters and scarcely a few kilometres from our trenches on the other side of the Meuse! The town clock continues to toll one by one its funereal chimes in the sinister silence. The sun is going to disappear behind the hill and we think that the moment is at hand; everybody is ready, finger on the trigger, to let fly at the slightest appearance. My section's senior corporal, with his wire cutters, has just cut the wires of several cattle pens, so that in the event of a sudden withdrawal we can get back on the path as quickly as possible.

Night is about to fall and we have the joy, the very great joy of finally seeing the first French aeroplane circle over the hills at very low altitude. He is welcome, that one, the only one since the start of this battle, who comes to fly his tricolour above us, while since the start we have seen thousands of planes but always with black crosses. It gives us back our courage to see him circling and following the contours of the hills and forests and there is nearly an ovation sent climbing up towards him. Night falls and nothing has changed in the situation. On the horizon, a large moon climbs. I am too thirsty, so I go down to the village fountain to fill some canteens with cold water. We have a snack for we haven't eaten anything since the previous midday, not having been hungry during these anxious hours. We eat nearly all our rations, then get back to our positions in the hedge. Nine o'clock in the evening sounds, then ten o'clock. Our old lieutenant makes a tour of inspection with an officer from the headquarters staff. Lieutenant Levrat has quickly seen the situation in our platoon which is virtually without command. He calls Staff Sergeant Vernhet who is in charge, in the absence of the officers. How is it, he says to him, that given you have been here since this morning you have not been better organised than this? The sergeant apologises, and immediately the whole platoon, in getting back its old boss, has recovered all its previous nerve. In a few minutes, the sections are separated out. The lieutenant chooses the positions for the light machine-gunners, then for all the men. He accompanies me to the position where I have to set up my machine-gun. I go down nearly to the last houses in the village, but high enough up the hill to be able to see above the roofs all of the road coming down from the wood. Furthermore, and this is my official duty, I must defend the place where the road goes into the village, a little crossroads formed by the road and a bare path where there is a watering place. He makes us, with my loader, go back into a bush at the foot of a large apple tree with drooping branches, and it is there that we have to dig our trench, for he tells us that the order has just arrived that there is to be no retreat, the order being to hold on to the regiment's last breath.

So here we are in the middle of the bush digging among the thorns that scratch us everywhere. It doesn't matter, work still goes ahead. At midnight we have dug down to 50 centimetres a hole of about 1.50m in length. At that moment I am overtaken by a serious fainting attack and only keep upright by a miracle. I cannot hold on much longer and my brave loader makes me lie down at the foot of the apple tree. We take off our packs and I wrap myself up in our two blankets, while my friend Doize watches over the machine-gun. I sleep properly for a moment, but a nightmare like those I have often had in my most frightened moments wakes me with a start. I look at my watch: quarter past two. I have not slept for long, and am cold. A thick mist hides the moon. At the gun, my mate is always vigilant. I get up and I have to insist to make him sleep for a little while. While my friend snores under the apple tree, I put myself back properly to digging the trench, not so much for the work as to warm myself up again. Day breaks and after having woken up my loader we observe

that when we manage to stand upright in our trench, our heads
scarcely stick out; it's enough to enclose us completely if there is a crisis. We camouflage the earth with branches, and the trench is
completely covered over. We clear away properly in front of the bush
for our field of fire, which is excellent. A path passes in front of our
trench. We camouflage the opening of the bush. An officer from the
company makes a final inspection; we are really ready. It's the same
for all of us, everyone who has kept on working throughout the
night. Telephone, communications, Red Cross, everything is in place
at sunrise.

What will come to pass on this day of Wednesday 15 May? The first
hours, nothing, but soon, towards seven o'clock, soldiers appear on
the edge of the forest. Should we fire? For us they are out of range,
but the big machine-guns adjust their fire, and then a patrol of com-
mandos, returning, announces that they're French. Indeed, soon
section follows section, white handkerchief or serviette tied to the
end of each weapon or baton to avoid mistakes on our part. At the
moment it's companies and entire battalions which are coming down
from the wood by the road, in complete disarray, they arrive in the village and pass one after the other behind our lines. Several sections
go along the little path in front of our trench, climb over the hill and
disappear in the direction of Beaumont. The regiments are mixed
up, various formations of different arms marching together, several
no longer having any equipment, many more no rifles, almost no one
still having the strength to lug a pack along. This is sad to see, especially for us who know these hard marches, but unlike them do not
yet know a grim retreat, with the enemy ceaselessly on your heels and
the planes which pitilessly roar above you. They tell us frightening
things, all nearly unbelievable. Some of them have come on foot
from the Albert canal, all the time in retreat; that's a long way from
the Belgian/German border. Others, and they're the most numerous, come from Luxembourg. They ask us for something to eat, to
drink; poor lads! But since the evening of the day before yesterday
since our departure from Létanne we have only had a tin of sardines
and one of tuna between two of us. The file-past continues, unremit-
ting up till now, it's pitiable. Ah! If the enthusiasts, who go to the
great boulevards in Paris or wherever to see these magnificent march-
pasts of the 14th of July, or other days, if they could see on this
morning this other army file past, the one that's real, that isn't on
parade, which hasn't any music, perhaps they would understand what
the suffering of a soldier is. The file past continues, now here are the
machine-gunners of the 11th, formed like us at Avignon, lads from

our part of the world. I look, and what a surprise and at the same time a joy it is to see a good friend, Maurice Ribes, from Gallargues. Poor him, he can do no more. They have been withdrawing right from the centre of Belgium, three days, three nights without stop, without even eating. I make him drink a little water with drops of peppermint essence, but I have nothing for him to eat, I am in a bad way as well. We speak for five minutes, then he has to go, the officers are hurrying us, the last groups are coming down the hill, and the enemy has been seen immediately behind them by a reconnaissance motor cyclist. One last clasp of the hand, we part, me encouraging him, he, who knows already what awaits us, telling me: 'I pity you if you have to stand up to a blitz like this.'

Just now the last groups are passing, a reconnaissance patrol goes off on a motor cycle, climbs the hill at full speed and disappears into the wood. Some horsemen at full gallop also leave on reconnaissance, but suddenly, while everyone is anxious about what might happen, full of anguish at waiting, a sharp burst of fire resounds. The shells fall, well-grouped, over the whole side of the hill. After the first minute in which we are taken by surprise, we realise that this is the French artillery, putting up a violent barrage. The ground is smoking everywhere, and shells of all sizes are bursting with a frightful din. Through the dust and earth which is flying everywhere, I make out a horseman. A 75mm shell has just burst right in front of his horse, which rears right up, but the rider – obviously no beginner – keeps his seat well. At the same moment a second shell bursts behind the horse which takes two or three jumps to the side. Is he hit? I can't tell, but like a meteor, such is the flash, I see him pass in front of my trench, without yet having thrown off his rider . . . my goodness, he has come close to death.

The artillery eases off a little and a group of soldiers appears at the exit to the wood, in rows and with a handkerchief or white napkin tied to the end of their rifles. The guns fall quiet immediately, the group comes down in perfect order, too perfect to be French soldiers in retreat, at least so the commandant must have judged, for the barrage starts up again even more strongly, the 155's rain down on the road and the entrance to the wood. On the hill I see the soldiers run from one shell hole to another; poor lads! There will be no one left. We are all there watching this drama and thinking perhaps that they are French latecomers. Now our artillery shortens its range more and more, such that a 75 falls scarcely 30 metres in front of my trench, and my mates from the other section who, on my right, are in front of us, the poor devils, how heavily they are going to cop it. I know that a lieutenant is 20 metres behind me, in a trench, with his field telephone. I get half out of my trench and I shout with all my might in his direction: 'Get them to increase the range, don't you see that they are massacring the company?' It is then that I realise that it is the lieutenant commanding the company who has established his command post there. Short-sighted as he is, and half-dead with fear, they really chose the right man for the job. The fire continues, still short, a shell falls on a small farm, which at once catches fire. I know that the 2nd Platoon is in the first houses in the village, and that they are all going to stay there, killed by our own artillery, if this continues. Then I see a mortar sergeant run as best he can towards the command post. And the fire lengthens its range and the shells fall again on the hillside. And not a moment too soon! It was fortunate that the sergeant, seeing like us the danger, had taken it upon himself to telephone, to the great benefit of the company. What's more, he stayed there until the end of the day, and through his precise instructions, received later the congratulations of the artillery officers.

In the meantime, on the fringe of the wood, to the left and the right of the road, the first tanks make their appearance in large numbers. Our artillery redoubles its fire, concentrating everything now on one side, now on the other. Two tanks are hit and burn, a mortar shell scores a direct hit on a third and that also bursts into flames. The others, facing this violent barrage, turn and shelter in the forest. It is here that the scene changes. The enemy artillery comes into play and a hail of shells starts to rain down. Too long to begin with, they burst behind us, but the range soon adjusts so that they rain down on us, I make myself small, as small as possible in my trench. Some fall so near that the trench trembles and the earth starts to collapse. It calms down a little and I stick my nose outside and spot a large tank, come from I don't know where, which is going to arrive right at the crossroads in my field of fire. What can I do? Quickly, I take out my normal magazine which I replace with one of armoured bullets and I wait for the precise moment when it is going to come onto the crossroads. I am not too confident as to what is going to happen, for I realise, and this is what makes me tremble, that if I miss, this formidable machine, spitting fire from everywhere, will come right over me and we shall be lost. I also know that even armoured bullets don't do very much harm to it. All this races through my head in an instant. In spite of this I'm still cool, and just at the moment when I'm about to let loose my first volley, a shell bursts on its front; immediately the engine stops and two men get off the vehicle. Half a minute later, some men from the platoon nearby take them prisoner without any resistance. It is a 25mm anti-tank gun, placed behind me and with the same field of fire as me, which stopped it. He really made me pleased, above all in not missing, for I had the impression that I was in for it.

The firing from the two artillery forces continues strongly, a French tank passes in front of my trench on the little path and stops a few metres away. I hear an officer who shouts at the driver who has stopped in a completely exposed position. The machine turns, mounts the embankment and gets stuck under the apple-tree, whose lower branches it tears off. It keeps on advancing and I in my turn shout after the tank's commander for he does not seem to realise that we are here, and he is just about to pass right over us with his huge machine. The trench half collapses. He stops his engine and from time to time fires on the enemy tanks, which are trying to get out of the forest to the right.

An order arrives telling me to be alert: some enemy soldiers have succeeded in getting into the little cemetery next to the village by the crossroads that I am defending. I look keenly out, but I see nothing beyond a couple of dozen cows gathered at that point around the water-hole. They shout to me again to watch out and I am obliged, to my great regret, to clear the square by raking the cows with fire. One falls stone dead, another one goes and collapses in the stream, finally the whole herd gallops off towards the village. Another order arrives: 'Hold yourself ready, pack on back, the counter-attack will start in a few minutes'. And we learn that the whole division is going to throw itself into the counter-offensive, preceded however by a company on reconnaissance which is going to launch the attack on the wood to weigh up the effect of our artillery's fire and the strength of the enemy's positions. Naturally, my company, which has no captain to look after it is chosen for this work. Poor us; no one will get into the wood, not least because what the liaison officer has just told us after coming back from the battalion C.P.[2], where the two prisoners have said that 80 enemy tanks are preparing the attack. At this moment the battalion chaplain, assisted by two male nurses who have put on gowns over their uniform, comes to give us benediction. They go along the little path from one group to the other, and make a tour of the company. I look on, dazed, without even making a gesture, or movement. We are equipped and we wait for orders, while the edge of the wood is shelled violently, no doubt because of the attack to come. Behind me, I hear the tank officers arguing fiercely, not wanting to throw themselves into such a risky business. Finally the captain commanding the tank section declares that he cannot execute the manoeuvre; one of his tanks having been destroyed, the second broken-down, he only has three machines left in good shape, which is far too little for an attack like this.

The enemy artillery redoubles the violence of its attack, we make ourselves small in our trenches, the shells cluster all around us. I am afraid lest the enemy spots the big tank which is there under the tree, and then what will happen? I hear a shout a few metres behind us. I look and see on the sloping field a soldier who has just fallen. It is Lieutenant Bergon, commanding the 1st Platoon of the company. Two medical orderlies are already lifting him up. The poor man is badly hit. A big splinter is, it seems, lodged very near his heart. The war is over for him. The company loses another officer, which throws it into disarray; there is only our short-sighted lieutenant left as an officer.

However the news goes round that the counter-attack is not taking place, the enemy force being too superior. I breathe again, for this venture, in which I seemed certain to get it in the neck, did not appeal to me. Some new attempts by the enemy to come out from the wood are pushed back easily enough by our tank-guns which spit out fire endlessly. Night falls. There's still firing from both sides. I am, like my partner in the trench, thirsty, very thirsty. Is that because of the smell of cordite, or really, as I believe, because of the fever that this battle is bringing on? I have never known such a thirst, even in the great heatwaves back home. We are not hungry, even though we have not eaten since yesterday lunchtime. Night has fallen and a mist envelops the valley, which means that we can see scarcely anything, despite the clear night. Ten o'clock sounds in the night. The pealing of the clock, which has kept standing while the surrounding houses are more or less all hit, seems like a tolling. It is even sadder because some of us are sleeping forever in this enclosed valley.

Despite the great danger, my loader wants to go to look for water at the village fountain in the square. I don't want to let him go, but after a pause he takes out two canteens and he goes off without saying anything. He makes a good job of it, and heavens how I drink and drink again the two litres in the bottle and in my turn go back to fill them for tomorrow, which promises to be hard. I even find a bucket which I fill right up. If we do not eat at least we will drink.

It is calm now. There are some shells from time to time from both sides. Despite myself, helped by fatigue, I sleep half-standing there in my trench, woken every few minutes with a start by a shell or machine-gun burst. One burst is fired from very near me. It is Corporal Fraysse of the 11th Platoon who, doubtless irritated by the sound of the clock, has just loosed a whole magazine off at its face, which has the effect of silencing it and its funereal toll.

Retreat

Three in the morning. The bombardment is stronger, but I should say the shells come not from the front like yesterday but from the two flanks of the hill. Four o'clock, the day breaks just the very moment the cannonade redoubles. We sense that things are going badly, very badly. Suddenly a lieutenant, I don't know which, and without any previous order, gives out a kind of 'every man for himself' direction. In five minutes, he announces, the withdrawal must have got over the hill. It's abrupt and immediately there is general panic, everyone thinking of his own skin. We have unrolled our blankets to keep us from the damp of the night, and our packs, our ammunition, satchels, everything is in disorder, us not expecting such a sudden order. In less time than it takes to write it everything is gathered up. It isn't the moment to see if our blankets make a neat horseshoe or if the flask or the *musette* are on the right shoulder or the left. In the twinkling of an eye we are out of the trench. I cocked my machine-gun for I feel that we are at a critical moment and right then a burst of machine-gun fire passes only a few centimetres over our heads. I still have a shiver of fear from it and I seem to be able to hear the bullets whistling past. We go forward until the end of the hedge so as to take the small path. The shells are banging down from everywhere. Just now, although it might not yet be broad daylight we can make things out in front of us very well. Soldiers are running from everywhere in all directions, but in the end they all converge on the little track for Beaumont, for the rumour spreads that we are surrounded. It isn't really quite that bad, but it must have been very close. The enemy's tanks, I don't know how, had used the cover of darkness to slide to the right and the left of the battalion and were almost taking us from the rear. In the streets it was the tanks which now took up the attack. I stood watching one of them which was already climbing the hill one hundred and fifty metres behind us. In front it was terrible, the tanks and enemy artillery were shelling and machine-gunning the little track which was fairly exposed right at the place where it climbed on to the hump of the hill and I saw some mates fall, scythed down in the only escape route possible. I thought for a moment. To go that way was certain death. Without even talking, my loader and I skirted the hill across several fields and meadows. At one place we went through water halfway up our legs, but it didn't matter. On the other side of the hill we rejoined the little path. Not before time. The shelling was even heavier behind us and we hurried on as fast as we were able with our load. On the path there was indescribable disorder, everyone trying to get away as quickly as possible.

I was completely out of breath, I could do no more. Two tanks overtook us, one pulling the other, broken-down one, behind it, with more than fifty soldiers hanging on. I did as they did and succeeded in hoisting myself and my machine-gun up on to the back of the broken-down tank. I sat myself down on top, and although only holding on with difficulty, at least I wasn't walking. I was there, carefree of the great danger I was in, for it was fully day now and the planes were beginning their infernal round. If they spot the tanks, that could all come down on us, one man said to me. That wasn't enough to get me down, but I soon had to abandon the tanks. The first tank, suffering from engine misfires and other troubles, was stopping all the time. We were just starting out again on the road, and to our surprise the French machine-guns in front of us were firing right over our heads. Soon we had an explanation for we crossed the lines of the Senegalese who were making a counter-attack and were already engaging the enemy at certain points; that is why they had hurried us so much, because the laggards found themselves caught between the two lines of fire. We see the Senegalese everywhere now, calm, resolute and even greeting us with a smile. In a few moments they would realise the truth, but they coped very well in this sector, where, after a few hours they succeeded in pushing back the enemy and retaking the village which we had lost, the enemy climbing back into the woods where they were the evening before.

However on the road the greatest traffic jam reigned. Some of the '75' guns were firing at point-blank range from the middle of the road; others, without being uncoupled from their caissons, continued to fire while all the time preparing to retreat. Some 155's, in open fields, without camouflage, were firing endlessly while the planes rained bombs down all round them. We were going forward with great difficulty, the road being impracticable for us foot soldiers as the artillerymen were passing with their horses at full gallop. The equipment convoy, the cars of the Red Cross and all types of vehicle that war necessitates were going in line abreast without the least pity for the infantrymen, who if we did not move to the side risked every minute being crushed. We crossed fields. For one thing the enemy aircraft never stopped bombing the road, which was becoming really dangerous. A shell or a bomb, I don't know exactly, fell alongside the company's little mortar carriage, the explosions cut through the shafts and the horse departed at the gallop only to collapse 50 metres away, fatally wounded. The driver had time to throw himself in the ditch and wasn't hurt. On the carriage a soldier, already badly wounded in both legs, was not hit; it was really lucky for being full of mortar shells the carriage could easily have exploded. In the end Beaumont appeared. From the first houses in the village the Colonel himself was directing the retreat and putting a little order into his battalions, all the time congratulating the soldiers as they went by for having held the line, for from the Belgian frontier we were the first division that had dared to stand up to the formidable German army. But this was not without cost, for at roll-call there were plenty missing. We crossed the town, where the greatest disorder reigned. With some colleagues I stopped at a fountain and joyfully swallowed a litre or two of cold water, afterwards soaking my head in the water, which really did me good. And then we go on, with the road always jammed and bombarded more than ever. We walk without exactly knowing if we are on the right road, for no one gave any orders, the regiments now being completely mixed up. At the edge of a big wood, a section from the company was stopped, with the remaining lieutenant surrounded by some sergeants; we do the same and sit down under the trees.

Some people were eating which made us think that it was by now a long time since we had eaten anything. Since mid-day the day before yesterday we hadn't had anything in our mouths except water. Suddenly I was hungry. Is it through seeing others eat? And my friends and me had absolutely nothing. It is now that I miss my pack, for being the machine-gunner I was not carrying it and I had left it in the company's lorry, full of emergency rations that I had thought it prudent to carry but which now meant nothing. By good luck I had two packets of cigarettes which I immediately swapped on the road with the artillerymen for a loaf of bread and three tins of food, to which we did real justice. But after half-an-hour we had to go off again, as the battle was raging not far away. We heard the guns and the machine-guns which were spitting out fire all the time. The road, blocked all the way and sprayed at irregular intervals with bombs, did not appeal.

Towards 10 o'clock, an officer of the headquarters staff stopped all the soldiers coming from the 1st battalion and immediately we were directed into woods a few hundred metres away where some officers were trying – with great difficulty – to get the battalion back in order. But more than half of the men were missing. They dribbled in continuously in little groups and straightaway did like us, stretching out to get some sleep, but it was impossible. Towards half past eleven the news runs round that the company's kitchen is there and is going to serve a meal. It is most welcome and we eat a decent enough dinner with appetite. A double ration of wine, that should have been triple for us since we had had nothing for three days. The meal over, I went towards the kitchen to see a Gardois friend from Moussac and to get a little coffee. I found him rather sad and he immediately told me some really bad news, that our common friend, Marc Joinville of Calvisson, had been left behind, wounded, maybe dead, we were not yet exactly sure, but the boys of the second company were sure that he had been left behind. This news depressed me the more as I knew him very well, and mates from the 1st Platoon confirmed it to me later that he had been left like so many others on the little path which was the route over the hill. I went back to my section and passed on the news to my partners who all knew Joinville very well, and then on to Polge from Sommières, with whom we discussed the problem for a while, but we were obliged to recognise that we could do nothing to try to get our friend out. Whatever we might have wanted, it was completely impossible for us, the place was now in the hands of the Germans or at the very least right in the centre of the battle.

Suddenly, while it had been pretty calm for a few hours, and the battalion, almost regrouped, was going to leave to get down to it again at another point not far off, the airforce made its entrance, if one can put it like that. Heavy bombs tumbled down from everywhere, it had never been so intense before. A large one exploded very near my section, but in the blink of an eye everyone is lying down in the shelters made by the artillerymen. Not bad this time, but the planes hammer away ever more strongly on this position. Immediately there is a general 'every man for himself' movement through the forest.

In my rush I forget the cover of my machine-gun. I go back to get it, but find no trace. As a result I lose my platoon and no longer know in which direction they have gone. Two more large bombs burst in the vicinity, and over the large trees there's the endless humming of what must be a large number of aircraft. Well, no longer knowing where to go, I tag along behind another section which is passing where I meet up with Polge, my mate from Sommières. The chief staff sergeant who is leading, is not too sure of himself despite his map, and he does not know exactly where he is leading us. We have to walk all the time through the thick woods for the road is not practicable, bombed and machine-gunned all the time. The clearings and the little paths through the wood are pitilessly pounded by air attacks. What a din there is! We have to go forward carefully for we are afraid of finding ourselves face to face with one of the formations of parachutists which have been reported almost everywhere. Bombs rain down ever more frequently on the road, where we learn, as we stay alongside it, that three of the mobile kitchens, with all their men, horses and equipment have been engulfed by a bomb of the biggest calibre, for everything is buried in the same hole. The Arab troops are already throwing tree-trunks over it, branches and bundles of sticks which were nearby so that the following convoys can get through. I am tired, my machine-gun is cutting into my shoulders, yet I don't want to abandon it even though I can't any longer manage this roller-coaster of a walk through undergrowth. My friend from Sommières carries the gun for a while, for he has left everything behind in the morning's chaotic flight. In the middle of the wood we meet a pretty important group led by an officer of the General Staff. We join up with them. A little further on, we find my old lieutenant in charge of a group which includes my platoon. I rejoin my platoon.

The drivers of some of the machine-gun carriages have also turned into the wood and they are having the greatest difficulty in getting along with their horses. In some places it is really boggy and we sink in up to our knees. In the end, towards five o'clock, we arrive at the edge of the wood, but it is impossible to get out as the planes are watching our every movement. We have to stay there and take a rest while waiting for nightfall. I am put on guard to watch the plain, where parachutists have been reported. Night comes without us being bothered. The officers of the group, after consulting each other, are not in agreement on the direction to take, because there has been no order to assemble the battalion or the regiment in a particular place. However we go on in indian file through the wood along very small, barely-marked paths, but we soon have to turn back on ourselves. It is impossible to get out of the wood that way, as the ground, ever more swampy, finally becomes a huge pond. After some detours, however, we finally get out of the quagmire. Now we go across fields, then vast meadows, then little woods. We climb, we descend, always across the fields. Towards 11 o'clock, on the edge of the wood we come upon a big farm occupied by a battery of gunners. The commandant of our battalion is there with a pretty important group of men.

There is a halt which gets ever longer. We unroll our blankets after having drunk some water collected in a reservoir that used to hold petrol, which accounts for the water's really bad taste. Several men are already asleep, lying across the road. Although wrapped in my blanket I am cold, in fact very cold. Is it the sweating from the afternoon which makes me like this? I get up and go around into the farm. In a kitchen, a team of gunners is making a great noise while preparing some coffee. A friend and I join them. They give us something to eat and we drink some coffee followed by a decent tot of rum. Now that is better. Night comes on and while I am dead with fatigue I cannot sleep. But the battalion, or rather only one part of the battalion, for although the commandant is there two-thirds of the men are not, has to move off. For a good hour we walk along a small track through the fields. Then we are on a main road where we meet all kinds of convoys, perhaps going up to the lines. We leave the road and are made to go into the undergrowth, which is in fact more like jungle. It is thick in there, you can see nothing. So much so that it is necessary to link hands and to make a chain so as not to get lost. The path is scarcely visible and all the time your head gets caught up in creepers and brambles. Fallen branches bar the way. It's with difficulty that we can go forward at all through this hell. And now the path rises, almost vertically, and the climb is very hard in the black night. Several men stumble and fall in hollows to the right and left of the path. In one place it is completely blocked. It's inexplicable, a big hollow, some big branches on the ground, some earth thrown up, twigs, everything bars the way. Grumbling soon starts, and the majority – of whom I am one – decide to lie down there. With my friend Doize, we wrap ourselves right up in our blankets at the foot of a tree and we quickly fall asleep.

I wake up. It is broad daylight and the sun already seems fairly high. Around there are only cut branches and wooden debris; I quickly have my explanation, for a huge crater, a vast funnel formed by a bomb of great size is only a few metres away. Some big oaks have been scythed down and others have been split down the middle, which proves to us the violence of these engines of death. They leave us almost undisturbed all morning. At the start of the afternoon they distribute a meal, our kitchen having been brought to the lower part of the forest. Impossible to find any water to have a quick wash which we badly need. We can't get enough sleep, we are really exhausted. But it is cool, almost cold under that thick cover that the sun never penetrates. Night falls. They make us do a few kilometres to set ourselves up, still in the wood, but near enough to where we can find the field kitchen, in one of the thickest parts of the forest. We dig our trenches but at scarcely 30 centimetres the water seeps up from below. To cap it all, it starts to rain. That takes the biscuit! However, we manage to set ourselves up as best we can, putting moss and leaves at the bottom of the trench, and covering them with our tent canvas. And well, we fall asleep just the same in this lousy bed.

The Regiment Re-forms

The next day, we still stay there. The good weather has come back and the cuckoos sing even more in the great woods where they are virtually the only ones to break the truly impressive silence. From time to time whole groups gather together. A few individuals arrive to join up with the battalion again. Some, recorded as missing, reappear but a goodly number are still absent at roll-call and in certain companies there are great gaps which are impossible to fill. The General Staff finds the solution. The three battalions are re-formed into two, still incomplete, which is to say that the equivalent of more than a whole battalion has been left on the ground as a result of the business at Yoncq. The General Staff has nearly regrouped and on 20 May we go back up to the line, which is not so far off. We are in reserve, among young trees which allow the sun through, which we are really glad of. The sector is calm, there is some firing here and there from artillery or machine-guns, which from time to time exchange bursts, but without much damage being done. A little rivulet passes through the woods, where we can have a much-needed wash. The enemy does not seem to be exerting too much pressure in this sector.

The first news reaches us since the storm started. Until now we have had nothing. Some letters, which are welcome, some newspapers tell us that the battle is raging in Flanders, where the weight of the army is engaged, which explains the calm in our sector, the enemy making his big effort on the North Sea side. Thursday 23 May, we go back a little towards the rear of the line. We march right through the night. We re-cross the Meuse right at the entrance to Dun-sur-Meuse, which seems a nice village constructed after the last war, built on a terrace which overhangs the Meuse, that one can see flowing at the bottom of the valley. The town is completely evacuated and you see nothing but soldiers from every kind of regiment. The sun rises and despite the harsh fatigue of the night I look at the countryside which seems to me really beautiful. We stop a little way from the town in a wood on the left of the road where we waste no time in getting some sleep. We are staying there for three days while an effort is made to re-form the regiment. Numerous reinforcements arrive. The Zouaves lost since Yoncq gather again, the three battalions are re-formed at full strength, and rearmed as many have lost their weapons, particularly the machine-gun company, which had not been able to carry its heavy equipment in the headlong retreat. At the bottom of the wood there is a small, pleasant, river, flowing right up to the top of its banks, and it is a great pleasure for me to bathe and at the same time to wash my shirt, which was starting to stick to my skin.

Sunday 26 May. The departure fever starts up again. Everyone is very well re-equipped, the lorry finally manages to join us, and we can take the equipment out of our packs, mine being full to bursting with washing and reserves of food that, alas, I cannot take away, being already too burdened down with my machine-gun and supplies of ammunition. It's at that point that I regret not being a rifleman and like them able to carry my own pack. I content myself with taking a change of shirt and with changing my shoes, for in these long marches my army boots are cutting into my feet. We leave at nightfall, go back again through Dun, cross the Meuse and here we are again knocking off the kilometres. From time to time a halt, and then away again. Daylight comes quickly. At the end of May the nights soon go and dawn finds us in full stride, descending one hill so as to climb back up another. The edge of the road is constantly marked with little monuments or simple memorial stones that mark the events of the last war, whether glorious attacks or just simple things, but the inscriptions have been all been smeared with red paint, probably so that we shouldn't see them.

Day breaks and it is very grey in a thick fog which hides the whole valley from us. At the moment we are on a steep slope, where a horse-drawn supply convoy has battled all night without being able to climb up. The poor beasts are really badly harnessed to their loads; thin donkeys, which can do no more, pulling old rattletraps that one should really call, in this day and age, prehistoric, for these kinds of trailers have nothing of the modern vehicle about them, somewhat resembling the Lyon mail-coach we saw in the cinema. Then they dare to talk to us about a motorised army; this convoy is truly sickening to see! At the top of the slope, a little village, Villers-devant-Dun. We go on a little further and enter a vast wood, known on the map as Bois de la Vache. It is horribly humid for the sun has not been able to penetrate for many a long year. The whole regiment takes up positions all around the wood and immediately each man digs his own

combat trench at the edge of the forest. My section is to be in reserve
and for this reason we go deep into the wood; on the other hand, we
have to maintain a post of six men to keep a lookout on a knoll one
kilometre in front of the wood.

We stay there until 30 May. Although hardly any distance from the
enemy, nothing in particular happens. From our look-out we see an
occasional observation balloon sent up from the opposing side. Some
shells fly hither and thither without doing any damage. We are pretty
badly supplied. Our company possesses a proper kitchen, but many
others don't, so ours has to provide meals for three companies. As a
result the number of courses shrinks. Also, to make up for this state of
affairs, there is quite of a lot of clandestine slaughter. It was thus that in
the middle of the wood we saw a group surround a superb, freshly-
killed heifer, completely skinned, hung to a tree and awaiting the
share-out of steaks. Many others were similarly slaughtered.

In the little valley on the edge of the wood is a pleasant farm where
a fresh spring runs into the washhouse and where we can get washed
and get some new supplies. The farm is completely wrecked. Has
this been done by the regiments that preceded us or is it the work of
the looters of our regiment, who have formed a team to grab anything that comes to hand? Whatever the explanation I am sick at
heart to see this devastation inflicted on dwelling-houses evacuated
only a short time before. The kitchen is completely turned upside
down, the downstairs bedrooms are in a pitiful state, the mattresses
have been torn open, the bed-springs and bolsters have suffered the
same fate, the wardrobes have been emptied of their contents which
have been thrown onto the ground. The pictures, whether religious
or otherwise, have followed together with the family photos, which
were probably kept in drawers and likewise a good number of letters.
Everything, higgledy-piggledy, lying on the ground. It's shameful and
it makes me sick at heart to see it through the windows which over-
look the courtyard. The numerous livestock run frightened through
the meadows; some little chickens, just born, some small ducks which
are going to die for lack of care, some pigs which are roaring with
hunger. The chickens, of which a good number are already missing
from the register, fly around in the trees, terrified. Some foals and
quite a lot of cows wander from one field to another.

One afternoon I meet my colleague Pau from Clarensac who I
haven't seen since the start of this set-to, he having left the company
to join the band and as a result become a stretcher-bearer. We talk
over the fate of our friend from Calvisson, over which I had acted to
inform the family, and without further problems we leave the wood

on the evening of Thursday 30 May. We take the road which brought us here. Towards 10 in the evening, in the black of night, we find the kitchen which serves us a meal on the side of the road. Once more we recross Dun-sur-Meuse, and with ascents and descents we keep on marching.

It is day. We have been marching for nearly 12 hours already and then someone says that we are only halfway. There is a handcart on which are quickly piled up all the rifles and packs from the section, everyone taking his turn to push. The column stretches out, but many give up, unable to do more, and thus we see on the road an infantry battalion which lugs along any means of transportation that it can get hold of. Children's prams, there are all kinds and models of them from the old type perched high on four wheels to the modern kind, lower on its wheels and aerodynamic, pushchairs, wheelbarrows and handcarts. The commandant doesn't seem too pleased by this but he doesn't dare to complain too much, for he can see men at their limit, who would otherwise just leave the equipment there, dumped.

Finally a village after numerous woods and it is Écurey. Another large part of the battalion gives up. Some grumbling begins; it is nine o'clock in the morning. We have been marching since six o'clock yesterday evening without, apart from supper, having been given a snack. I march some more kilometres and then, at the edge of a little wood, unable to do more, I too lie down. All those that remain of the section, a dozen in all, do likewise, the rest being far behind. We rest for a moment, then, from the little food which we possess, we share out a snack. One comrade, in the course of the march, has succeeded in refilling his flask with wine. For my part I have in my flask the section's rum reserve. We have a light meal.

But, while we are preparing to go off again, a car coming along at high speed stops at our position. The colonel in person gets down on to the road. He is furious and lets fly all his invective while getting the officer who accompanies him to take down the names of all the laggards. But he has so much to write that he cannot manage it, for a cyclist acting as liaison tells us that the first to arrive at the end of the march with the commandant number not even 100. It's not bad out of the 1,200 men that make up the battalion. At last we arrive in our turn in a little wood where a halt is planned. The colonel is still there. A captain bends his ear, telling him that the men have been marching for more than 15 hours without even getting a snack. Straightaway we lie down but it is impossible to sleep in this wood which is more like a marsh with mosquitoes swarming. At the centre of the copse is a German cemetery from the last war that we visit, going up and down the pretty well-kept avenues, with several hundreds of black crosses lined up, the whole thing dominated by a kind of monumental chapel.

At midday a parade, which hasn't happened since the days of calm. The events of the morning are the reason. Various tough sanctions are announced for the next group of laggards. But tomorrow we shall be in the front line, so prison hardly makes us afraid. The sun is going down when the battalion is once again ready to depart. Many have not yet rejoined from the stage of the night before. That makes no difference, we start off again, but very tired. The march is slow. In fact we do not march too much, six or seven hours bring us, around two o'clock in the morning, to the wood of Grand Failly where we rest the whole day in the thickest part of the big forest.

We start off again at the going down of the sun, cross the vast wood throughout which are camouflaged all kinds of vehicles. Everywhere there are just shelters, telephone wires criss-crossing, batteries in firing positions, which makes us think that the front line cannot be far off. However we march until midnight where we arrive at an anti-tank line. A final stop for the horses, carts, lorries, nothing goes beyond this point, which just means that the poor infantryman, he who is authorised to go further, must carry everything on his back. They hand out a second load of ammunition, grenades, some emergency rations and all the equipment for the company. The machine-gun company in fact needs a hand because it is so heavily loaded. The machine-guns, and trench guns, are very heavy. With some mates from the group I have got a good supply of sugar found in an abandoned van. We go through a small village already three-quarters demolished by enemy artillery. It is sinister at night, these half-ruined houses, where you can only see sections of walls, with windows and doors hanging from them, with some furniture still on the first floor, only partly come down. Now we are going down a narrow road with the greatest care, without a word or lighting a cigarette, with the least noise possible, for being in open country, the least mistake would risk getting the artillery going, and that could turn out badly for us.

Flabeuville

Finally the noise of a small river comes to our ears: it is the Chiers which runs into the bottom of the valley. The night is pretty black, you can't see far in front of you, a good night for relief in the line. We stay on the little road for a while. The section commanders have gone to reconnoitre the positions, while the relieved sections prepare for their departure. They are happier than us, for it is surely better to depart than to arrive in holiday resorts like these. After a maze of trenches where there is an endless going up and then down, after stumbling a hundred or more times over roots, stones, planks, crates, walking two or three times in water and the rest in mud, I finally get to my position which is at the bottom of a trench more than three metres deep. A kind of cavern dug under a rock, reinforced by railway lines and sleepers. A candle is burning in this cave of death. We shake hands with the tenants of the place who are happy to see us arrive, and the gunner quickly gives me instructions, as he can't wait to go. They leave us some provisions, quite a lot of ammunition, a full bag of coffee, and among other things an enormous sow, killed the day before and hung up virtually whole in a neighbouring cavern. We put our guns in firing positions. Two men go to take over guard for the group and we try to lie down in this shelter, which is truly a cold store. It wouldn't be colder in an icebox, and we arrived all sweaty from the march, my teeth are chattering in there although our predecessors have piled up quite a few eiderdowns, mattresses, and bedcovers, some of which seem to be rather too good for the place, no doubt stolen from the neighbouring village, which, it seems, is 200 metres ahead of us, at the end of the valley and on the very edge of the river. No, it is too cold and I don't want to peg out in there. I leave the cavern and the trench itself by a kind of ladder which is there, and after attaching myself to my machine-gun by my belt, I sleep under a copse of trees to the side of the trench.

I wake up. It is fully day although it is only five o'clock in the morning, and at once I look around the countryside of our new abode. The view does not stretch very far as the hills are near. We are halfway up the slope of one of them. About 200 metres below is the hamlet of Flabeuville (Meurthe-et-Moselle). The Chiers, which laps up against the houses, is not very wide, five or six metres at its widest, and very different from the Chiers that we knew near Sedan. On my left is a mill with its lock. Immediately over the river, a railway line that links Longuyon, Montmédy and beyond. On my right, five or six kilometres away at the most, is Longuyon. In front of me, another hill, but that is the property of the enemy who are occupying it. That's to say we are virtually on top of each other. For this show we will really be in the front row, even though we haven't reserved our places. Between two hills we see a small village, that is Villette, where the German flag has been flying for a few days now. On my right, the line goes into a tunnel and the remainder is in the woods. Behind, here and there, are some small camouflaged blockhouses, some ready, some scarcely half-finished.

Everything is very calm even if we are in the furthermost front line, and the cuckoos sing even more. In the trench, life gets organised, and we tour our area. Some trenches are dug and lined with timbers in which the riflemen and suppliers are set up, each one opposite his lookout slit, which is a combat position. The trench is very deep all the way along. At one place, which is nearly a cul-de-sac, a particularly large trench is covered with corrugated iron. A table, formed by two planks, surrounded by benches is doubtless the refectory of the group. And it's true, our predecessors have left quite a lot of crockery, a superb filter coffee-maker, the grinder, several casserole dishes, some plates and dishes coming from a marvellous dinner service, and crystal glasses. Now we only need some good bottles of wine, some novels and old newspapers, and the whole thing arranged on shelves dug into the trench.

In a nook of the trench, we set up a nice enamelled stove, all new, that our predecessors, not expecting to leave so soon, had gone to get from the village the night before. We are having difficulties with the chimney, but someone who is a specialist in these things arranges it so that the smoke does not show. Already the two blokes from the group who have been appointed cooks are preparing some coffee which we gulp down. It is really good and well-sugared. My turn on watch arrives, and via a narrow passageway which goes down between bushes as far as the middle of a great clump of hawthorns scarcely 50 paces from the river, that's where the section's forward look-out post is. Moreover the post is doubled at night. It's nice weather, in fact very nice. With the field-glasses I look at the line of enemy trenches which is nearly on the summit of the hill. From time to time you can see a few forms stirring, but mostly no one on either side moves or fires.

At midday there is the first meal that we have in our dining-room. The section, now nearly complete, is seated. Big Pop, hosier by trade, grenadier in the section, has become cook. He serves up a kind of potato stew in which a large piece of pork is cooked, then the leftover beans from the departed men, with two cans of beef, the whole thing well seasoned, and we eat with appetite, for the thin fare from the evening before is already a distant memory. We still have a little wine, cheese from who knows where, and the coffee that we have in abundance for the time being complete the meal. It is really a long time since we have had its equal, eaten on plates, with silver spoons, all on a table, really this is a touch of luxury that we have nearly forgotten.

In the afternoon things cloud over a little. I was taking a siesta lying down in a bush on the edge of the trench, when the dance began. Four or five shells are fired at the same time and the ground trembles. One leap and I am in the trench, at my position. Once the first moment of surprise is over, we see that it is our side which is firing. The shells are leaving, and we thought that they were arriving. These are the big guns from the last defences of the Maginot line, near Montmédy, which are firing. Everything trembles. We hear shells passing overhead in an uninterrupted rustling to burst further on in Belgium or in Luxembourg, since we are nearly level with the junction of the two countries. The artillery replies and the duel lasts for a little while like this, without doing any harm to us, then everything returns again to calm.

The first night is fairly quiet. Towards 10 o'clock two men from each group go to get some provisions. This can only be done by night as our predecessors had suffered some losses in trying to go by day. The smallest roads, or tracks, being observed, the enemy artillery comes back into play at the least sign of movement on them. I am on guard at one o'clock in the morning when the meal-carrying party returns. The poor lads are done for, they have made eight or ten kilometres across fields to bring back a plate of rice, some scrag-ends of meat, enough bread, and some flasks of wine. That is all we have to keep a dozen men going until the following night.

Day breaks quickly in June, dawn is scarcely apparent when I decide to go to the village with a mate. I take my soap and towel, for I should really like to have a quick wash. Everything is quiet when, by the side of a hedge which hides us a little we get into the first houses in the village. It is not a pretty sight, like all the villages evacuated in haste and immediately pillaged by those coming up behind despite the notices which threaten those caught in the act with death. A group of Arab soldiers comes down out of one house with a large bag, which looks as if it is full of potatoes, and water. We go in in our turn, by necessity, but I go into these devastated houses only with repugnance. Here as in many other places there is only horror to be seen. The looters have passed through and nearly everything is ripped open and lying on the ground. In the kitchen, there is a pump; we clean up in the sink, and I even wash my shirt. After filling a bag with spuds we take two buckets of water and then get back rapidly to the trenches, because we are not too relaxed in the houses, where an artillery round could surprise us.

Like the day before, the day turns out to be nearly calm, the silence occasionally broken by bursts of artillery fire. It's the night which is frightening; at every moment we fear being surprised: both sides are so near each other. This forward listening post is scarcely a few paces from the river; on the stroke of one or two in the morning, when sleep tortures you, you doze for a second and then jump up thinking you hear the tanks coming, then you are reassured a little, it is only the water pouring out of the lock. How we curse this lock for its sporadic noise! Then to the right and the left machine-guns from time to time let go bursts of fire. It only takes one shot for the whole line immediately to start spitting forth. There is firing for five minutes before silence resumes. Then it is the artillery which has a little fun. Some shells falling pretty close give us a fright. At last, at half past three, dawn is coming and the day is greeted with the greatest joy, for in situations like these you like to be able to see yourself.

Nearly every morning, although it is scarcely daybreak, I go out with a basket to make a tour of the gardens in the area. This is my kind of line, and I enjoy this duty. I gather asparagus, leeks, onions, and anything I can find which is halfway drinkable, while two or three companions go into the cellars for daily provisions of potatoes and of water. One morning, I go up and down all the village streets. Several houses have collapsed. In the square, I go into the church, which, by the way, is still open. It has suffered no damage and so far has been respected.

One morning a group from the company which had gone down to the village even though it was not yet quite day, bumped into a group of German soldiers who had also come for provisions. The two armed groups, virtually equal in strength, looked at each other and no words were exchanged; the incident went off very well, each one regaining their lines without a single shot being fired. But all the same it put a damper on things and now we go down to the village with some caution.

The trench life is fairly well-organised; our cooks do a pretty decent meal of everything that we bring back from our morning sorties; the coffee is still good, and the pork, that we don't find so good, is eaten all the same, boiled up in the soup. We discover an explanation for the bad taste of the meat, as two mates have found eight piglets hardly a few days' old in a farm, dead of hunger, all of which leads us to conclude that we are eating the mother, our predecessors having surely killed her while she was suckling her little ones. We are, moreover, very badly resupplied. A neighbouring company has lost some men who went off on meal duty, every road and path being observed by the enemy. However some letters arrive, but no newspapers. We are completely cut off from the remainder of France, we who are the closest to the war know nothing of it. Are we withdrawing? Advancing? A mystery.

Our old lieutenant comes to visit us and congratulates the platoon on its defensive position, but he is not so happy when he sees our cooker which is working away merrily. We have to work hard to explain to him that for three days we have had nothing to eat, he treats us as if we are mad. Another morning, it's an artillery officer who, down to check the range for the guns, happens upon the stove where there are two or three cooking-pots boiling which he tries to send flying. But in a minute the whole group is assembled around the cooker. Big Pop threatens to throw the artilleryman out if he so much as touches one of our pots. He threatens us with worse punishments, a report to the colonel, to the division, to the general, but nothing is of any use, from the moment that the midday meal was put in question. Our colleague Enquet explains with a stammer that it doesn't matter if we die from a bullet or a shell but we don't want to die of hunger first.

The following night is eventful. An enemy patrol penetrates our lines and there is a general firing of all our weapons; calm returns in the morning. On the night of 7–8 June, towards midnight, while I was sleeping deeply, I am woken with a start by the lieutenant. 'Quick, quick, we are surrounded.'

Already he has grabbed my machine-gun so as to put it in my hands. He leads me to the upper trench and places me with my weapon facing the rear. I don't understand anything any more of what is going on; it's true that I am not yet fully awake. We listen. Yes indeed, people are chatting in a low voice along the edge of the small road, above our heads, along the copse. What am I supposed to do? The sergeants have briefed the other two groups of the section, one to my right, and the other to my left. The voices, which I can't make out, get closer and immediately I let fly a burst of about a dozen rounds; my two mates to right and left do the same and that is enough to start up the whole arsenal. The blockhouses where the machine-guns are installed reply and this continues for part of the night, while the enemy artillery sends some well-aimed shells to dampen our ardour. In the end everything is quiet, but we have the certain knowledge that someone is hidden behind our backs. We are afraid at the same time of being attacked from the front, so the whole platoon is anxious and at action stations for what is going to happen. The lieutenant wants to clear the matter up and he orders a patrol.

Naturally I am chosen, together with one of my friends. I tell the lieutenant that to go as a pair is really risky, even with the light machine-gun and some grenades; there are lads out there waiting for us, because I'm sure of it, as I've heard them talking. A sergeant and another man are added to the patrol. The lieutenant himself ends up by joining the sortie. I'm the first out of the trench, my loaded gun under my arm, ready to fire. The others follow, grenades in hand. The lieutenant, clutching his revolver, walks in the lead. It is not yet quite dawn, but we can see a little better. We walk spread out in firing positions, up a field, scouring each bush on the edge. We go down another; no one. However, I did hear talking, as did the lieutenant, I am sure of it. We search several hedges and groups of trees and we are going to return when the sergeant climbs up onto the little road which goes along above the trenches, and wasn't he surprised, weren't we all, to see camping utensils full of beans, meat and rice, flasks of wine, dixies of coffee, a bike, all of it put down in a hurry! On the other side of the road, below in a thicket of hawthorn, we have the explanation: one by one a dozen Zouaves emerging from their unfortunate plight, all from the 5th company, which, coming back from dinner had got lost in the night and had stumbled on our position. The poor devils were really afraid, they heard the bullets whistling by all night. Happily, no one was hit, apart from a few mess-tins, as the men, being a good metre below, were not at risk from the bullets, which must have skimmed over their heads all the same. The incident ends well and we go back.

The Dun-sur-Meuse Sector

Sunday evening, 9 June. We are unexpectedly relieved, while waiting for a fierce attack at any minute, our recce patrols having noticed major preparations on the other side of the Chiers. We leave our trenches a little after midnight and march fairly quickly towards the rear. Quite late in the morning, we arrive at Grand Failly Wood. The kitchen has preceded us and at noon a decent meal is served. We get a fair amount of mail and we enjoy reading the news from home.

In the afternoon the battalion gets a significant reinforcement, all the sections are brought up to strength. In the wood I meet my chum Pau from Clarensac and we chat with him for a moment; besides it is the last time that I am to see him. The evening meal is served at four o'clock and immediately afterwards we are on the road after being issued with some iron rations. That bodes ill: reinforcements, iron rations. Nevertheless we keep on marching. Night comes, we are really tired, but we keep on going forward all the same. Towards the middle of the night, the road becomes badly congested. Several batteries, perhaps from the same division as us, are following the road. At one stage a motorcycle liaison soldier mows down one of the section's loaders, and sends him rolling into the gutter. There is a general traffic-jam, you can no longer go forward, horses, guns, caissons, lorries, plus our own carts. Several battalions mingle. We stop in a vast field, near the village of Écurey. At the end of half an hour we start off again. We can only drag our little cart, on which are arranged all our packs and the section's ammunition, with great difficulty, on this jam-packed road. We drag, each in turn, the trailer, but half the platoon has disappeared while leaving their equipment on the handcart. What's more, a wheel of the heavily-laden vehicle threatens to break into pieces. A new convoy of artillery passes us going the other way, it's two o'clock in the morning. The fatigue is terrible and for the first time since the beginning of the war I give up, not being able to do any more. All that remains of the platoon does the same. We retire into a meadow and under a

92

clump of trees roll ourselves up in our blankets and waste no time in getting off to sleep.

The sun is already high when we wake up. It's seven o'clock. We are alone in the middle of this vast plain, all the congestion from the night before has disappeared. That's not all, no one among us can even remember from what direction we came here. Somehow we have to rejoin the battalion. We gather up the equipment while two or three fix the wheel of the trailer and we leave in a westerly direction, which seems to me to be the direction that we were following. A clear and cool stream appears just at the right time. We strip down to our shirts and there on the side of the road have a wash of the kind that we haven't had for a long time. That done we start off again, but the pace is not very quick, the cart drags and the road climbs. A big village whose name I was never told. In the square, a militiaman tells us which direction our battalion took. A battery which is coming down from the line passes by. The gunners also seem very tired, they tell us about having fired ceaselessly until their stock of shells was exhausted, that's to say 70, 75 and even 80 hours without pause for some of the guns. As for information on the operation, they hardly know more than we do. A lieutenant tells us, however, that the enemy might be in retreat along the whole length of the front, which makes us happy, but the same evening we have to acknowledge that the tip was wrong.

At the exit from the village, we meet the remainder of the section which was waiting while getting anxious for their packs which had remained on the cart. And starting off again, as it's heavy, stormy weather, it's a great struggle to march. We go past a tiny but very pretty cemetery. A monument recalls that it is there that in 1914 the small garrison of Verdun met the first advance guard of the German army; the whole garrison lies there after having fought bravely. We pause, really we had to; we have a snack, and use some of the iron rations.

And we start off again in sultry weather. We drag ourselves along rather than march. The road climbs endlessly. On a bend is a huge mastodon of a gun, a 420mm drawn behind a tractor, lying on its side in a neighbouring field after missing the bend, and with everything abandoned. Further on there is a lorry which has caught fire. Several horse-drawn vehicles, one with its horse dead in the shafts. These are truly the images of war. On the edge of a wood, five or six gunners dig a trench and unhappily we soon come to understand why. Four other artillerymen carry on stretchers four of their comrades killed the day before by an aircraft bomb while they were watering the horses in the neighbouring village. At an intersection Sergeant Vernhet, the platoon's deputy commander, waits for us. The lieutenant, finally realising that his section has almost completely disappeared, has left one of his NCOs here to bring us in. The poor man is even more tired than us, he is at the end of his tether and can only hold himself upright with the greatest difficulty.

Right now the planes are joining in and they spiral down on us in tight-knit groups. One among them suddenly comes down on us in a dive. Immediately we throw ourselves into the ditches, which are not very deep at this point. After a few seconds I realise that I am lying near an important pile of shells, stored there on the very side of the road. Between two aerial passes we get out, for the area is too dangerous. Again we cover a few kilometres, pass through another village, half-ruined, and are forced to stop under a copse of trees, the sergeant no longer able to keep up. The weather, while overcast, is even heavier, what fatigue! On the plain, completely exposed despite the constant attention from enemy aircraft, the artillerymen bring the guns into action, urged on by their officers, and immediately some of them start firing relentlessly. We see guns arriving from everywhere, which immediately makes us think that down there in front it can't be too good and that time must be pressing. Our officer cadet comes to meet us, brought up in a side-car. He doesn't say too much, but takes the light machine-guns and goes back to put them all together while we quietly carry on. Towards midday we are on the banks of the Meuse once more. Again we see Dun-sur-Meuse; one thing is true, we always come back into this sector.

We go forward along the river beyond the town, for at least four or five kilometres. In one place, various big roads cross. The railway crosses the Meuse at this point on a superb metal bridge that we see blow up with a frightful crash, while plumes of water come up from the river. We advance two or three hundred metres downstream of the bridge which has just collapsed and find our company already there in position. However, everything is calm. We find our combat positions, mine is right on the bank of the river, between it and the main road which goes from Dun-sur-Meuse towards Sedan. We have come, so we hear, in a frantic march, to take position there to help a regiment of the Legion disengage, as it was threatened with being completely encircled. While waiting, it's calm and we gladly rest on the grass of the bank right next to the trench. Some people plunge completely naked into the Meuse. I feel that a good bath would do me good and a moment later I cannot resist the temptation to soak myself, in this Meuse of which I have heard so much spoken and which I would never have believed I would bathe in. At midday the section's wandering gypsy, Aquatino from Nice, turns up with a full basket of carp and some superb pike killed by the detonations of the explosives which have been used to blow several bridges downstream of the river. In fact we have a choice of fish for with a pole from the bank you can take one at will. They drift quietly in the current, belly upwards, within arm's reach.

In the afternoon the sky darkens, a storm menaces, and it becomes close, in fact very close right on the edge of the water. At four o'clock the enemy artillery, which up to that point had stayed quiet, starts to send over its shells. Long at first, they explode on Dun or its immediate surroundings where one of our battalions leaves quite a few of its men. Night falls. I profit from it by eating some still half-green cherries from a tree by the side of the road. The engineers mine and bring down some very big trees which fall down across the road; that is not a very good omen for us. At night the enemy artillery begins to shower us copiously while dropping its range. Several shells fall near us, some fall in the river or the canal alongside and the explosions produce sprays of water to a great height. At nine o'clock, while the onslaught is raging ever more strongly, the order to withdraw arrives.

By bad luck I bump into the lieutenant commanding the company who puts me on guard on a small bridge that crosses the canal parallel to the Meuse where a lane leads to the village of Sassey. I have to stay there with a soldier of the engineers who is charged with blowing up the bridge immediately after the passage of some sections which are positioned on the plain on the other side of the canal. I have to warn the sections so that they do not step on mines put on the roadway of the bridge and identify the sections so as to signal to the engineering corps that no one remains on the other side. The shelling redoubles in violence. At this moment the storm which has been menacing since the morning joins in. It thunders some way away, but the flashes of lightning cut across the sky which makes it all appear even darker after they have disappeared. Meanwhile, the first platoon of the company gets over the bridge. Only three sections remain on the other side. A shell arrives, whistling with that peculiar whistle signifying the end of its journey, which should never be mistaken. I throw myself on the bridge and I really believe that my last moment has come. The shell misses the railing by a whisker and bursts two or three metres downstream in the river. I had a narrow escape. However, others burst in the immediate surroundings. Time presses and the three sections still do not come along. At last, the first section of the sergeant-major, Manière's, platoon, I chat for a second with my friend Polge from Sommières who is there. The other two groups finally get over too. I was going to follow them, to withdraw as well, after having passed the order to the soldier from the engineers to blow up the bridge, when the shortsighted lieutenant comes along, again telling me that he was losing patience with the Manière platoon. I had to tell him until I was blue in the face that everybody had gone over. He hadn't seen Sergeant-Major Manière and he continued to argue that they were still on the other side. Some shells went off again quite near while a roll of thunder mixed with them and some drops of rain started to fall. The soldier from the engineers was indecisive with his fuse already lit. However, I got into a rage arguing that I had spoken myself to the sergeant-major as well as to several soldiers from the platoon. In the end he gave in and we left at speed, to join up with the company, by now quite some distance away. We had not gone more than 200 metres when the bridge went up. We were marching blindly across fields for the big fallen trees across the road made marching on it impracticable. From time to time we had to lie flat for the shells were falling in clusters. The rain was taking a hand, and was coming down in torrents, while the lightning and the thunder were repeated endlessly one after the other, yet without dampening the ardour of the enemy artillery which mixed its explosions with the sounds of the storm. To the end of my life I will never forget that frightful night.

At last, at the edge of a village, I catch up with the 4th Platoon of the company, who were also late because nobody had warned them of the retreat, and it was only after quite a while that a sergeant remembered them. And finally I happen on my platoon. The poor men have had real trouble with their hand-cart that they had to carry at various stages to get clear of the congestion. The storm is redoubling its violence. We stop for a moment in a farm building exposed to all the winds. Two shells land with a tremendous crash on the houses close to us. Despite the rain, we have to go for we don't feel safe in these parts. In the end a fine rain succeeds the storm. We march along, up to our knees in water in places. Some shells explode again but they are losing their accuracy, because they are dropping too short.

Day breaks, the dawn arrives in a rainy sky typical of the days after a storm. Some big clouds still scud along really low, but we have the sense of having left the firing zone. We all look at each other, counting our members; our platoon is nearly complete, while others have lost a few men. We are no longer men, it's deplorable, full of mud, our greatcoats are heavy and run with water from everywhere, our shirts stick to our skin, and it's in silence that we march through the woods, each one thinking of this nightmarish night that we have just lived through.

In the deepest part of the wood we make a stop at the side of a kind of clearing where a line of blockhouses is under construction. The kitchen is waiting for us there and serves us a mug of hot coffee, which does some good, after which, all soaked, we lie down under the brushwood completely drenched and our teeth soon start chattering. The cold forces us to remain standing, despite our exhaustion. A very strong smell bothers us a great deal. Each of us tries to find out where it is coming from, and we don't take long to discover that, near a copse, under barely two centimetres of earth, were sleeping – forever in their case – four or five soldiers buried in haste some days ago. Two gaitered legs were sticking out of the ground, which makes us think that they must be artillerymen who had copped it there, almost certainly from the air.

At 10 o'clock, a timid sun appeared through some big trees and everyone wanted to bask in it. At last they serve us some food, a copious helping that must have been the last official meal of the campaign. While eating, the rumour goes round from group to group that we shall be embarking by boat. Some people, who say that they are well-informed, claim that we are leaving for Tunisia, our division being made up nearly entirely of north Africans. Others claim that we are leaving for the Rouen–Le Havre sector which is, according to the latest news, very threatened. No one knows anything, when the order to depart arrives at midday and immediately the artillery, which had left us in peace all morning, starts up again, pounding relentlessly and with precision the area where the battalion had spent the morning, which proves that we had been closely observed. The air force flies over us, without however dropping any bombs. Rain starts to fall once again. At the top of an incline we pass a regiment of legionnaires who are going the other way up to the positions, bringing with them a great variety of equipment; cows and goats make up part of the escort.[3] We leave the road to them and take the one along the big woods, which does not make any easier the progress of our trailer, on which is piled up all our equipment. The wretched thing had to suffer cruelly.

Verdun, Memories of the Other War

As last, at five o'clock, we reach a pretty important junction. Hundreds and hundreds of cars, lorries and other transport are arriving on two different roads. Along the main road the division's artillery has already finished its loading, the horses in the lorries, the guns, the gun platforms in trailers behind, the men in the coaches, and there are lines of vehicles as far as the eye can see. They take us forward another two kilometres on a small road to the exit from a village hidden in the hollow between the hills. It's there that the battalion has to embark. The coaches have been waiting long enough, the enemy reconnaissance planes are overflying us all the time, making us fear the worst and we don't need orders to get into the ditches, despite the water, and to use the clumps of trees or the cowsheds in the fields to camouflage ourselves as well as possible from the view of the planes, for by now everyone understands what it costs to play the brave man. At last an interminable column of large buses moves off. Order is very well maintained by the officers of the battalion, and quite quickly, without rush or scrimmage, each company gets into the coaches. My platoon is lodged in a big tramcar from the centre of Paris.

While all this was happening the horses, the machine-gun and equipment companies have embarked in transport lorries, the mastodons of the road, each one of which takes 10 or 12 horses. A quarter of an hour afterwards, the column moves off quickly, but the planes don't let us out of their sight, even though they don't machine-gun us. No doubt they have been ordered to keep an eye on the column's march.

We leave the firing line which is now a good 25 or 30 kilometres behind us. We pass some villages of the Meuse Department where, apart from soldiers, you do not see a living soul. We climb, go down again and then forward at a good pace. On the edge of the road you see a succession of lorries stuck in ditches and coaches smashed open. Others, having burned, contain black carcasses. Often enough there are horses lying in the road, fallen and never to get up again. All kinds of machines lie useless in the ditches and then, which is even sadder, right on the side of the road, in the neighbouring fields, there are two or three square metres of freshly dug earth, surmounted by a cross made in haste out of two sections of wood, from which hangs a helmet and often a bottle containing the papers of the poor boys who copped it there.

Now we're crossing the great battlefields of the other war. We see very well, however crumbling, and three-quarters filled in, the layout of all those trenches and tracks. In places the barbed wire still shows the combat positions clearly. In the coach an old reserve officer who had been in the previous war and who, what's more, is from Verdun, lists for us the names of the hills of which we've heard so much talk, of the formidable battles which had unfolded there. At the summit of one hill we look out over the whole valley and on the facing slope we can see Verdun. The officer, that almost everyone in the coach is listening to, with no one saying a word, continues his story. On the left, Douaumont, to the right, the fort of Vaux, the keys to Verdun. Our eyes want to see everything at the same time, to the right, to the left of the road where nothing has yet grown, there are only trenches, dugouts, and shelters three-quarters collapsed. The tower of the great monument of Douaumont rises up, overlooking the valley. Down in the valley, where the worst fighting must have been, a small village has been reconstructed, pretty under the setting sun. At the exit from the village to the right there is an immense cemetery with lines of white crosses. Some newly-made graves mean that there are men who lie next to those who have been sleeping there for 20 years.

At last we go into Verdun. The first thing that strikes us is seeing civilians, women, young women, kids, things that we haven't been used to seeing. This return to civilisation, if we can call it that, is a shock to us all straightaway. But what's happening now? The people seem to be thronging the roads, panic-stricken, despite the late hour; it's not yet night, but it soon will be. The women, the kids, the old, lug trunks, suitcases, bundles, wheelbarrows, carts; everything jams up the roadway and forces our coaches to slow their pace and in certain places to stop completely. We try to chat to the civilians and immediately we understand. The people are half mad, they don't even reply to what we ask them. There is only one word in their mouth: evacuation, evacuation. This is all that we can find out about events. We go at a slow pace over the bridge which overhangs the station. Some trains are drawn up there in formation and everyone embarks in inextricable disorder, higgledy-piggledy in the cattle trucks. We do not really understand the reason for this hurried operation. The line is a fair way distant from Verdun, a good 80 kilometres.

We keep on travelling, now on the glorious road bedecked with milestones topped with helmets, and again some cemeteries to the right and to the left. But night falls suddenly and we can no longer see very well. A little fine rain starts, and soon there's a complete stop. We will wait for the first glimmers of dawn because such a convoy cannot travel in a night as black as this. I have kept back a small tin of tuna that I share with my loader, seated on the same bench. A mug of wine for two completes this poor meal and we sleep pretty badly despite the great, very great fatigue.

At the first rays of dawn, things start up and immediately the question returns to the order of the day: where are we going? Nobody knows. What is today, the 13th of June, going to hold for us? The future would tell us that it was one of the hardest of the hard days of the campaign.

However the sun rises in a morning mist that is quickly dissipated. We go through some villages, everywhere there are only tears and lamentations, everyone is evacuating at top speed. At the moment the road is full of refugees, and there is a general traffic jam. The column can hardly go forward quicker than at the pace of horses. On the crossings, despite the gendarmes who are keeping order, helped everywhere by the militia, it's with great difficulty that one can manage to get through. However, one understands that the police force has been ordered to give priority to the troops for they head off all those awful columns of refugees mercilessly into the neighbouring fields. That makes us think that if they are in such a hurry to get us forward, they must have a serious motive. And it continues like this right across the Department of the Meuse. There's an endless succession of villages; in the central square of one, people are collapsed prostrate. Indifferent and haggard, they watch us go by. They have seen so much, these poor people, coming from deep in the Ardennes, from Flanders, from Belgium, from Luxembourg! The majority are on foot, and have been wandering for more than a month without knowing where they are going, always pushed forward by the advancing front. Groups of hundreds and hundreds of people are lying down along the woods, copses, some surround an army mobile kitchen which gives them a little soup, broth or coffee. But what is most pitiful, is to see entire families on the road, with their livestock that they force to follow them, but that they finally have to leave in some cattle pen. We see wagons drawn by two, three or four beautiful mares, some with their young foal which follows at the risk of being crushed every few metres. The wagon is driven by a woman, often in tears, but most of the time it's a kid of eight, ten or perhaps twelve years old who leads the horses. On the wagon, on which furniture, trunks, cases, linen, the most precious things, or rather the most indispensable things, have been hastily piled up, the grandparents have also taken their place, holding in their arms a very young child, even a newborn baby. What a spectacle that is! The children look at us one by one as we overtake them, holding in their hands the little dog, the little cat or the cage of canaries which they didn't want to be separated from on departure. Poor people, one can never pity them enough. I remember when I was very young in the other war; these convoys of refugees which came down to our village, certainly they were helped on arrival, but in my opinion not as much as they needed. They were often put up in old shacks when in many cases one might have been able to do much more for them without much effort. The people of our place had an excuse, for you had to have seen it to understand what these people could have suffered.

Champagne

However, the morning goes on. We see in the distance Bar-le-Duc which we leave behind on our left, and it would seem that we are going back up towards Reims. We go on more quickly at the moment, and the road is less congested. Finally, towards 11 o'clock we overtake the lorries that have been bringing the division's artillery. They unload in the fields all along the main road and very soon we see, not without fear, that the horses, harnessed immediately after unloading to the caissons and to the guns, are leaving towards their positions at a canter, which makes us think that time is pressing, which bodes no good. We go on again for a few kilometres and are stopped at the entrance of a village short of Vitry-le-François. I find myself right by the colonel who is arguing fiercely with the battalion's commandant. I hear a few words: the colonel does not know exactly what we are going to do here, and gets endless orders and counter-orders. Various false reports pass from group to group.

Already looters are beginning to take over, the village having been cleared out in the night or even in the morning. Aquatino, the section's gypsy, arrives with four or five large jars of preserved cherries, plums and grapes and makes a generous distribution to all in the platoon, who hold out their mugs. Heavens, we have had nothing or nearly nothing to eat since yesterday morning, which is about 40 hours, and our heads are beginning to droop after 18 hours of travelling in these coaches.[4]

The company is reassembled and we leave by the road that we came on, but we soon leave that to take a small secondary road to our right. We go on for a kilometre through some light woods. We arrive at the edge of a largish river, the Saulx. A nice little bridge separates us from the village. Here we stop and camp on a small beach, on the edge of the river, under the big trees. It's good weather, but I am hungry and there is nothing to eat. I relieve myself of all my gear, and wash barefoot in the company of a few of my comrades in the river, where the cold water does us good.

Here again the looters from the section are already coming back from the village loaded up like mules. They are pushing a little hand-cart on which there is a barrel containing around 100 litres of wine, two hams, a large goose, several slabs of fat and rind, some bread and various other things. They have not yet stopped and the barrel has already been tapped. The first to drink declare the contents terrific. I drink a full mug of it, it's really good; it's cold despite the heat, a white champagne type of wine which sparkles as much as one could wish. It's a long time since I have drunk anything so good. Now everyone drinks; 100 litres, we'll never see the end of it. I drink a second mug and allow myself to try a third, and I have never managed to drink so much wine, particularly without eating, but the fatigue of the journey, the midday heat and this wine so cool, so seductive . . .

But what's happening? There's a kind of stirring in the other companies positioned all along the Saulx in the meadow. Soon the news breaks. A motorcycle dispatch rider brings a message: the enemy advance guard are two or three kilometres from the village. At a stroke, our appetites disappear, just as Big Pop, a pigsticker in his hand, was starting to attack the biggest of the hams to share out some large slices. Is this possible, just as we were going to have such a nice meal? But yes, already some men from the 2nd Platoon of the company under the leadership of Sergeant-Major Manière are leaving on a recce patrol. Immediately there is a general bustle, while a scuffle breaks out among the men of the 4th Platoon, and it needs the intervention of some officers to calm them. They give us orders: 'Equipment on, and get on the road quickly.' Straight away there is a general rush towards the barrel of nectar. I drink a fourth mug of it and succeed in refilling my flask in the general scrum, although most of it spills on the ground. The hams and all the other food-stuffs are left where they stand and everyone hurries for the first bursts of machine-gun fire have just crackled not very far in front of us. We get set up one after the other in the ditch facing north on the side of the road. They give me a position for my light machine-gun in a stream behind the parapet of a small bridge. Immediately I load and mount the gun, but there we go, my machine-gun no longer works. The moving parts will not work with the gas cylinder. I am flushed, very flushed, the champagne is beginning to have its effect. My old lieutenant from the platoon passes by, stops and gets down from the motorcycle to get some rifleman better placed. He sees immediately that I am in difficulties with my weapon, which I now remember having knocked when falling on a rail during the night of the storm. He quickly gets the weapon put back in working order and goes off again at speed, map in hand, after having given us some new heart.

The patrol, which has not gone very far, comes back just at the moment when the firing redoubles. They bring with them a man who they put down on the road near me. It's Carpentier, a good lad in the company, very much liked by all of us, who has just had his shoulder smashed by a bullet. Another man falls on the road. It's the captain commanding the machine-gun company which is newly arrived in the battalion. One or maybe more bullets have pierced his stomach and it is a dying man that the stretcher bearers carry away. The senior captain, deputy to the commandant, gives the order for one company to go forward, deployed in extended order, and to hold the line at any cost, while the battalion, which is far from being ready to engage in combat, organises itself. Here and there, on bends in the road, we set up anti-tank guns. The order is given, it's our company, as usual, which has been chosen for this mission of sacrifice.

As soon as we cross the road, my platoon is placed in the middle of the line which has to advance. For the first two or three hundred metres we advance easily enough in a meadow planted hither and thither with some big trees. The platoon goes forward with unusual vigour. Is it the effect of the champagne? But no one drags behind, such that at the end of a quarter of an hour we are forming a well-advanced arrowhead in the field in relation to the other platoons, despite the heavy enemy fire which is now relentless, for we have been observed. We reply even more strongly, round after round, firing at random for at the moment in front of us there stretches a really huge meadow where the hay is more than a metre high. After the meadow, the edge of a wood tells us that the enemy is there. Some of them are even lodged in the trees and fire at us from up there. We now only go forward in rushes, section by section, or even by half-section. The mortars give a hand. Happily their range is too long and the shells fall between us and the road which is now pretty far behind. I watch it while turning round and can see some tanks and automatic guns going down it. We are caught between two fires.

A huge explosion indicates to us that the bridge over the Saulx has collapsed. The battalion has surely withdrawn behind it and we are abandoned to our fate. Now we only go forward on our bellies, while firing burst upon burst, in this hay which is saving many of our lives. A stream or rather a ditch as they say back home[5] crosses the meadow. We throw ourselves into it despite the water which comes up to our knees and we fire even more fiercely, but we can no longer go forward. The enemy doesn't seem to want to retreat either. The duel lasts like this for a good half hour; from time to time a burst of fire looking for the position of the machine-gun cuts through the grass a few metres in front of my nose. We make ourselves small in the ditch and reply immediately. No, the platoon has never been so coura- geous. The ammunition suppliers bend their backs well and the loaders resupply my machine-gun without complaining furiously and according to my needs. They even compete to fire with their rifles. The effect of the champagne has truly worked miracles. With a clear head we would never have done that at only 20 or 30 metres from the enemy, in open country, for to keep such a battle going would have been beyond our power. A voice rises out of the middle of the grass, cut short by the bullets which whistle by. My loader Doize recognizes immediately the voice of Solau, the company's liaison officer. I lift my head above the grass and see Solau, brandishing some paper, scarcely visible above the grass (for he is very small, happily for him), but he immediately becomes the target of several enemy automatic weapons. I shout to him and he comes over to us: 'Withdraw, keeping the stream on your left as far as the screen of trees which borders the field'. Then off goes Solau shouting at other groups. Would he get back from such a mission? However, firing all the time, we execute the order, but we feel, from the bursts of fire which are coming over, that at the rate and extent that we are giving up ground, the enemy is gaining it, so much so that now only 50 or 60 metres separate us. To crown it all, this rivulet is only a blind stream which finishes there in the middle of the meadow and we still have at least 100 metres to reach the screen of trees on the edge. We stay there for a few min- utes, not knowing what decision to make. A new burst kicks up the earth 50 centimetres from our heads and straight away our minds are made up. In two or three bounds we reach the trees, while the enemy advances by the same amount.

Nearly everyone has already withdrawn there, we being among the last and straightaway the battle starts up again. A good stream, deep enough, serves as a trench. I fire two or three bursts so as to forestall any nasty surprises, and let them see that we are there, then I feel thirsty, terribly thirsty. The gunpowder fever overtakes me again as at Yoncq a month ago and I realise that I no longer have my flask, my flask full of champagne which would have been so good to have right now. My colleague Doize tells me that he saw it when he was crawling behind me in the grass. How could it have slipped off my shoulder? Only one thing is possible: the strap must have been sliced through by a bullet, it couldn't have broken, it was new. I drink all the same some water from the bottom of the stream. The lieutenant turns up; the enemy, more numerous than us, is outflanking us on the right and on the left and soon we will be encircled. We have to withdraw, and quickly, but it is very difficult being driven to the river flowing two or three hundred metres behind us. As for the bridge, there is no point in even thinking about it any longer. Firstly because it has been blown up, and then because we can clearly hear the enemy tanks firing with all their guns from there at the battalion, which has to be on the other side of the river.

We are going to try to get over the river. This is our only chance of getting out of here, or we are all going to get killed.

I am designated with another machine-gunner who arrived two days ago as a reinforcement for the company to cover the retreat whilst we are crossing the river and slowly withdrawing. The company, or rather what's left of it, for it's really quite small, goes off immediately. There are four of us left: the two gunners and the two loaders, the latter withdrawing 20 metres before we do. We fire almost without stopping, first one, and then the other, all the while retreating, but the enemy has brought up a heavy machine-gun which seems to have us under observation. I fire lying almost flat, while my mate, even though I tell him that it's not prudent, fires standing up. Three minutes later a bullet right in the middle of his forehead puts an end to his bravery; he collapses at my side letting out a great cry. Already the blood is streaming down his face. I did not know his name, it was the first time that I had seen him.

That cracks my resolve. To feel myself alone at this time! I run for 50 or 80 metres and catch Lieutenant Athenoux who is among the last to withdraw. I inform him of the death of my colleague. He shouts at me because I haven't taken the identity disc off him and orders me to go back to get it, which is completely impossible. The enemy is already near my mate's body. I fire again, supported by a sergeant who, full of courage, has already been firing burst after burst for some time. He has problems with his weapon which has just jammed. 'Pass me yours', he says to me, 'and get yourself back to the river' which is anyway no more than a few steps away. I pass my weapon to him, he gives me his own. In my confusion I take it by the muzzle but immediately I let out a loud yell, the white hot barrel has just burned my hand horribly to such a point that the sergeant told me some days after that it smelled like grilled meat. I blanch and an awful faint feeling overtakes me. I fall to the ground for a moment, but a burst of firing two paces away from me brings me back to reality. In two bounds I get down from the embankment and find myself on the edge of the water on a tiny beach. There are only four or five men left there and they are getting into the water. Several others, in the middle of the river, are making superhuman efforts to escape the pull of the current, which has just carried away two Zouaves who are drowning, without any one being able to help, the water having dragged them 100 metres downstream. They are the two new arrivals who came to reinforce the company in the last few days. I get into the water last but one, only the sergeant remains behind me and he is still firing. The first few metres are almost alright, but soon the water comes up to my neck and I have not yet reached the middle of the river. The current is strong and I can scarcely hold on. Now the water is up to my helmet and it makes me drift a little but I hold on strongly and nevertheless manage not to let go of the machine-gun. At one point I lose my footing and I am completely submerged, but it is only a hole and I get upright immediately, but not before time for it would not have taken much for the current to drag me away. The water seemed to do some good to my burn for the pain eases. At last I get to the other bank which is a perpendicular overhang of three or four metres over the river. Two men are there who help us to climb up grabbing us by the hand. One of them is my friend Polge from Sommières. They catch me and hoist me up along the bank which is clay and sticky from all the water that my mates deposited in climbing before me.

In the end it is done and we are all reassembled under the bushes and thick copses which border the river. We look at each other without speaking, each one counting. But alas we can easily see that the company is far from complete. An entire platoon, with its lieutenant, has disappeared, the first of the company, in which was one of my friends, Inginoux, from Aigues-Mortes. Two sections of the 4th platoon have completely disappeared as well, the 2nd platoon has lost some men. The third, that's mine, is fortunate enough to be complete without having lost a single man. However, we cannot delay, for a series of mortar shells bursts near us, happily a little over and to the left, but we must get out of there for their range will soon become more accurate. Three or four marksmen stay on the river whilst the company tries to get away. But where are we going? A huge field, tilled and freshly harrowed without a blade of grass, is in front of us. We are hardly going to be able to camouflage ourselves in there. We hesitate; however there are no alternatives and time is pressing. We go into the field spacing ourselves out as much as possible, and as quick as we can we go on. By good luck the curtain of undergrowth and few trees on the edge of the river hide us from the view of the enemy who is firing more than ever on the place that we have just

left. Some planes turn around over our heads; one of them, in a
spiralling dive with the speed of a meteor, dragging behind it long
flames, crashes into the ground and immediately explodes scarcely
300 metres from us. Is it the result of an aerial combat? I know nothing of it, not even its nationality, for we didn't have time to look for
such details. Then we reach the end of the huge field without being
further caught out, but a new problem awaits us. Having climbed the
embankment we are opposite the Marne-Rhine canal. To cross once
more, is to run the risk of some men drowning, because many don't
know how to swim. The Lieutenant is opposed to it and he goes to
follow the tow-path. It has to be done quickly for we are in the open
and clearly in view. We go in a westerly direction, for towards the east
the enemy has already reached the canal. We are out of breath but
even so we advance very quickly.

At last a lock appears and we can cross on the small footbridge
which is part of the lock. We cross below the embankment and stop.
Here everyone reassembles, the stragglers do not take long in
arriving. All along the canal they have organised a defensive line and
a company of the 15th Moroccans from the same division as us is
charged with its defence. A little further on, on the road which crosses
the canal, the artillery have placed a 75 battery which has to fire on
sight, in the anti-tank role. Some groups which have become detached
from their various infantry regiments are joined up with the Arabs, the
officers of the latter having immediately gathered them together to
help in the defence of the canal and of the village which is 200 metres
behind it. Our officer tries to find out what is happening on the telephone and to get some orders from our Commandant. But it's
impossible to contact the battalion, communications have already
been completely cut.

During this time we rest, stretched out on the grass in bright
sunshine, which however starts to fade. What are we to do? The only
remaining lieutenant puts his head together with the officer cadet
from my platoon. They are both, the one as much as the other, incapable of finding a solution. Then a lieutenant from the Arabs arrives
and he, at least, makes a clear and prompt decision. He quickly takes
everything under his command and we soon learn that although
very young, his orders allow no argument. He gives out some orders,
a big revolver in his hand, and everyone must execute them speedily
without answering back. All marksmen are placed along the canal.
My machine-gun being jammed, he leaves me there for the moment.
Within my section we stay resting, eating some ripe cherries which
hang within reach.

Suddenly, the inevitable happens. The artillery fire which precedes an attack starts up. Before we realise it, some shells have already
burst in our immediate vicinity. We throw ourselves higgledy-piggledy
into a shallow trench which can scarcely contain five men and there
are more than 30 of us that throw ourselves in there. I am one of the
first stretched out at the bottom and five or six others are lying on top
of me. A shell falls scarcely five or six metres away and throws up the
earth and splinters all around. A second falls level with the trench.
There are several screams as some men are hit. Big Pop is the first,
blood is dripping from the sleeve of his greatcoat, a splinter has
made a large gash in the arm underneath the elbow. A corporal has
got some splinters in his leg. Several others are more or less hit but
no one badly. Happily the firing moves a little to our left while also
shortening its range. Everyone takes the opportunity to get themselves better positioned for it could soon come back on us. The Arabs
who have been there since yesterday at noon have made large and
deep trenches where they are well sheltered from the grenades. They
are waiting motionless next to their machine-guns.

Suddenly the artillery stops and not two minutes have slipped by
before the machine-guns come into play. At first it's the enemy that
sends over burst upon burst. They attack, and advance pretty quickly
towards the canal and the village. You can make them out easily; furthermore they don't even camouflage themselves, advancing along
the paths and the road, and even bunched whilst crossing the fields,
while uttering terrific battle cries that make us shiver. They are no
more than 80 or 100 metres away and a hail of bullets crashes down
on us. Suddenly while the first of them is coming up to the canal, the
automatic weapons come into play. There is constant firing from our
side, the Arabs firing continuously with their machine-guns, and
shouts can be heard that last a good quarter of an hour. Then everything becomes calm, the attack has been repelled and the enemy has
retired beyond our view. Some dead and some wounded are gathered
up by the Arab stretcher-bearers.

Le Buisson (Marne)

Everything is calm at the moment, night falls, no order arrives, we don't have any more officers, no one knows where they have gone. In the shelter of the embankment of the canal, we move away from the village just as the machine-guns start firing down on us again, but the bullets pass over our heads or are lost in the embankment of the canal. We are advancing, mostly on all fours, when an adjutant, having come out in pursuit of us, catches us up and leads us back to the village. It is nightfall when we get into the village which seems fairly big, a pleasant town with some quite nice houses. A sign informs us that it is the village of Le Buisson (Marne). A house is burning, which brightly lights up the very wide street that one or more machine-guns sweep ceaselessly from their positions on the low slopes outside the village. We have to hug the houses so as not to get ourselves killed. We have reached the centre of the village and have to cross a small square to get into a tiny alley. No one among us dares to commit themselves to the square where death is almost certain, for in the night which by now has fallen, we see tracer bullets endlessly going by at a man's height, marking their passage like the sparks from a firework. Some of us have nestled against the corner of a house. Suddenly the fusillade redoubles in strength and in the midst of this din a team of four or five horses bursts onto the square pulling a mobile kitchen. The horses have bolted and in a terrified gallop pass in front of us; one horse, mortally wounded, falls which doesn't slow the pace of the others who, carried on by their momentum, drag everything along, so as finally to crash at the end of the road into a barricade erected in haste by the Arabs who have piled up higgledy-piggledy, threshing machines, harvesters, rakes, reaping machines, carts and all kinds of agricultural instruments. The team sinks into this with the mobile kitchen.

However the bombardment eases off, which we immediately put to good use by crossing the road which leads us to the entrance to the village, the side by which the main road joins. We go into the first

110

farm at the entrance to the village. A vast courtyard surrounded by large buildings, which leads us to assume that some big landowner owns the place. In a shed the officers had set up their headquarters. Immediately we spotted once more the lieutenant from the Arabs who was giving the orders. He was organising in a masterly way the defence of the village which he wanted, he said, to hold until the last man. A fair number of sections had withdrawn into the farm, and nearly all of those who were left of my company were there. The lieutenant, in a few words, explained the situation that he now found improved. 'I feared at one moment', he said, 'that we might be finished. The first attack has been just about repelled, but now things are going better, and we have all the night to organise ourselves.' All the time, while congratulating everyone, he was giving out new orders; he allotted positions to each group, accompanied by an NCO or simply by an Arab, who was about to go to his position.

The Arabs had been installed all around the village and the men gathered there were going to act as a second line of defence. I was given a new machine-gun and I followed the lieutenant who was leading my whole section himself. We didn't go far. Having left the farm by a door at the rear, we crossed a small garden, then an orchard, getting into another property to stop at the end of a courtyard, along a dead end of a canal or a large stream serving as a duck pond, scarcely 50 metres from a vast barn. It's there that my platoon has to set itself up, the three sections along the stream, with scarcely 10 metres one from the other. As we were pretty numerous it allows us to have one automatic weapon every 10 metres. The moon rose while calm returned. The majority of my mates were at the end of their tether, unable to do more. They lay down under the trees and the hedges on the edge of the stream and immediately fell asleep. I was also at my limit, and my hand was making me suffer although I was wetting it constantly in the water; but I had the strength to take my boots off so as to get out of my socks and get some air to my feet which, after the soaking at midday when my boots had been filled with water, were giving me a bad time. I leant back against a tree and wasted no time in falling asleep. You have to have lived such moments to realise what sleep is, scarcely a few metres from the enemy on the other side of the stream, while we knew very well the danger we were running; it was stronger than us, it was impossible not to fall asleep. I sleep for a quarter of an hour, perhaps half an hour in a terrible nightmare, and was woken up with a start by a machine-gun firing a few paces away from me. Suddenly reality seized me and I realised the danger. I wake up my loader and good friend Doize who having fallen into a deep sleep, had not even heard the machine-gun which was firing just a stone's throw away. 'That's not all', I told him, 'we have to dig a trench, otherwise tomorrow morning we'll be cut down there, under those trees.' He was very tired, and I was as well, but despite that we were of the same opinion. Yet we did not know how to make ourselves get up, we felt so tired. At last I took the pickaxe and he the shovel, and we started to dig on the edge of the stream under a thick bush. The earth was fairly manageable but it wasn't long before we were at the end of our tether. My mate lay down again, while I continued quietly on my own until one o'clock in the morning when I went to sleep under an apple tree.

I woke up, dawn had come and with it some machine-gun fire which, as it happened, woke me up. My mate must have been already at work for a while, as I was happy to see that the trench had advanced quite well. Ten minutes of joint effort and we were easily able to hide ourselves inside it. We got ourselves into firing positions, cutting some small branches from the thicket with a knife, to enable us to see and to fire. It was just in time, the sun was scarcely coming out when the dance started up again. Now there were shells which arrived pretty tightly grouped but, being all beyond us, exploded near the centre of the village. We were crouched in our trench, awaiting events. The shells were now falling nearer and some burst between our position and the barn. A shell fell on the barn which immediately burst into flames. Flames began to come out of the shell hole. The bombardment of the village increased, houses were ablaze all over the place and huge clouds of smoke were climbing towards the sky, obscuring the sun, which by now was high. Suddenly in a huge roar, the vast roof of the barn collapsed and the flames thus freed climbed up very high, hitting us with a powerful blast of heat in our trench. The overheated air was unbreathable and we were thirsty, very thirsty, as always at such moments. We had emptied my mate's flask. I had lost mine the day before, but I had found another one around the artillery encampment. It was full, but of eau de vie, good certainly, but of too great a strength to be able to drink; we just had some drops at the bottom of the mug that we then refilled with black water, full of tiny beasties, from the stream which passed in front of our dug-out. The conflagration was now at its height, the position was becoming untenable, we were sweating rivers. The whole of a piece of wall 50 or 60 metres long and five metres high caved in and some stones rolled down nearly as far as us.

At last the fire died down, the heat grew a little less, but the artillery started up again ever stronger. This time we were clearly the target for the shells were all falling on this corner of the village. Several burst in rapid succession in less than two minutes in the immediate area. The curtain of fire had been intended for us, for it is around here that were massed the most automatic weapons. In the unbearable din I hear some loud cries and immediately I shouted to my loader: 'Denjean is hit'. In the frightful noise I had recognised his voice. We couldn't get out, for the barrage was falling even stronger around us. One shell fell scarcely a few metres away, a big splinter hit my machine-gun in the middle, while the trench half collapsed and the water from the stream came in to pay us a visit. We made ourselves small, as small as we could, tightly packed one against the other, not exchanging a word, our eyes popping out of our heads, both half mad. It lasted for five or six minutes like this and it seemed to us a century. Then the shells became more intermittent and the range longer. I came out of the trench covered in mud and earth and ran straight to the position of the first section of the platoon which was only 10 metres away to my right.

I saw a horrible spectacle that I will never forget in all my life, although I didn't understand too well what I was seeing. Sergeant Denjean, who had been a real mate of mine since the beginning of the war, really well-liked by the whole platoon, was uttering terrible cries, lying on his stomach losing blood from his side. To the side of him, in a sea of blood, a man that I identified immediately as Toulouse, had had his head severed. Poor Toulouse! As if his father hadn't had enough of it in the other war, where he had had his left arm and right leg amputated, a major disability, and now waiting with his daughter-in-law for the return of his son, he having married scarcely a few days before the declaration of war. The third had his stomach opened, this was Corporal Fraysse, married during special leave at the beginning of May, barely a month ago, and coming from around Bédarieux. Another body near them, frightfully lacerated, was Picou, the loader of the group, brave Picou, a married man and father of three children. To the right and to the left, in the undergrowth, the rest of the group had also copped it. Manier, the grenade thrower of the group, was terribly wounded in the thighs. There was another man who was not of the section or the company, belonging rather to the machine-gun company, and I always wondered how it was that he was in the village, not having been with us on the patrol the day before. He had stumbled over my dugout a few minutes before the balloon went up and asked me about his mate Picou, both of them coming from the same village of the Basses-Pyrénées. From my hole I had showed him his colleague's position, where in a few

minutes he was to meet his own death. He had his two legs severed at
the thigh and was losing a huge amount of blood. I didn't know his
name, having often seen him in the platoon as he came to pay frequent visits when we were at rest. The remainder of the section had
disappeared and I still wonder now what could have become of them.
The ammunition suppliers and the riflemen Boiron, Blanc, Breysse,
notwithstanding that they had been with them, had disappeared and
we were to see them no more. This whole incident lasted no more
than three seconds, for time was pressing. Doize joined up with me,
we lifted up Denjean. I took him under the shoulders, my mate took
him by the legs, he then hung on to my neck and embraced me crying, shouting with all his force: 'Carry me, carry me'. I can still hear
his voice. We really wanted to carry him but it wasn't easy. We made
him suffer horribly dropping him roughly at times or to the ground
so as to throw ourselves down, for all the time shells were coming
from all sides. At last after great difficulties and flat on our stomachs
having got over two or three garden fences and crossed a small
meadow we put down our friend in the living room of a house which
was still standing and where there were already several badly
wounded men brought in by the Arab stretcher bearers. I made him
drink, just as I did several others who were there, a little of the alcohol from my flask, and immediately we went off to look for someone
else, for we couldn't count on the Arab stretcher bearers who, being
few in number, had been wholly overwhelmed by their own people.
What's more, with the village being completely surrounded, we were
isolated, without ambulances, without telephones, without any possible form of communication; we could only count on ourselves.
Happily there were with the Arabs two doctors, officers from their
battalion, but despite their devotion they could not be everywhere at
the same time. They had established their position in a cellar where
the seriously wounded were piled up. Moreover, they couldn't do
very much, having no dressings or equipment, still less any pharma-
ceutical products. An Arab medical orderly was crawling around
making a tour of positions to ask the able-bodied men for their
packets of personal dressings so as to care for the others.

However we returned as quickly as possible to the position.
Between times, Riquet, aided by another friend, had brought in
Manier. There remained Tonnelot and Picou's friend who was continuing to lose a great deal of blood. Tonnelot implored us to take
him away, but the other case was much more urgent. We lifted the
terribly wounded man up. He wasn't speaking but he hadn't lost
consciousness despite his horrible wounds, his two thighs being

nearly severed; he drank all the same from the flask that I put to his mouth, a good throatful of eau de vie, looking at us with frightened eyes. We carried him as well as we could. His blood soaked our great-coats and trousers, I was covered in blood mixed with mud. During the journey he lost consciousness and he died in our arms, although I had tried to stop the haemorrhage with a curtain snatched from a window, having laid him on a sofa in the room now overflowing with wounded. We were walking in the blood which was covering the floor. A real butcher's shop, or rather I should say an abbatoir. Riquet turned up, carrying Tonnelot with great difficulty for he was a very heavy man, weighing nearly 90 kilos.

We were standing there stunned, watching this massacre, when a lieutenant jumped in through a window, revolver in hand. He gave the order to all the able-bodied men to return to their posts. The enemy artillery had now ceased firing, and they were launching the attack which was bound to be critical. I passed round a drink in the sitting room, but had the greatest difficulty in the world in making my mate Denjean come to from his faint. The officer virtually jostled me outside. I told him that I no longer had a weapon, my light machine-gun having been hit in the shelling. A few seconds later he gave me another and ordered me to go back to my position, then he thought better of it, wanting to send me to the edge of the village on the road where five men one after the other had been shot down at their machine-gun. I met the lieutenant from my company, and he sent me to rejoin my platoon or what was left of it. I was very careful to pass on to him the order that I had received from the lieutenant from the Arabs and I went off across the gardens, followed by Doize and Riquet who belonged to my group. We didn't go very far. It was impossible to reach our trench. The attack had been launched and the enemy had reached the opposite edge of the stream where we could hear them shouting orders very loudly. They were all shouting I don't know what kind of battle cry, but it was really unnerving. At the same moment their sub-machine guns sprayed us copiously and it was only by a miracle that we escaped death under such a hail of bullets. A hut serving as a chicken coop was there, and a rifleman from my group was already inside. All four of us threw ourselves onto the ground under the chicken dung, seeking to bury ourselves as much as possible. The enemy saw us go in and a hail of bullets rained down on the hut perforating the brick wall like a slotted spoon. There was a lull for a second, Doize and Riquet left the position, and I stayed there alone with Beker (that was the name of the rifleman). We were afraid. 'If they come into the courtyard we're lost', I told

him, 'they know we're inside and they will throw grenades', of which
I was more afraid than bullets.

However the Arabs were holding on well and our machine-guns
were sweeping the ground constantly. The last section from my platoon, the only one which was still intact, with Sergeant Roure who
really was the only one in the middle of all this not to lose his head,
was firing all the time, joined by one or two sections formed in haste
from the artillery, the engineers, and the pioneers, who being lost
had withdrawn to the village, as we had done the day before. There
were Arabs to the right and to the left, at the machine-guns, ignoring
the very great danger, who never stopped passing up ammunition
belts. Five minutes later, the attack had been driven off once more,
but we had a real fright. Some enemy troops had even crossed the
stream in a few places, but had withdrawn leaving quite a few of their
number on the ground, the weight of the attack having been unable
to follow them in support. We also had some deaths, so we collected
the wounded, but the dead stayed where they fell. I rejoined my position and, profiting from the moment's respite, we made good our
trench again, realising that the artillery would soon restart. Contrary
to what I had thought, we were virtually quiet for a good while. The
artillery was firing, but not with the relentlessness of the morning.
Moreover it was the west side of the village which seemed to have
become the target. Now the whole village was in flames, no house had
been spared, and in the majority of cases the fire was spreading from
one house to another.

And now there was a comic event, if it is right to use such terms in
the middle of a disaster like this. Private A . . . who hadn't been seen
since yesterday, although we had looked for him in the early hours of
the morning, since as supplier of my section he was holding stocks of
quite a lot of ammunition for my machine-gun, finally turned up. He
was as drunk as a lord, or rather he hadn't sobered up since yesterday
lunchtime. He came forward, dragging his pack which, by the way
was empty, or rather contained two or three bottles that he had
swapped the ammunition for. Even so he had not lost his rifle. We saw
that he had just woken up from a long sleep and that he had been
aware of none of the events of the morning. Right in the middle of
the courtyard he looked, stupefied, at the fire raging in the village
and seemed uncomprehending. He went to sit at the foot of an oak
and started to argue the toss with Sergeant Roure who wanted to
make him take cover. But, knowing there is nothing that could be
done, we abandoned him to his fate and started to empty one of the
bottles, although only by sips. Some shells were still arriving, one

among them hit the oak full on and decapitated it. A pile of branches, leaves, dead wood, tumbled down. We looked around anxiously. We thought A . . . must be done for. But after a few seconds we saw him, safe and sound, coming out from underneath the branches. The luck of the drunkard! He was afraid, for without anything being said to him he quickly dug a trench in a pile of manure 20 metres behind me. The barrage of fire started up again more strongly, but on the other side of the village; it's now nearly as bad as in the morning. Another attack, as violent as that of this morning, starts. We can hear it building up; in a moment we will be truly submerged. I fired some cartridge clips straight off. Now, stopped, my finger on the trigger, I waited anxiously, for I saw four or five men crawling through the bushes seven or eight metres in front of me, it was just a fleeting glance, but I couldn't fire, a fold in the ground hid them from me, and I sensed that they were searching for my machine-gun, for I've seen grenades in their hands. If I fire, my gun's position is revealed. That is surely what they were waiting for to throw their grenades. My loader saw the danger. 'Don't fire, don't fire', he tells me in a whisper, 'or we're lost.' This situation lasts scarcely two minutes and suddenly one or two of our machine-guns to one side, which we didn't know existed until this moment, start to sweep the ground. Immediately the enemy beats a retreat and withdraws, the attack has once again been repulsed.

A lull followed, which lasted quite a long time. The occasional shells which came over now fell on the other side of the village towards the west where, an hour afterwards, a new attack took place, weaker this time, and was thrown back without too much damage. We were tired, or to be more truthful we were absolutely out on our feet, being hardly more able than the dead to stay upright. I had a fever, indeed, like all the others, a fever, my windpipe burned, my eyes could no longer see anything outside my own head, my hand was causing a lot of pain, we no longer had anything to eat, we had had absolutely nothing since the meal taken in the wood on the banks of the Meuse on the morning of the storm. I was thirsty, always thirsty, I was overtaken by a serious fainting fit and I collapsed at the bottom of the trench. The loader took the weapon and acted as lookout. An Arab crawled from one position to another. He carried a pitcher of cold water mixed with I don't know what. I drank a good litre of it and that revived me a little. We stayed for some minutes on the *qui vive*, fingers on the trigger, a grenade in the hand; a sound in the water seemed suspect to us. We held our breath. There was no mistake, someone was walking quietly in the water a few metres away

from us, hidden in the bushes. The sound came nearer. I leaned
forward gently and there, two metres from me, a troop of geese came
out, preening themselves and squawking right in front of me. The
poor beasts, like all the village poultry, had fled away across the fields,
understanding from the first that something abnormal was happening in their ordinary and normally so tranquil village. Profiting from
the moment of respite, they regrouped, coming out from the bushes
which lined the stream.

When the young cadet commanding the section came to look for
us some shells were coming over once again. We followed him in
silence. We were changing position since now it was the south side of
the village which was threatened. We passed three or four houses
which were completely in ruins. A large number were still burning
and they made the air very difficult to breathe. We were all unrecog-
nizable, covered in mud, haggard eyes, with a beard of three or four
weeks. The platoon was really reduced now, a good number being
missing. Of the Denjean section, nobody remained from the ranks, all
were dead, or wounded and the rest disappeared. From Sergeant
Roure's section, three or four men had also been noted as missing. By
contrast my section was still complete. In all, eighteen of the thirty-two
of us remained from the platoon's strength on the evening of the day
before. We came to the edge of a huge field of corn which bordered
on the orchards behind the houses on the south side of the village.
The lieutenant showed us our respective positions. Fortunately some
deep trenches had been prepared, for the first shells were raining
down on us and there was just time to jump inside. Without a trench
it would have meant certain death. Our friends from the Denjean section had had a bad experience in the morning, for lying down behind
bushes or trees had not been enough to save them.

Right now the shells were falling in groups of eight or ten, with a
few minutes of respite between each salvo. A small plum tree protected the trench. A few metres away a large cherry tree was groaning
with fruit, beautiful cherries. How good they would have tasted then
but it was impossible to leave the trench even for a minute. A
machine-gun had been placed 10 metres away from me, two Arabs
were operating it, they were firing burst after burst, replying tit for tat
to the artillery which was clearly looking for this automatic weapon.
One fact however surprised us a great deal. The enemy, who had
formidable armoured elements, had not thrown any tanks against us.
Certainly the village had to be difficult for these vehicles, for from
one side the canal was protecting us, while the sizeable stream,
running quite high, acted as an anti-tank trench for a good part of

the perimeter of the village. There remained the south side, and it was precisely for this side that our commanders feared right now, making many of us set up positions all along the cornfield. Some planes had machine-gunned us badly, even dropping sticks of small bombs, but without too much damage on our side. Our officers, who had been full of hope the day before and again this morning, believing in a counter-attack by our troops to try to relieve us, began to lose hope, all the more given that our total strength had received a hard blow and ammunition was beginning to run low. Just now it was a mortar, a trench mortar, which was pounding us. Its large-calibre shells were searching for the machine-gun. But we didn't allow ourselves to be intimidated by that, replying in kind. They really had a strong spirit those two Arabs who were manning that weapon.

Suddenly my loader found the mystery which had been worrying us for a while, for we had been persuaded that someone was directing the enemy fire visually, judging from the accuracy of the shells which were dropping all around the machine-gun, yet without succeeding, since it was firing even more strongly. My loader discovered, on a large poplar three or four hundred metres in front of us, a soldier who was making signals with a small flag in his hand, surely to the man firing the mortar. Immediately all the marksmen nearby were informed, as well as the machine gun, and it was a real hailstorm which descended on the poplar with the result that after the burst of firing was over, the man and his signals had all disappeared. For all that, the mortar didn't stop, but it did lose its accuracy. The bursts of fire, which were falling short of our machine-gun, sprayed us copiously. At each explosion the trench shook and crumbled a little more. We made ourselves small, counting the departures of the seven or eight shells; the last had left before the first had yet fallen; that was the moment to huddle together. They came tumbling down all around the trench, making the earth and the branches of the trees fly around. The last one fell, we breathed again, and looked at each other without speaking, as if to say to ourselves: 'We are not dead yet, this time.' For a few seconds we inhaled this heavy atmosphere deeply and then it started again, we held our breath while waiting for death. I looked at my watch for perhaps all of 10 seconds, but it didn't seem to want to turn quicker and the night which we so much desired for a little respite, seeming to us to be our saviour, seemed never to want to come. Still, the sun went down, but not as quickly as we would have all wished.

Towards half-past seven, between two bursts of fire, Riquet turned up suddenly and gave me a message. I read: 'Hold yourself ready, at precisely 9 o'clock we will try to get out of the village on the west side, along the canal.' But just as I was reading, I heard a new group of eight shells leaving. I had the very clear impression that this one was for us. For quite a time, they had been falling thick and fast around us. Riquet was still on the edge of the trench, and since he also had the sense of danger, he dived into it without thinking. We were three. For two it was alright, but for three we had to really huddle close together to get back in there in a crouching position. All three of us formed as tightly packed a group as possible; the whole thing had lasted a second or two. The first shells were raining down, bursting all around, less than five metres away from us, the trench was crumbling in. A shell, I believe it was the last, fell right against the trunk of the little plum tree covering the trench. A frightful moment followed; I cannot describe it. I was the first to regain my senses and my first words, coming from a mouth which could now barely speak, were 'I'm hit.' Doize replied immediately. Riquet, for his part, did not reply. We were three-quarters buried. Riquet was completely covered with earth. I released myself quite quickly, pulling out Riquet, who was coming to, by one leg with the help of Doize, and I left like a madman, running across the orchard, stumbling over all the shell holes. I went around 100 metres and collapsed on the hay in a ramshackle barn. All that had scarcely lasted a few seconds. I felt the blood streaming down my back and inside my trousers and I lost consciousness.

When I came round again, night was nearly fallen. Doize, helped by Beker, was giving me something to drink and the gun was still firing all the time. Beside me, Riquet was stretched out, he had not yet regained consciousness. The wounds were not very serious, but the shock had been very great. All the time I felt blood running down my back, but nothing seemed seriously damaged. Riquet had a pretty big splinter in his right breast and a multitude of little splinters over his whole face which was bleeding from everywhere. Doize, the least hit, had nonetheless received a small splinter on the upper left part of his chest, where a light trail of blood was seeping out. We stayed there a little while, while the artillery pounded away all the time, only wanting one thing, to die as quickly as possible. However, some Arab stretcher bearers turned up. One corporal, while we had passed out, had gone off to get them. I got upright but my legs refused to hold me up. I was trembling over my whole body, I was still feeling the effect of the explosion which had taken place scarcely a few centimetres away from my ears. I didn't want to get on the stretcher, leaving it for Riquet who seemed to me much worse than I was, but a second stretcher arrived and I lay down on it. They took me like this through the ruined houses. Many of them were still burning and, by night which had now suddenly come, that was still more horrific. In the road, there was an inextricable tangle of wires from telephone and electricity cables, with beams, planks, windows, doors and debris of all kinds. A machine-gun was still firing over all the ruins and I saw again, as on the day before, the tracer bullets whistling by. We met two men who were carrying a badly wounded man and immediately I gave my place on the stretcher to him. In a burst of energy, my legs, which were still trembling, succeeded nonetheless in holding me upright. After many detours across the ruins, I arrived at the shelter serving as an infirmary in the cellar. It was packed full of badly wounded lying on the ground. Those who could, and they were quite numerous, stood up, although after being bandaged they lay down where they could. I arrived just at the moment when one of the medical officers was grouping all the wounded who could walk to follow the column, which at that moment was seeking to get out of the village. I asked the doctor to give me a dressing as all the time I could feel the blood running down my back. He didn't have the time and what's more there weren't any dressings anyway, and despite my great weakness I undertook to follow the column; we couldn't be responsible for those who were going to stay there. Only the badly wounded stayed in the cellar where a doctor, considering that it was his duty, didn't want to abandon them, despite the fact that the place was becoming dangerous as the house began to burn.

'In this huge cornfield . . . '

We departed. I followed the column of wounded which was lengthy.
The able-bodied, who were less numerous, had already left the village
before us, going along the canal under cover of the embankment.
One section of the advance guard was patrolling forward, preceding
the small column, while four volunteers had stayed in the four
corners of the village, firing all the time to put off the enemy, who
must have thought us still in the village, and the four volunteers were
not to withdraw until two hours later. We stayed for a long time lying
down in a cornfield under cover of the embankment, while the patrol
looked for a path across the fields so as to be able to get out. The
night was pretty black and the manoeuvre succeeded without a shot
being fired.

And now the village was far behind us. We took a break on a small
hillock and from there we could see the village which was being
engulfed by fire. I thought of all our mates that we had left down
there in that furnace. To the right, to the left, in front, behind, everywhere immense fires turned the sky red. How many villages we had
seen go up in flames that night! I was at the end of my tether, I could-
n't start off again, the least movement made my wound reopen and
the blood started to flow again, I fainted once more and I stopped
there for quite a time. However my mates did not abandon me. Staff-
Sergeant Béliard (from the same village as Riquet, under his real
name Lalanne) did not abandon me, making me drink regularly
from a concoction that he carried in his canteen. He himself had
been wounded, having taken quite a big splinter in the leg. With
five other men, he represented all that remained of the 4th Platoon
of the company. We marched for a long while, I was not too aware of
time, along a road. I fell down and lost consciousness again. Big Pop,
whom I had met up with again in the infirmary, was sitting down near
me when I returned to reality. He made me drink a mug of wine that
completely knocked me out. I no longer wanted to leave and I
begged my friends to leave me there in the stream. But despite my

protestations they took me under their arms, even carried me for a
while, and I restarted the march. I was carrying absolutely nothing,
all my equipment, gun, haversack and other things being left buried
at the bottom of the trench, but I had the utmost difficulty in following. Four Arabs, who changed places frequently, carried a
stretcher on their shoulders on which was laid the officer who had
masterminded the resistance. His head, where a bullet had lodged at
the base of the skull, was virtually hidden by bandages. We crossed
some fields of potatoes, cabbage, beetroots, stumbling over everything without me being too aware of it. We crossed a main railway
line, which must have been the Reims–Dijon line, where all the illu-
minated signals kept up their vigilant watch, although the trains no
longer passed by. Dawn was coming. We were groping around the
crossroads. Should we go left, or right, when we heard the loud noise
of approaching engines. In my delirium, it seemed to me that it had
to be the Anglo-French columns, going onto the attack. But the officers themselves were not deceived and they quickly made us get back
into the woods, and then before our very eyes an interminable column came past on the road of tanks, machine-guns and all other
kinds of vehicles, cars and lorries passing endlessly. We went deep
into the woods so as not to be discovered and we had a rest. I redis-
covered what remained of the company, scarcely 40 out of 160 from
the day before yesterday. Again I happened upon my friend from
Sommières who, having learned in the night that I had been
wounded, assumed I had been left in the furnace. We were happy to
shake hands. His section had also copped it badly, but less than mine
all the same.

   The few remaining officers being in agreement, an immediate
move was decided upon, in an easterly direction across the woods. We
marched through woods with some fairly boggy places, where we sank
in right over our boots, stirring up clouds of mosquitoes. And so we
came to the edge of a canal[6] which we went along. As soon as we were
on the towpath, a plane spotted us and circled all the time over our
heads. We continued to go on. A lock: we crossed the canal and followed the other bank, the woods have come to an end. Now there is
nothing more in the middle of the huge cornfields than the two lines
of tall trees which border the canal. We come across a woman who an
officer asks if the village that we can see is occupied or not. The wash-
erwoman got confused, didn't reply, then changed her mind and said
that she had seen some German soldiers, but not many, on the outskirts of the village. We couldn't trust our fate with her and continued
on. A group of planes flew over us, everyone hid himself as best as he

could but we had been spotted, for the small observation plane didn't let us out of its sight. In this area the ground is littered by newspapers, hats and all kinds of debris that come from troops having halted. It was the English who were stationed there, say some NCOs, and casting caution to the winds we go back onto the towpath.

A road crossed the canal and goes into the village which is on our left. The first groups from the little column, some Arabs, arrived at the junction of the road with the small path where there was a farm, and suddenly a burst of fire crackled out, breaking the silence, soon followed by others. And in the twinkling of an eye fighting broke out, everyone camouflaged themselves as best they could, whether against the embankment of the canal, or in the field. The few machine-guns that we possessed, carried by the Arabs and ready to fire, were quickly in position and immediately there was firing from both sides. I threw myself with some mates into the fields where we were copiously sprayed with bullets. Some German soldiers were firing from the portholes of barges halted there.

I crawled under the bursts of fire in the field so as to get away as quickly as possible from the area of the fighting. Unarmed, with my shoulder and hand hurting, I was completely useless. One burst cut through the field only a few metres from my head. Near me, I heard cries coming from several mates being hit. A plane flew over us at quite low altitude and over every group of soldiers resisting in the fields sent down a parachute flare which opened above our heads, staying there for a good while, which was enough to direct the fire of the machine-guns immediately onto us. I kept on crawling, making the least possible movement of the corn. I had lost my mates in this big field, not daring to lift up my head for that could have been a fatal mistake. It must have been about half-past six, there was a heavy dew, I was soaked, covered with mud picked up when dragging myself along the ground. I came to the end of the vast field on the edge of a deserted road. I looked to the right, to the left, finally I saw a colleague from the 2nd Platoon and both of us, without exchanging a word, crossed the road and went into the cornfield on the other side. On the horizon in front of us at the end of this huge plain lines of vehicles stood out. It seemed to me that if we got down there, we would be saved. Some motorised vehicles passed on the road near us, they were still firing quite close at hand. We lay down for a few minutes and I looked over the corn which was not very high at that place and saw some German soldiers, who rifle or machine pistol in hand, were advancing in formation as if hunting for hares in the corn. The situation was very critical. I quietly informed my colleague; they had

seen us go into the corn, perhaps there were others. We had only the
rifle of my colleague to defend ourselves with, it was very little against
five or six machine pistols and as many rifles; we only risked being
killed, the best thing was to surrender. They were no longer firing on
the edge of the canal. We were waiting, anxious about what was going
to happen, when two tanks passing on the road were attracted by
some cries and gestures coming from the cornfield. They climbed up
on the bank and started to patrol in the corn. One passed scarcely 20
metres away from us as we held our breath. Once he had gone by I
crawled towards the road. My friend followed me, abandoning his
rifle. We went out on the road at the moment when a small lorry full
of soldiers was passing. They slowed down and were going to collect
us, but they saw a soldier on the edge of the cornfield to whom they
gestured to escort us. He came forward, coldly keeping us in his line
of fire. We raised our arms. My left arm was hurting me for my wound
had once more opened and a slight trail of blood was running down
my back. I lowered my left arm, which was an imprudent gesture
which could have cost me my life, for the soldier five paces away
from me shouldered his rifle again and made as if to fire. I was not
afraid however, for over the last few days we had become used to all
kinds of emotions. He made us march in front of him in the direction
of the village with arms raised; I made him understand that I had
been wounded in the shoulder but he didn't want to hear anything
and led us pretty harshly along for about 300 metres. There he met
another soldier who took over. This one knew a few words of French,
he was very kind with us, offered us a cigarette which I took mostly to
please him, for I had hardly any wish to smoke at such a moment. We
arrived at the bridge which crossed the canal, the place where the
fighting had broken out and which had produced numerous dead
and wounded despite having only lasted a few minutes. Some large
stains of blood were still spreading, while stretcher-bearers were
rapidly gathering up the dead and wounded.

We learn from a placard that we are about to re-enter the village of
Orconte (Marne). We were coming to the main square by the
church, all my mates had already been there for a while. Everyone
lined up on the pavement, on the edge of the small cemetery which
surrounds the church, they went on to the first formalities which
consisted of a search. I had neither weapons nor ammunition nor
belongings, only my pocket knife and my torch in the pocket of my
coat, to hand over. Then they made us go back inside the church in
the door of which a soldier, bayonet fixed, was on guard. We were
prisoners and a new life was going to start; for us the war was over.

One of my comrades in the group, Beker, originally from Metz, although he had lived in Marseille for many years, spoke German fluently. He was immediately taken on as interpreter. He held a short parley with an officer who was there and succeeded in getting me taken to the infirmary which had been installed in the presbytery, whose two ground floor rooms were full of wounded. Two French doctors, aided by some nurses, were distributing first aid. I saw some mates lying down there who had not had any help for a long time. There was a young cadet who was commanding my platoon, his lower stomach shot through by a bullet from a tank which had given him the order to surrender, he not responding. There was the battalion Sergeant Major Manière, commanding the second section of the company, an arm and a thigh smashed, who'd lost consciousness. I took off my coat, a doctor stripped away my shirt which was red with blood, cutting it into four. I told him that it was the only one that I possessed. He told me that you never put shirts like that back on again. He made me a bandage, my wound was judged not too bad, a nurse who was rummaging in a wardrobe got me a shirt which no doubt about it had to be one of the *curé*'s and I was taken back to the church where all my mates, joined by some other stragglers from various regiments, had sunk down onto the benches.

The first moment passed, we started to look around us: alas, in this last affray, many had remained where they had fallen. The second section had been hit badly, one of my friends, Corporal Vernet of Béziers, had been killed in the cornfield. My friend from Sommières had been pulled out of there, and we were happy to see each other again. Of the officers, there was only the short-sighted lieutenant left. A sergeant took the company roll-call. At that moment we were 35 of the 160 that we had been on the morning of 13 June. In two days the company had lost 125 men, dead, wounded or disappeared, three officers commanding platoons and I don't know how many NCOs. Of the 35 remaining, another 15 were lightly wounded.

However the morning went on and we were still there, collapsed on the church seats, absolutely at the end of our strength, but all the same unable to sleep, for the emotions of these last three days made us react against rest. Towards midday a German NCO, with a voice that resounded under the vaulting of the church, shouted out I don't know what order or command, but they made us all go out and get in threes into a column on the road and go forward down a main *route nationale*. The march was very difficult under the midday sun and suddenly we remembered that we hadn't eaten for a very long time. It was now 15 June, at midday, our last real meal had been taken early on the 12th, the night of the storm on the banks of the Meuse. What events had happened since, with nothing in our stomachs! If only we could have had something to drink, but it was impossible, the sentries were guarding us closely on the right and the left of the road. From time to time there was indeed a fountain, a stream, a drinking trough for cows where the cold water flowing in front of us made us really suffer, but it was impossible to drink since whoever left the column even for a few metres was brought back in line harshly on pain of his life. We were going through areas which had seen some violent fighting, everywhere telephone wires and electric wires were dragging along the earth, higgledy piggledy. The road had just been cleared by a tank of the barricades made of agricultural machinery of all kinds, which did not seem to have hindered the enemy much. Some bridges had been blown and had already been reconstructed for the passage of troops. From time to time groups of prisoners joined us and the column became ever more swollen. At the front of the column, a delivery van was going slowly, carrying some soldiers to the rear who were joyfully swigging champagne and setting up the bottles by the side of the machine-gun aimed at us. We came across a big village which we went through. I would have really liked to have known the name of this large community, or rather the little that remained of it, for the houses were almost completely burnt out.[7] Perhaps it's tiredness? We had arrived in the middle of the village and I wondered at what I was seeing, for all that remained, scattered hither and thither, were high columns in the middle of a vast area of smoking debris. Soon enough I had the explanation: these were the chimneys of some of the houses which had been built in freestone, while the houses of mud or of wood were turned to ashes, they stayed upright in the middle of the rubble. This was a true vision of war, this wasn't some cinema mock-up. The beautiful trees, with chestnuts and plane trees forming a magnificent avenue on the road which was at the same time the main street of the village, were burnt to the trunks. That was the most horrible vision of devastation that I had during the whole military campaign.

Saint-Dizier: From Theatre to Stadium

All the time we were going forward. Occasionally some men collapsed, at the end of their tether, no longer able to do more, some others carried, or rather dragged them, for no one was allowed to straggle behind. By a superhuman effort of will I held myself upright, I don't know how; despair took hold of me, and it seemed I would never get to the end of this march, but I kept on going. Then we were overtaken by a motorised column. Right under our eyes they went by endlessly, in impeccable order and discipline, lorries carrying troops, tanks with machine-guns ready for attack, side-cars, motorcycles, pontoon bridges ready to be thrown over rivers, buses where every soldier seemed very relaxed, tractor-driven artillery, kitchens on lorries, ambulances and equipment of the most impressive kind. For hours and hours it filed past under our gaze. We had been deluged with German soldiers taking photographs, for nearly all of them had a camera and wanted to take endless views of the interminable column of prisoners. In the middle of each crossroads a gendarme gave precise instructions to divert the flood of vehicles of all kinds. The German army had a truly proud bearing and the soldiers, those close to us anyway, didn't seem tired. Comfortably seated in deep armchairs, they made war almost as tourists, while we, on foot all the time, had wandered for thousands of kilometres over all the roads of the north and east.

We went ever onwards and always the impressive file past of motorised troops continued, protected by the air force, which followed the convoy at treetop level, skimming the trees above our heads. We had been impressed by such a deployment of force, which showed the German army in all its colossal power in the invasion of our country. We had by then become convinced that this attacking army, well-trained and prepared, was impossible to stop, with the arms and equipment which the French army had at its disposal.

Meanwhile we were entering the suburbs of Saint Dizier, around which there had been some very hard fighting. Some bombs from the air had damaged houses here and there. The artillery had also done some damage. On the outside walls you could see in places numerous marks of bullets, but the fighting had unfolded outside the town, for where we were at the moment, it had not been damaged. Yet, on the roads there was the greatest chaos, a sign of the drama which had just occurred. Some looted shops spilled their merchandise onto the pavement, several stove-in windows let material of all kinds flow onto the roadway, with curtains, chests, chairs and debris all mixed up. We arrived in the town hall square and collapsed onto its steps, capable of no more, at the end of our strength in a way that I had never been before. On the square, some tanks were halted and the crews had sat down on the terraces of the big cafes where the greatest confusion reigned, each one serving himself, for the proprietors had abandoned everything and taken flight. A torrent of bottles came out, of all qualities and labels, from the cellar and from behind the counters. However the German soldiers, who for the most part were very young, were kind and distributed plenty of bottles amongst us. I nabbed a bottle of madeira, which I shared with two or three friends, and that did us a power of good. They shut us in the theatre, where I wasted no time in falling asleep on a folding seat.

They assembled us again outside an hour later. Some other columns of prisoners had arrived and they kept on coming by all roads. Some of the badly wounded were lying down on the steps of the theatre, displaying horrible wounds from which blood was escaping. Some nurses and Sisters of Charity were busying themselves near them. Some prisoners, completely at the end of their tether, overcome by a perfectly understandable feebleness, collapsed on the spot, unconscious. The file past of the German army kept on going. Now there were the troops of cavalry followed by the horse-drawn artillery, then formations of cyclists, while a senior officer in the middle of the square, helmeted, gloved and with whip in hand, was directing all of it, giving orders to everyone in a thunderous voice. Finally they thought of us; at that moment we might have numbered between two and three thousand. They led us down various roads, walking on the pavements because it was important not to hinder the German troops who were continuing to go past. Then we saw some civilians who were coming out, having stayed deep in their cellars or in shelters during the fighting and the first hours of occupation. Many women were crying and the men lowered their heads while watching this lamentable shambles of the French army, covered in mud, blood, with their clothes in tatters, pass in front of them; it was pitiable to see. At last they made us go into a vast barn where, in the courtyard, guarded by a machine-gun placed on high, a second search took place. Then they invited us to lie down, and stay completely quiet.

While crossing the town, I had been given two bottles, one of wine and the other of liqueur, by a brave woman. We emptied them, which bucked me up a bit and, like a log, I let myself fall down on the straw in the barn where, with great difficulty, I had been able to find a space about the size of a towel. Completely curled up, my head on the boots of one friend and my feet on the stomach of another, I was asleep before I hit the ground despite the infernal din made by armoured vehicles going down the road.

I woke up again on the morning of 16 June, a Sunday, when the sun was already high in the sky. I had slept a dozen hours at a stretch and that had done me a lot of good. For a long time I had not slept like that. You have to have lived such days to realise the value of sleep and above all of one's own bed. My bed at home, how much I thought of it at that time! I had certainly suffered cruelly at times from hunger, and yet more from thirst, but what tortured me most in these frightful days was fatigue and above all the lack of sleep, and that's how I realised that despite the hardest privations, those who stay at home, knowing neither evacuation nor war, can count themselves lucky to go back to their own bed in the evening, from my point of view it's enough just resting in a shelter, even with a half-empty stomach. Is it the effect of sleep? I certainly felt better and I regained my taste for life a little. In one of the farm sheds, I got the worst of the mud off my greatcoat and my trousers, which were in a deplorable state, with a miserable broom. Towards nine o'clock a medical officer, taken prisoner like us but at work at the hospital, came into the farmyard and asked for the wounded. A line formed, he looked at the wounds, cared for some people on the spot and put the worst hit on one side for hospital. He can't bandage me up and he takes me with a dozen others to the hospital, followed by a sentry with a bayonet on his rifle. We go through virtually the whole of Saint Dizier again. The civilians, less numerous than before, and not yet restored from the traumas of the preceding days, help with cleaning up the town, for the occupying army is making a wholesale clear-up of the streets, which was badly needed. The town, which I hadn't really noticed the day before, is attractive enough with pretty roads bordered by some very nice shops, which in normal times must embellish the centre. There is a lot of shade to be had under some superb trees. I notice a lovely church, the central square with its town hall, the theatre opposite, the statue in the middle and on each side some large cafés, forming a perfect ensemble. We arrive on the east side of the town on the banks of the Marne, where the Paris–Strasbourg road crosses over a magnificent bridge. To our great surprise they make us enter not the hospital, which is occupied by the German wounded, but the mental hospital where some buildings have been transformed into a hospital for French troops.

We were very well received by the Sisters of Charity and the nurses from the hospitals. While the doctor opened my wound with I don't know what, I was overcome by a bad fainting fit and they had to give me a pick-me-up. Many of my mates also collapsed, and the doctor quickly understood what was the cause of it. We were all in a state of extreme feebleness. At the same time as looking after the latest arrivals he supervised the nurses, who quickly cut us large slices from a big loaf of white bread that they spread with a moist paté. I ate one in three mouthfuls. It went down well, for over the last five days I had had absolutely nothing to eat and I had driven myself hard. The second and the third slice followed the first, all washed down by two full glasses of wine. The meal only lasted three minutes, for the sentry was showing signs of impatience. They took us back to the farm; they couldn't keep us at the hospital for lack of space. However, thanks to one of the good Sisters, I was able to get myself given a whole loaf of bread and a tin of paté, but I didn't break into them because my mates were dying of hunger, poor blokes. With my shoulder now well-bandaged, the doctor told me that it had proved to be trivial, a little splinter which nonetheless went in pretty deep. My hand is giving me much more pain, tiredness contributing to it but the untreated burn had gone over the whole hand which was badly swollen. Finally I left there pretty much put back to rights. They had given me a shirt, sandals and some new socks, for I had put out my own to dry and had left them at Le Buisson. I had made those final marches with bare feet inside my boots and had arrived at Saint Dizier with my feet torn to ribbons.

On arriving at the farm I was quickly surrounded by friends who saw me get out this really nice white bread. Alas there wasn't enough of it for everyone and in less time than it takes to write it had been wolfed down, together with the paté. Towards the middle of the day they put us back into a column and led us into the attractive church that I had noticed on going to the hospital. We were all piled in there, perhaps 3,000 of us. I waited for somebody to speak to us, perhaps some leader would take the floor, but no there was nothing, they simply shut us up in the church. The first hours passed in silence. Nearly everyone respected this holy place, and we were exhausted as some started to lie down on the ground while the *curé* went hither and thither between the altar and the door of the main entrance, seeming to guess what was going to happen if they persisted in leaving this tide of half-dead soldiers inside the church. They brought big coppers full of water to two or three places in the church, where everyone could drink and where many people soaked their heads. The evening drew in, we had been immobile for six or seven hours on these seats in the semi-darkness which was only palely lit through some rosette windows. They were going to make us spend the night there and we had to get organised for it. That's when a complete rearrangement of the church took place. From everywhere the noise started at the same time. We put the chairs in a pyramid so as to be able to stretch ourselves out on the floor. Soon the church resembled an exhibition hall where the stands were marked out by chairs, each team reserving its place and demarcating it by chairs that your neighbour moved so as to have more space for himself. In no time there was an uproar in the church from the noise of chairs and benches that were being moved around. Together with a mate, I was seated in a *prie-Dieu*,[8] where, all curled up, we finished up by lying down. The officers occupied the high altar and started to lie down on the steps, while the small side chapels were the domain of the Arabs and the Senegalese. From everywhere hung the beautiful church linen but nobody touched anything and thus we passed our second night in captivity.

On the next day towards 10 o'clock they authorised us to go out in front of the church in the shady square and we enjoyed stretching ourselves out under the trees. We were guarded by the gendarme. I went back to the hospital, not so much for my wound, for the doctor had told me only to come back in two days, but to try to get something to eat. I succeeded again in getting a small amount to eat and on the way some civilians distributed some rations to us, but there were many of us to share them. When I went back to the church, the column re-formed on the boulevard. Where were they going to take us now? We marched for quite a long time through the town and then we went out towards the station. There was a long halt on a road, we crossed a canal and they made us go into the town's stadium.

Some other columns were expected and that very evening we had nearly 15,000 in the stadium. The only stand was black, not with spectators but with prisoners. The surrounds of the pitch itself were full of prisoners. To crown it all, it started to rain and there was no shelter for the great majority, and that saw the start of an authentic campsite; people made little huts, some with their packs, some with their tent canvasses or their greatcoats, fixing them to the posts of the railings which go right round the running track, but it was no better off than being outside in the rain. I succeeded in stretching myself out under the stand, very tight-packed, but at least under cover for the night.

In the evening a loud voice demanded and obtained silence, then it announced that the Armistice had been signed, although that may not have been true because this was 17 June. They told us to stay calm and that in a few days we would be going back home (there were three years of that). Prolonged applause greeted the end of this little speech.

We stayed in the stadium for four long days, while all the time other prisoners arrived and the crowds got ever bigger. It was only with difficulty that you could get a little water to drink when there was a rush towards a kind of tank dragged along by a few prisoners coming back from water fatigue. The cask was besieged by all the men who were thirsting to drink a mug of water, undrinkable water at that, pumped as it was into a petrol tank, which must have filled with water during the last storm.

I asked once again to go for an examination, thinking that they would take me to hospital where I could eat something, but the organisation has changed, and they have installed an infirmary in the stadium's changing rooms. They put a new bandage on for me, and the doctor tells me that my wound, and above all my burnt hand, is going septic. I am overcome by a dizziness, like all those who are being cared for, and I collapse like all my mates. They make us drink some hot alcohol to bring us round.

Finally on Friday 21 June they give us a little to eat, but not much! We have now been prisoners for seven days; to start with they give us a half-mouldy French ration loaf to share between 25. It's just a scrap, just a little mouthful that they distribute to us and I witness some terrible scenes of violence to get even that. In the evening they give out a ladle's worth of soup to each of us, but half or even more have nothing to eat for their meal. You see the most unbelievable utensils taken out to serve as plates, the bottom of a helmet, the bottom of a broken bottle, a brick or a piece of wood hollowed out with a knife. Each man looks after himself, clinging to life which makes us suffer so much but to which we hold on all the same.

To the Lemoine Factory:
These Mad, Tireless Workers

The same evening there were almost 30,000 of us in the stadium which in its whole life, even on the day of the greatest festivals, must have attracted far smaller crowds. Now it's so inadequate, it seems it's necessary to move on again. They put us back into columns and we take the road out on the west side of the town, near the electrical factory. Immediately after crossing the canal we leave the road and on the left we enter the huge Lemoine Factory complex by a no-through-road.

In a few minutes, all the prisoners have invaded the huge courtyards of the factory and some workshops which are open. My burnt hand is hurting me a good deal, the swelling has spread to the arm which is enormously enlarged and a swelling like a huge boil has formed in the middle of my hand. After a tour of the factory, and its yards, we look for a place to spend the night but it's impossible to find an unoccupied square metre. Already a good number of people have made shelters with pallets, bricks and cloth, some others have installed themselves in lorries or some broken-down cars which were in the yards, yet others have stormed the railway wagons which were on a factory siding. Like everyone else I am looking for a shelter because there is the threat of rain and I would really like to spend the night lying down. Prowling around everywhere, I see, in the corner of a yard, a man who is bringing a horse out of a small hut made out of pallets that was serving as a stable; he is evacuating the place, which has to be left for the prisoners. Immediately I rush in and succeed in being the first occupant of this little refuge. With my mate Polge, we become the proprietors of the place. Not before time, for immediately several men come to look in at the door, but the place is taken and we would defend it dearly if some intruders came to disturb us. We are there on a great pile of manure that we cover over with old planks so as to lie down.

I sleep very badly, my arm hasn't stopped swelling, and my hand is hurting me more and more. At daybreak I go for a check-up. For they have set up an inadequate infirmary in the offices of the factory. A

French doctor, backed up by some orderlies, is providing care. The major looks at my wound and consults with another officer who has come to help him. They decide to take out the splinter that is in my left shoulder, but they can do nothing for my hand. They say they will open it up when the time is right. Once again I collapse, overcome by a terrible fainting. They lie me down on thin straw, in a little building where there are about 30 of us stretched out. I suffer a lot with my hand throughout the day . In the end, towards midnight, the doctor on the last round uses his lancet to open up my hand. It then discharges for a long time. At once I feel some relief. The next morning, Saturday 22 June, the doctors on their rounds mark me down for hospital, not having what they need for further treatment. A German ambulance takes five of us to the hospital. We go right through the town and finally the vehicle stops in front of the building on the edge of the Marne where, the week before, I came to get myself treated. The ambulance went into the huge complex which is nothing more than a lunatic asylum. It's right on time for the midday meal. They take us to the refectory and give us dinner. The tables were lined up in a shady courtyard, in the open air. We took our place at one of them and they gave us a pretty good meal which went down very well. It had really been a long time since I had had anything like it. Vegetable soup was followed by a good plate of green beans, a nice piece of meat, some fresh white bread, a dessert, everything washed down with a big glass of red wine. This meal coming after such privation, such a fast, was a right royal spread; I was nearly ill, for my stomach had not been used to anything so rich for many days now. But the height of joy was after the meal, when they took us into the dormitories, one small room shared by 10 of us. I took possession of my bed, a real one, such as I hadn't seen since leaving home. A big iron bed, with springs, a mattress, white sheets, pillows and pillowcases. It was really too good for lads used to hardship! Without further delay I drank deep of the pleasure that you can guess at, the joy of a good sleep on a full stomach. When I awoke it was well into the afternoon and I was much better. This meal and this sleep had been for me the best restorative medicine. I went out to look at my new residence. Around the buildings were huge gardens, extensively planted. The scents of vegetables and fruit trees – all very well looked after – mixed with baskets of cut grass and flower-beds. It was really good. Some nice walkways divided the various parts of the garden into big squares of equal size and, from each side, the Marne flowed gently along, dividing here into several branches, and it was between two of the branches that this huge estate had been laid out.

I met a few colleagues who had been wounded in the little affair
that had preceded our seizure. Several from my regiment were there,
alas many with an arm or leg missing. I met a colonial soldier with
whom I quickly struck up a friendship, because he was from very
close to my home. He was a Cévenol, from Collet-de-Deze, by the
name of Fort, a very brave lad what's more, and the two of us were
inseparable during my stay at the hospital. He had been there for 10
or 12 days and he took me around the various buildings where they
had everything needed to supply themselves. The bakery, which produced a very good white bread, was opposite a huge laundry where
all the workers were young girls who he told me were mental defec-
tives but I frankly couldn't believe it because they were working
normally and with gusto. Further on there were immense modern
kitchens where some Sisters of Charity were in charge. We went on to
the linen room where without further formality I was issued with a
shirt, some sandals, handkerchiefs, scarves, socks and various other
bits and pieces. We saw the chapel, and we finished our tour at the
farm, which was at the bottom of extensive gardens, and possessed
numerous kinds of livestock. The whole thing was cultivated, superbly
organised by the guards who looked after, and put to work, a whole
team of inmates who obeyed orders without any fuss, but all the same
quite a few of them asked us questions which led us to believe that
these were poor, unhinged people. At this time there was a lack of
staff, for their complement had been reduced. In the panic some of
the inmates, men or women, had profited from the chaos to flee
from the asylum and get into the fields. Every day the police or some
German soldiers would collect groups of these poor people that they
had found wandering in the surrounding countryside. The clock-
tower sounded the evening meal as we finished our tour. We arrived
at the refectory where there was a decent meal, as at midday, with a
good salad what's more to which I did the fullest justice, for I had not
had a nice lettuce for a really long time. I went to bed immediately,
although it was only five o'clock and the clock went completely
around before I awoke.

At reveille I felt better, the rest had given me back my nerve. I got a
towel and some soap, and instead of going to the washrooms, which
actually were pretty well set up there, I went back to the Marne again,
right at the bottom of the gardens, and there, completely naked,
despite my hand and my bandaged shoulder, I had one of those washes
that you really need, up to my waist in the cold water. Then I shaved
myself and cut my hair, although that slowed me up me because I had
a month and a half of beard which had really been irritating me for

SOLDAT de la IIe ARMÉE

La guerre a commencé, et, pour vaincre, c'est toujours ton moral que l'ennemi veut atteindre. Dans ce premier choc, sa tactique, ses ruses de guerre, ses armes mêmes n'ont qu'un objet : TE DÉMORALISER. L'ennemi ne compte pour t'abattre que sur la peur. Il faut d'abord que tu le saches.

Sache aussi que les bombardements massifs de son aviation, si impressionnants qu'ils soient, font peu de victimes, tu as pu déjà t'en rendre compte. Nous connaissons le total des pertes : ELLES SONT MINIMES. Abrite-toi, quand l'avion passe, et reprend aussitôt après, ton poste de combat. Ne crois jamais être à l'abri en reculant ; tu risquerais d'être rejoint sans pouvoir te défendre.

Notre aviation te protège, MÊME QUAND TU NE LA VOIS PAS. Sache que nos avions ont abattu plus de mille appareils en moins de huit jours, et que, chez l'ennemi, nos bombardiers rendent coup pour coup.

Sache que contre l'infanterie, le char ne peut pas grand chose si tu te terres, il ne te verra pas. Laisse le passer, sans te démasquer, puis tire sur les guides qui l'accompagnent. Sans eux, le char est presque aveugle : tôt ou tard, il devra abandonner le terrain pour se ravitailler, si nos canons anti-chars ne l'ont pas abattu. Ceux-ci sont d'une efficacité certaine ; ils en ont donné maintes preuves, au cours de ces derniers jours.

Ne te laisse pas influencer par les histoires de parachutistes là où il y en aura vraiment, UN HOMME ARMÉ POURRA TOUJOURS LES ABATTRE. Garde-toi des dangers imaginaires. Jusqu'au vif combat, tu as à te défendre contre des FAUX BRUITS qu'un traître ou un imbécile pris de panique, suffit à répandre ; si on les écoutait, ces rumeurs pourraient provoquer de graves abandons. N'écoute donc que ton chef direct ou ceux que tu connais.

Un homme peut éprouver la peur. Son devoir est de la surmonter et de la combattre chez les autres. S'il la propage, il ne commet pas seulement une lâcheté. IL COMMET UNE TRAHISON.

Sache enfin que l'ennemi n'est pas aussi fort que certains le croient. Oppose lui ta volonté : c'est elle qui l'emportera. PARTOUT OÙ NOUS AVONS CONTRE-ATTAQUÉ, NOUS AVONS FAIT DE NOMBREUX PRISONNIERS. En tenant bon, tu es sûr de vaincre.

N'oublie pas ce que tu défends. Si tu laissais passer l'ennemi, tu perdrais plus que la vie. Tu serais impitoyablement séparé des tiens pour subir loin d'eux un esclavage pire que la mort.

LE GÉNÉRAL COMMANDANT
LA IIe ARMÉE.

1. This poster, signed by the commanding general of the French 2nd Army, on 18th May 1940, was a desperate attempt to bolster morale. It contains several statements which Folcher's diary renders ironic, such as 'Our air force is protecting you, EVEN WHEN YOU CANNOT SEE IT' and 'if you let the enemy through . . . you will be ruthlessly separated from your family to suffer, far away, a slavery worse than death'.

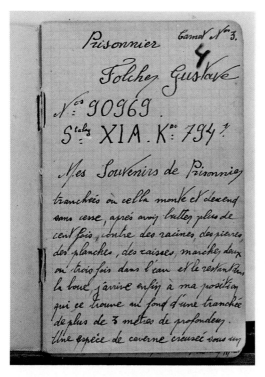

(Left) 2. The opening page of the third of the notebooks in which Folcher kept his diary, written whilst a prisoner of war.

(Below left) 3. Folcher in the uniform of the 12th Zouaves.

(Below right) 4. Three views of Schorstedt.

5. Folcher (second from left) and fellow prisoners with a potato sorting machine.

6. Folcher (standing, fourth from left) watches his fellow prisoners playing cards, their perpetual amusement, but one he took up his diary to avoid.

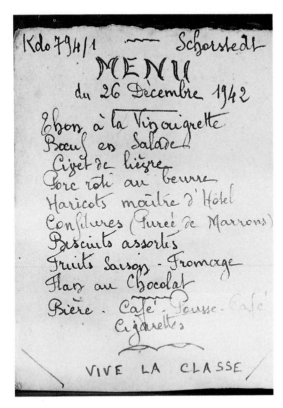

7. *The Christmas menu for 1942.*

8. *Folcher (in the middle) with some of his fellow prisoners.*

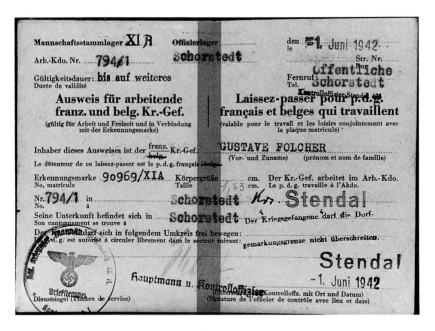

9. & 10. Folcher's identity card as a 'working prisoner of war'. He was forbidden entry to shops, restaurants, public festivals, cinemas, stations and churches.

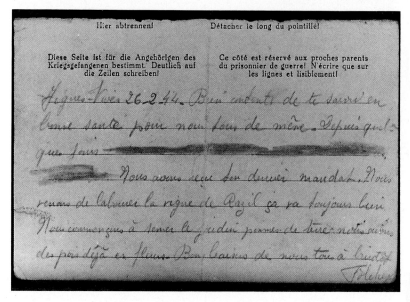

11. & 12. *A postcard sent to Folcher by his father, Augustin, in February 1944, and showing signs of German censorship.*

13. *The section of Folcher's diary that describes the consequences of the Allied bombing of Stendal Station (see pp. 220–221).*

FICHE DE DÉMOBILISATION

RAPATRIÉ D'ALLEMAGNE

N° de la fiche 4128   Exemplaire n° 1

CENTRE DE DÉMOBILISATION de Centre Départemen...
(1) de Libération des Prisonniers

Arme : Infanterie   Grade 2° Classe

NOM : F O L C H E R

PRENOMS : Gustave

Né le 24 Août 1909 à GAVEIRAC (Gard)

Nationalité (1) : Français de naissance naturalisé en vertu XXXXXX (article 3 de la loi de recrutement)

Situation de famille (1) : Célibataire XXX, Marié, XXXXXX, enfant.

Profession exercée avant les hostilités : Cultivateur

Adresse avant les hostilités : AIGUES VIVES (Gard)

Adresse où se retire l'intéressé : Rien

L'intéressé a-t-il du travail dans sa profession à l'adresse indiquée : oui

Bureau de recrutement NIMES

Numéro matricule de recrutement : 359

passé le conseil de révision :

Centre mobilisateur, ou unité, ou dépôt, rejoint au moment du dernier appel sous les drapeaux (1) :
9 MI. AVIGNON 155

Date à laquelle il a rejoint cette formation : 3 Septembre 1939

Dernier corps d'affectation (3) : 3° Cie 12° Zouaves

Emploi au corps : tireur   Spécialité :

Fait prisonnier à ST-DIZIER (Hte-Marne) le 15 Juin 1940

Dernier camp de prisonniers où l'intéressé a séjourné : Stalag XI A
Date d'arrivée en France : 10/5/1945

Numéro d'immatriculation au camp de prisonniers : 90969

(1) Rayer les mentions inutiles.
(2) Département.
(3) S'il s'agit d'un affecté spécial, indiquer l'établissement employeur.

14. Folcher's demobilisation certificate.

15. The 19th century statue of a Zouave soldier, on the Pont de l'Alma in Paris, which is traditionally used to gauge the rising level of the River Seine.

several days. That finished, I was no longer the same man. I was put on the round for clean bandages and I was ready for a walk. Lying down in the long grass on the edge of the water, in the sun in the morning, but in the shadow of the big trees at midday, I spent my time in siesta, interrupted only by the clock which announced the mealtimes, which I hurried to obey. During these days, lying down on the edge of the water, I read novels of all kinds, all the time watching the columns of German lorries go by on the Paris–Strasbourg road, which crossed the Marne here. My comrades played interminable games of *belote* on the grass, others had made up lines and fished for minnows the whole day long. In my entire life I hadn't had such lovely holidays; it is also true that I richly deserved them after my experiences.

From time to time I wandered around the gardens, for gardening interested me wherever I was. I spent a long time discussing them with the head gardener. I even helped the bursar of the hospital to work his own garden a little, and one evening he invited me to dine with him where we had a very good meal. Every day I went to see my lieutenant, as well as Sergeant-Major Manière who, after several days improvement, when I was able to chat with him, had once again taken a turn for the worse. By contrast my lieutenant was getting better, beginning to take food, and we talked for a long time on the recent events which had nearly cost us our lives. On the other hand how many badly wounded there were in these huge rooms, with arms and legs cut off! Many from my regiment were there, having lost a limb. Every day someone died from it. The lieutenant who had so valiantly directed the defence at Le Buisson had just died, after having been unconscious for several days. He had been hit by a bullet at the base of the skull and it was impossible to operate on him. The officers of his regiment and of mine who were interned in the camp had been given permission to give him full military honours while accompanying him to his last resting place.

However the days passed. By now I was completely back to normal, fully recovered. My hand was nearly healed and it was no longer hurting me. As for my shoulder, after bandaging it up a few times, the nurses had abandoned me and nobody talked to me any longer about getting the splinter out. What's more, the lightly wounded were no longer even visited, the two or three doctors being constantly busy with the badly wounded. There were several second lieutenants, very young doctors, who thought more of running after the young nurses than of busying themselves with the wounded. I continued to read and to walk in the huge garden all day long. Like so many of the others I could have escaped. It would have been very easy, but I decided that my home in Gard was really a long way away. A captain in the neighbouring bed assured me despite my doubts that we wouldn't be going into Germany, which was all the more plausible given the fact that the Commandant told us in a short speech that after some days at the camp we would be going home.

Saturday, 6 July 1940, after a general round of doctors, I was marked down to leave the hospital, and on Monday 8 July I was taken with a dozen mates towards the prison camp which was still in the Lemoine factory. We left after the midday meal and once again we were separated, always difficult after having made some friends. We go through the town which is beginning to get back to life. Many houses are in use again, a number of civilians having returned. Others are occupied by troops but even so the town is clean and cleared of all traces of the débâcle which it had endured.

We arrived at the camp, now protected on the outside by a network of barbed wire. On going through the door I found three of my mates from my section who I had some difficulty in recognising, for if the stay in hospital had really benefited me, they by contrast had got even worse. Their cheeks were gaunt, their eyes surrounded by dark shadows and I could immediately see and understand the great suffering and privations that they had had to put up with in there. At my request they put me into group 58 where all my mates from the 12th Zouaves were, and guided by my friends, I went into the huge workshops of the factory where they were forging and assembling various kinds of springs. They led me through furnaces, presses, vats full of oil or of water, piles of coal, of scrap metal of all kinds, wood, benches, planks, doors laid down on the ground, crates, everything made into beds. I arrived finally at the place where all my colleagues were, in a pretty poor state. My first job was to find a place to sleep, which was very difficult, the smallest pallet, sheet of corrugated iron or of metal being occupied by an entire group. Several groups had lain down on the coal and as you might say were real negroes, others were on the ground covered over by a thick layer of oil, yet others, more ingenious, had made forms of hammocks with inner tubes cut into ribbons from the cars that they had found broken down in the courtyard. I was one of the last to arrive and it was impossible for me to find the smallest unoccupied corner. I went into another workshop and found a section from the 2nd platoon of the company installed there. My mate Polge from Sommières was there and tried with all his strength to make me share the bit of wood that he had set down in a corner that formed the rear of a furnace. 'Nobody bothers you there', he told me. Well, I stayed with them, not least because my best mates from the platoon had been left behind in the fight.

We talked for a long time while waiting for the evening meal which was served at five o'clock. It consisted of a round loaf of about three pounds shared seven ways, which didn't do much for anyone. My mate gave me a bit of cheese taken from his meagre rations which he immediately shared with me.

Once this frugal meal, followed by a cup of water, was over we went to walk around the factory, where there was a great uproar. The busiest yard was that to the west of the factory. There, under the watch of a machine-gun placed at the top of a tower in the centre of the huge square, five or six metres high, there was a real throng, a bit like market day in a county town. It seems we are now 30,000 prisoners in the camp formed by the factory, and as always, the ingeniousness of some people has quickly got the upper hand. And that's how all kinds of dodges and ways of making money originated. There is a veritable Monaco installed in the open air, with some crates supporting planks for a gaming table, and a bicycle wheel marking the numbers. Further on is a dubious lottery, run by a team of Arabs who are playing for cigarettes. Then there was a professional individual skilfully doing a card trick, always with money changing hands. There was bartering, tobacco or cigarettes against bits of bread or a pitiful bowl of dubious soup. We made a tour of the fair without, however, participating in the games which are more than games of chance. We continue on our tour. The various races have formed different quarters in the camp. The Arabs have formed a real village of mud huts made with bricks or pallets, and covered over with old tarpaulin, bits of cardboard, oil paper or scrap metal. They preferred to sleep outside which reminded them of their African houses. Further off there were the men from Indo-china, sat down with legs crossed talking amongst themselves in their staccato way. As for the Senegalese, they stayed inside since, being more susceptible to the cold, they feared the night chill. At the entrance to the camp, the lodge served as billets for the management and that was where they put up notices for the day's orders. That was where there was the infirmary and where the camp's loud speaker was set up which all day long gave out its various announcements, whether summons, orders, duty requests or various records, and in the evening news from the German radio.

After our tour, we went back to lie down on the wood that my comrade really wanted to share with me. But there you are, like a real greenhorn, I had not brought my blanket which would have given me a lot of pleasure right now. Happily my friend had a big enough one which covered both of us. The wood was very hard and made me long for the hospital bed but all the same I slept pretty well. However in the morning I was cold, for the huge workshops were open to draughts coming through the various openings made by shelling in the glasswork, which had been blown in numerous places, or in the walls. Despite the hardness of the bed, I get up really late for there is no hurry and, after washing my face, I wait for mealtime, equipped with my metal plate that I brought from the hospital.

Towards midday they serve group 58, about 160 of us. Two men go to get the meal in a great iron vat that they carry by its two handles, put it down in the middle of a piece of ground a little to one side, and the whole group immediately makes a circle around it. A quarter-master-sergeant serves it out, ladle in hand. He gives one ladleful to each man as he comes to the pot. The food is immediately bolted down, but it is eaten only because we are so hungry, as it is worse than bad, and we look on enviously each day at the happy men who help themselves to the remains at the bottom of the pot, what is left going each day to a different section, which means that every eight days you get the right to what's left. The thin meal is over, and that's it; you have to wait now until evening to get a ration of a little bit of bread. It's really not enough and we see the big eaters suffering terribly. Hundreds of poor lads, tin or bowl in hand, stay for hours pressed up against the fence which surrounds the open air kitchens to wait for a little fatty water, if that's the right way to describe what the sharks of cooks get from the bottom of the pots and sometimes deign to hand out. That was such a sad spectacle, masses of men stricken by hunger. I saw some men from my company, two in particular who were big eaters, tortured by the shortage of food to the point where one of them had a nervous breakdown one night, and we couldn't restrain him. These two men got up at one or two o'clock in the morning, waited close to the kitchens for several hours so as to help carry some haunches of horse-meat, which brought them an extra morsel of bread with a little bit of meat.

Around the camp there was a road which wound through gardens on one side, and along a canal on the other. Some civilians used to pass by. Taking pity on us, most of them threw a bit of bread, a cigarette, a bunch of radishes, a lettuce, or a piece of fruit over the railings. Then you saw some terrible scenes. Even before the object had touched the ground 20, 30 or even 50 people immediately threw themselves on it pell-mell. No one benefited from the windfall, which was squashed, but quite a few men came out of these scrums with a bloody nose, an eye completely blackened, an injured arm or leg, it was terrible. One day, walking close to the fence I caught a bunch of miserable radishes in middair. At once more than 10 Arabs jumped on top of me all at the same time, trying to take away my precious booty that I held on to with all my strength. I was about to be crushed under their weight, and I would surely have been really injured by them, if a few friends of mine, who had seen the attack, hadn't come to my help and fallen on the Arabs who reluctantly gave up their assault. Despite the strict orders and the sentries threatening them, women, young girls, a few kids all came to sell us little cheeses – which weren't too expensive to start with but which rose in price as the days passed. I had some money and I succeeded in buying some of them, which set up our evening snacks nicely. I also succeeded in buying (from the traders who were coming back from their duties in town – and I had to pay a king's ransom to do it) some raw steaks and a soft white loaf that I shared with my mate Polge, returning to him the favours that he had done me earlier. From time to time we were able to buy a little beer. Thanks to the Prefect of the Haute-Marne two or three cups of wine were handed round, but when they got to us they had been copiously watered down by the men who were employed to run the camp services, nearly all of whom were from Alsace-Lorraine, preferred by the Germans when they chose them because nearly all of them spoke German.

One day followed another. The month of July itself was really miserable, as nearly every day it poured down and it was rather cold. Is it the effect of being weak that it seems so? We were shivering, and in the vast halls here and there they lit stoves, cookers and even just fires, and everyone got round in a circle, listening to and telling stories like on long evenings in the depths of winter.

The sharper characters were always reviving many little crafts, to pass the long hours of inactivity here , and to walk around meant that you could call in on numerous artisans. To begin with, the main fashion was the making of lighters with discs, bronze or copper push-rods which were there in great numbers for the spring-mountings; the real artists made nice lighters. There was a queue before the various lathes in the factory, where everyone wanted to make or turn his products. Two men turned the electric motor of the lathe with a crank while a skilled workman got some real gems of lighters out of these lathes. The great demand for this industry kept a great number of prisoners busy, riveting, turning and endlessly filing all day long. Files in hand, they made some real trinkets of all shapes and sizes, infinitely complicated and of varied designs. Others who flourished were the saddlers, cobblers and blacksmiths. They liked nothing better than cutting up the large, new drive-belts which were on the machines in numbers and, with the aid of this leather and the lorry tarpaulins which were in the courtyard, they made satchels and very nice bags, besides belts of braided leathers of all kinds. Further on again were woodworkers who carved the most complicated designs on cane or little trinkets. As for the Indo-chinese, they worked with bone, and with a rare ability they made it into bracelets, rings, necklaces, with the aid of their bare feet, which held the trinkets that they filed as tight as if in their hands, whittled and inlaid with all kinds of designs. Some open-air hairdressers, who tore the roots out of the poor lads who trusted them, completed this pleiad of craftsmen. All the various crafts employed a large number of prisoners who, well before daybreak, took over a lathe, an anvil or a vice that they then guarded jealously for the whole day, to the point that finding a vice near me one night I took it down and threw it into a tank of oil so as not to be woken by the mad filers who started their work in the small hours and carried it through until it was completely dark, which was not the most attractive thing for us, neighbours of the bench-vice . It was a common occurrence, when night had long fallen, to hear one of these crazy, indefatigable workers banging on an anvil with an unequalled enthusiasm, bringing forth a roar of protest from the lads in the great hall who wanted to sleep. The noise redoubled in violence in the four corners of the hall for five minutes, some moving wood, others metal, and then everything returned to peace and quiet. All the objects which were made found a buyer, whether with money, or by exchanges of tobacco or rations, all at the highest prices.

And so the days went by without producing any great change in our miserable situation. July 1940 came to its end and truly it was enough to make you despair. During my stay in hospital they had formed companies of different groups of trades which had to leave to work in the surrounding area. Throughout the day the loudspeaker asked for one or more prisoners to go off to work, whether in town or in the outskirts. Different professions were required. From time to time they asked for countrymen to go, whether alone or in little groups, to work on the farms. I had decided to leave as I had not been put down for any group of workers and they were always asking for the uncommitted. I was afraid of being left alone and of seeing my mates – who were all enrolled in different groups – leave. In the midst of all this my friend Polge was sent off. Enrolled as a mason, he left with several of my mates. It upset him to leave us, but on the other hand I made him understand that this situation, which was becoming critical for all of us here, could yet continue for a while.

A dysentery epidemic was taking over and it was aggravating the condition in which we found ourselves. In a few days the whole camp was in the grip of the epidemic. There were some serious cases, several prisoners were taken off to hospital. I was affected like all the others. I wasn't one of the sickest, but all the same it was inconvenient to have to run, often even to race, to the ditches dug right round the yard and where there were always hundreds of poor lads suffering a martyrdom.

The mate I had left in hospital also rejoined the camp in his turn. I found him in a shed, searching for a place to sleep. He fell right on his feet. Since my friend from Sommières had left me, his place next to me had become vacant and I was glad to share the boards with him. Many prisoners tried to escape, quite a few succeeding in absconding by one means or another. One poor Arab was shot immediately after getting out and was left exposed for the whole day at the entrance to the camp, as an example. A Frenchman was also shot down.

A team of Arabs made their meal with a bone that they had dug up, to which they added herbs gathered around the camp, among which there was, it seems, some hemlock. Three died of poisoning while several others were taken off to hospital suffering atrociously. The situation got worse day by day and then came the inevitable . . . what I dreaded most for I'd seen some men scratching themselves oddly for a few days now, others seated on the edge of the track or behind the wagons, or more simply like nearly all the Arabs in the place where they slept, looking for the little beasts we call lice. I had not yet caught any, but it was not long before more or less everyone had some, and then the scratching sessions began.

The month of August arrived, and the rumour circulated that the camp was going to be evacuated. Our total complement was already reduced a good deal, for many prisoners had gone off to be labourers. On 2 August they formed up the first convoy which was leaving immediately. Where were they going, these several thousand prisoners? We had already seen in *Le Petit Haut-Marnais*, the newspaper that appeared from time to time, that some camps were being transferred to Germany. We still did not want to believe it. However they were putting trains together which led us to suppose that a long journey was in store. The next day, 3 August, my group in its turn was enrolled for departure. My word, I was happy to leave. Where were we going? That was the mystery. But to depart, to get away from this camp where we had been so unhappy![9] Only one thing worried me, like nearly everyone, I had been without news since the first days of June, the 8th to be exact when, in the woods of Grand-Failly, I had received my last letters. Since then, nothing more. What was going on back home? Naturally the war hadn't reached there, they had not had to suffer on that account. But they must surely think by now, while hoping every day for news, that I am in the next world. I had done everything possible to notify them, I had written via the Red Cross, I had written ordinary letters from hospital, sent cards. Right at the entrance to the camp there was a big box of letters where the mail was piling up, but when was it going to leave? For everything, the postal service, the trains, had been stopped and although things were now starting up again it was in slow motion. Like my colleagues I had the impression that this big box had been placed there to make us be patient and nothing more.

III

FRANCE LEFT BEHIND

The Journey to and from Captivity

On the Way to Germany

At last, on Sunday 4 August, exceptionally good weather; when the sun rose hot, the rumour went round – and was straightaway confirmed – that the convoy prepared the day before was leaving at midday today. I went to Mass like every other Sunday since I'd been in the camp, because there were a lot of chaplains, who'd been taken prisoner, holding services either in the open air when the weather permitted or in the basement of the command post when the weather was too bad. When we left Mass, it could have been nine o'clock, they were preparing for departure in a big way. The meal was served up earlier than usual. There was a roll call of the groups. They distributed a snack of the small bread ration and, maybe to celebrate departure, we were given a small portion of dripping on the bread, and two mugs of wine were distributed. By the way, they were taking no risk that that much would go to our heads, because it was wine in name only. They went as far as distributing two pipelets with lighter-stones to each person. Every man, with his ration on his back, and mine quite a small one, took his place in the group and, in single file, the groups headed out towards the camp exit where the register was ticked off and everyone was given a ticket. We are lined up group by group in a yard outside the camp. It's very hot, it's eleven o'clock in the morning, and we stand there against a wall, in the full heat of the sun, for an infinitely long time. At midday, the column sets off, there must be about 2,500 of us. We go through the suburbs of the town. People come out on to their doorsteps and sadly watch us march by, guarded by sentries who, with bayonets fixed, escort the procession placed at every 10 metres to right and left. We reach the station, the goods station of course, and all the way down a huge platform a line of goods wagons is waiting for us. We are given the order to get in, which we do without any form of organisation, so that while some wagons are overfull, others are less so. There are 35 of us in mine which isn't one of the biggest.

So there we were, once again loaded up like animals. There were

147

very few days when that hadn't happened. The eternal question comes up again: where are we going? No one has the least idea. Some girls come up to the train, in spite of the guards who become more and more threatening, but all the same don't dare to harass them. One, bolder than the others in spite of the harsh threats, manages to take a few addresses. I give her mine, perhaps that way my family will get news of me, because I have the feeling that they haven't heard anything yet. We stay there for quite a long time. When we question a French worker who is shunting a string of wagons, he answers that he can't tell us the exact destination of our train, but thinks it probable that, according to the few papers that he's been able to get a look at, we are bound for Sarreguemines. This name spells danger to me, because I know that this town is very near the Franco-German border.

At last the train starts off, slowly and steadily we are leaving St Dizier where we had a hard time. It's one o'clock in the afternoon, the weather's good, even warm. An extraordinary thing, they left all the doors open, and so the doorways are stuffed full of prisoners sitting with legs on the steps, as is usual with troops on the move. All the same we are well-guarded, because at the front and back of the train there are armed guards, and some more in the brake boxes every two or three wagons. To my great surprise, we go down towards Dijon, when I was rather expecting to set off in the other direction, which seemed to me to be the direction of Germany. Perhaps it's only a way of getting onto another line. But no, we are still going towards Dijon, which I know because I've travelled down this line quite a few times already. We soon reach Joinville where we see a lot of scrap iron wagons full of all sorts of implements. Many are crashed or half burnt-out aeroplanes ready for resmelting. We set off once again after a half-hour stop and soon we are at Chaumont which we glimpse on the left, quite high up in comparison to the track. The train comes to a long halt on the superb viaduct which comes before the town, and in the valley bottom, amidst the meadows, you can make out tiny little houses, garden sheds as we call them at home, where the townspeople are taking a rest because it's Sunday. Women and girls who have recognised a train of French prisoners from far off wave to us with their handkerchiefs. Chaumont station is very well guarded, and we can see German soldiers on every side. German nurses make an impeccable job of cleanliness in the hospital cars, restaurant cars, and sleeping cars that are being used by the occupation troops. On the platforms, a good many French civilians are waiting for the hypothetical trains which should take them home, because a lot of people evacuated during the battle are still hanging around, longing to get back under their own roof, but services are far from regular, many lines are not fit for use and the few trains running are reserved for troops.

We set out again, still in the direction of Dijon. In the fields, despite it being Sunday, the country people are at work, because work is very much behind for several reasons. Just about everyone is harvesting and we can see prisoners setting up cones of sheaves. Everywhere you looked, there was nothing but stands of sheaves. I'm quite happy because we are getting near Dijon and, my God, that doesn't seem to me to be in the direction of Germany at all. We have just gone through Chalindrey when, at a big junction of the tracks, it seems to me, as I remember it, that we left the Dijon line. After a few kilometres I am sure that I have never been that way. The train is bowling along quite slowly at the moment and I am able to shout to a crossing-keeper to ask him in which direction we are going. 'It's East, towards Nancy', is what he shouts back. At this blow, our spirits sink a little inside the wagon. The train continues along beneath the last rays of the sun.

Night begins to fall now and we work out that each time the train crosses a wood or little thicket, it noticeably slows its speed. It seems almost intentionally done to invite lads to jump off. And, in fact, everybody in the train has now clearly understood that, given the direction that we've taken, there was no longer any doubt, we were going to Germany. In spite of the guards, several jump from the wagons. One of them goes under the train, while another, in jumping, is impaled upon a stake. From my wagon, two jump in their turn and at once disappear into the copses that border the line. Another jumps into the arms of a German sentry crossing-keeper and is thus immediately retaken prisoner. By the time we reach Neufchâteau it has already been darkest night for some time. I, too, very much want to cut and run. Even though I don't have a map, it seems to me that I could easily find the course of the Saône which shouldn't be far away and, from there, following the course of the river, get down to the Rhône. I go through this plan with my mate Caplong from Montpellier with whom I've become friendly since Polge from Sommières left. He points out to me the deplorable state of our clothes. Unwashed, unshaven for some days, we'd look quite sadly out of place. Well, come what may, we stay on the train.

The night on the train is very long because we can't even lie down, remaining crouched up close together in often very cramped positions. The train goes quite slowly, with a lot of stops which are turned to good account, because, in spite of the journey, a tenacious dysentery has hold of us and a good number of the prisoners are very frustrated in the wagons. The day breaks pale in the morning mist. We get into Toul station, very quiet at that hour. There are still some trains transporting refugees who are returning home looking very weary and extremely low in spirits. My mate who, I now realise, is a smart operator, walks down the platform in spite of the restrictions, goes out of the station and, I don't know exactly how, comes back a few minutes later with a nice snack given him by a station employee who has taken pity on us. Straightaway he shares the railwayman's breakfast with me and many envious eyes fall on us, because since midday yesterday, since the thin soup, no one's had anything. No one says anything in the wagon, everything's quiet, each one dwelling on his own misery.

Very steadily, around midday, we came into Nancy. The station, being down below, doesn't allow a very good view of the town which seemed to me to be very large. On the platforms, and in the sidings where the train halts for a long time, the civilians do all they can to alleviate our great misery, but what can they do, these poor people who are themselves so hard done by? And then there are so many of us. Women, girls, kids, even men working there, give their snacks and drinks that they'd brought for their own lunch, while others give out apples, bits of bread, cheese, wine, in spite of the guards who do everything to move on the people who are feeding us, but they won't let themselves be intimidated and hold out towards the thousands of hands that come out of the wagons all sorts of different foodstuffs which are immediately swallowed up and wolfed down. I write two or three letters that I give to three different people. Will these at least, get to my home?

All afternoon we cross these last departments of France, through constantly changing scenery. In all the villages, everywhere people come running up as the train goes through and they always give something to this pack of starving people. The afternoon is wearing on when we approach the French border. The train slows down again because the track, which had been blown up in a number of places along with every bridge, is now being repaired. The train often goes quite slowly over the makeshift tracks. Many prisoners dressed in blue overalls take advantage of the way they're dressed to quickly set to work, pick-axe in hand, mixing in with the labourers and so leaving the train to move on without them. We reach the war zone. Here and there are houses, even villages half or partly destroyed. We reach Sarreguemines about five o'clock in the evening. At the bottom of the quite narrow valley, as far as can be judged from here, the town doesn't seem to have suffered too much, but there are no civilians here apart from some station workers.

After this town, the track – which had been completely destroyed – has only been repaired one way, which necessitates long stops for trains to get past each other. We cross the battlefield where the small French offensive of October 1939 took place. From the wagons, a lot of prisoners recognise the places and explain how operations unfolded. To right and left, some graves, on which the grass and brushwood have already pushed through, mark out the battlefield. A little ruined house, which had once been a halt, marks the very border of France. One last French workman, who as it happens speaks German, shunts the train in the falling dusk. And that's how the second night of the journey comes on. I sleep quite badly, woken up all the time by a foot in my stomach or by somebody else who, exhausted, stretches out full length, no longer able to help it, or by the jolting of the wagon, which is not exactly padded.

Pale daylight is breaking when I put my nose out of the door. A thick fog prevents me from seeing very far. The train stops in a little station and, before my eyes there's a little building that looks rather like our WC at home with the words 'Für Frauen' on one side and 'Für Manner' on the other.[1] These two words I had to guess, because I didn't know what they mean at all, and they made me sick at heart, really sick, because then I looked into the abyss, we were no longer on home ground.

The train went on and after a few minutes we came into quite a pretty little station called Kaiserslautern. The whole town, which didn't seem too bad, could be seen from there. On the platforms, where there was quite a bustle, the passengers looked at us but without showing any hostility. But this place was not France, whereas yesterday at Nancy and right across Lorraine people had shown a ready sympathy for us, here it's cool stares and you can really feel the marked gulf between victors and vanquished.

Now we are travelling through the whole of that Rhineland region that I've heard so much about and read so many books and articles on. The countryside is quite beautiful. Wide valleys follow steadily upon hills, well-tilled fields, nice villages with houses surrounded by flowers and nice little gardens, wide open spaces freshly harvested with sheaves stood in little stacks lined up as far as the eye can see. With a smile on their lips the country people watch the train go by. For them, on the one hand, it's the best possible victory propaganda and the certainty of a cheap source of labour around here in a few days' time. Kids call out silly things to us as we pass by. I don't know what they're saying but it certainly isn't congratulations. Sometimes, in the distance, at the top of the hillside, or beside the stream in the bottom of a valley, girls wave their eye-catching coloured scarves, but in a moment they become aware of their mistake, these are not German soldiers, and very quickly they let their arms drop.

We are making headway all the time. Now the hillsides are covered with vineyards. But what vineyards! They're certainly well-maintained, in terms of upkeep, but there's not a leaf on the short and shrivelled shoots. I didn't need to ask to find out the cause of this disorder. I knew all too well about what must have happened and I saw straight away what must have happened at home too. Now my eyes saw nothing but the vines at Aigues-Vives which, for want of copper, which in France as in Germany had been required for other purposes, were perhaps in a similar state.[2] The grape harvest will be over quickly if it's like that at home, I thought.

We were making headway all the time. Now we were not very far from the great river. Worms is where we cleared the Rhine which was flowing quite steadily in a fairly wide riverbed, but without the speed of the Rhône. The little towns and villages soon came one after the other along the river which must have fertilised and enriched this beautiful valley. It was nearly four o'clock in the afternoon when we got to the banks of the Main and it wasn't long before we could see the town of Frankfurt-am-Main, which seemed very nice to me with lots of shade all along the splendid waterways where lots of barges tied up along the quays were loading and unloading their goods. I made a note of a magnificent stadium and some very beautiful boulevards on the outskirts of the town.

And the train still kept going, taking us ever deeper into Germany. In the wagon, with the weariness of such a journey, in such uncomfortable conditions, without being able to stretch out, without eating, without drinking, without even being able to sleep, given how weak we already were. About six o'clock in the evening, I no longer remember at which station, the voice of the loudspeaker came over in the purest French. We were required to stay calm and told that at the next station we were going to be given refreshments. The next and then again the next station passed, like Sister Anne,[3] without us seeing anything happen. And for the third time since our departure from Saint-Dizier, night came on.

On the Wednesday morning, when day broke, we were really very weak, and wondering then if this journey would ever end. We've been in this wagon since midday Sunday, there's been enough to drive us to despair and we've really had the impression that the journey would never end. About 10 o'clock, we get to the outskirts of one of the biggest towns we've seen on this long journey. We get into the huge covered hall of the station. It's Magdeburg, where we stay for a long time without moving. Since the station is situated above the city, which seems really big, from the station, and when leaving the town, you can see some pretty, very lively streets as well as some most beautiful boulevards. We wonder if we've reached the end of our journey. But no, we set out again in the direction of Berlin according to the few big charts put there, after quite a long stop in this bustling station, where there are crowds of people quietly going about their business on the platforms, with agents of the Gestapo walking in pairs to keep order.

We rumble on once again over the vast plain interrupted here and there by monotonous villages. The land stretches out of sight, at the moment we can only see fields of sugar beet or of huge patches of potatoes like the vast vineyards back home. My God, what a lot of spuds! In my whole life I couldn't have imagined fields of potatoes like it. Fields and fields which, to my eyes, are as big as the huge vineyards of twenty, thirty and even forty thousand vines. What could you do with so many potatoes? I wonder. Here and there, are a few fields of big red flowers or rather some kind of poppies; it seems this is to make oil and I found out later that it was the sort used for painting. Cottages, some cleared of their sheaves of rye and others with their little stacks of 20 sheaves in straight lines stretching out of sight; rye especially and quite a bit of oats, but very little wheat and not much barley either. In all this vast open countryside there were numerous busy hands, shifting the sheaves, hoeing, tools in hand; a number of Frenchmen, prisoners already at work, stood and watched the train go by and gave us a wave. Everywhere the countryside hummed with toil. Those who like me were used to hard work in the fields looked on this quite favourably. But, amongst us, there were some townies who didn't raise a smile at the sight of prisoners loading up the great carts of sheaves. And I was thinking: if only they'd send me to a job like the ones we've seen beside the track!

Now, the flat open country had changed, it was nothing but pine trees and yet more pine trees. We passed one last station, where, as in all the stations or towns that we've been able to see, we notice that they hadn't yet taken down the garlands of flowers, some of them wilted, or the bunting which crossed and intertwined with loads of German and Italian flags with which all the buildings had been covered to celebrate the tremendous event which, as I would have occasion to see later, had created a great stir amongst the German population. Beating the French and quickly at that, civilians told me several times, when they were expecting terrible things if the last war was anything to go by. That was why they had put out the flags every-where. Whole streets glimpsed from the wagons were covered with flags and pennants. Huge swastika flags covered the entire fronts of houses. Down to the smallest villages and hamlets the country people had put up decorations and they told us later that the bells had rung for eight days, morning, noon and night, to celebrate this astonishing and tremendous victory brought off by German soldiers. I'm straying a bit from the account of my journey, but I'll finish by telling about how, everywhere, people came running from the villages farthest from the main line to see pass by, and to visit in the main stations, the Armistice carriage from 1918 which had been brought to Germany, making many stops to the great delight of the Germans, who came flocking in crowds to see the historic carriage go by.

Meanwhile, we were leaving the main line and set out on a single track line which wound through the pine woods. The train drew up alongside a big platform and, five minutes later, the order came to get down from the wagons. At least we were at the end of the journey, we had arrived. Everything comes to an end, even long journeys. My watch showed three o'clock in the afternoon. Since midday Sunday, and now it was Wednesday, that made a journey of about 75 hours without food or drink, piled in cattle trucks where we couldn't even sleep or stretch full out. This performance must have been a record of a sort. At the actual time of writing, I don't even know what's in store for me, but for nothing in the world would I want to undertake again a journey like that in those sort of conditions. It was at the extreme limit of suffering that, half dead with fatigue and hunger, we let ourselves be put in columns of five men in a line on this huge embarkation platform. A loud command rings out in German at the head of the column and we set off marching. A short while later, at the end of a nice boulevard planted with magnificent trees, we were skirting a big fence of triple barbed wire and a big gateway was in front of us on which was written 'Altengrabow, Stalag X1-A'. It didn't take long for us to get through: we had arrived, we were inside the walls of our new residence.

In the Stalag

At once the barbed wire closed in behind us. The sentry took his place again on guard duty in front of the locked gate. We were real prisoners this time. The arrival formalities drag on for a bit, they can't even get round to doing the roll-call. Seeing this, the officer in charge simply counts out the men in companies of 200. That's done quite quickly. I'm a member of the 7th company of the 6th battalion. A German sergeant takes immediate command of the company, a colossus of close to two metres in height, smiling a bit and no longer young. He is aided in his duty by two other senior soldiers, also fairly old, and three Belgian prisoners, who've already been in the camp for some time, and who probably serve as interpreters, speaking the two languages fluently. In a column of five abreast, the company marches briefly through the camp and we are made to go in under some tarpaulins as at a circus. Four rows of duckboards are set out down the length of the huge circus tent; it's there that we must set up our billet, temporarily it seems. Each man takes a place that he marks by putting his rations/bundle at the head of the duckboards that must serve as beds.

Scarcely two minutes after going in, we hear the powerful voice of the sergeant: everyone outside and into a column, the order in German, straightaway translated into French by one of the interpreters. Immediately, everyone is given quite a big, deep earthenware bowl and a spoon, and forward we go still behind our big sergeant. After a few turnings through some huts, we find ourselves in front of some big kitchens which seem very clean and well-appointed. One by one, like in a station booking office, we file up to an enormous cooking pot, and two men armed with big spoons give everyone a spoonful which almost fills the bowl to the brim with very hot, quite thick, soup with lots of potatoes and little scraps of meat chopped up in it. All that happens very quickly. In five minutes virtually everyone is served. It's really surprising that 200 men could have been served in so short a time. No pushing, everyone going forward in an orderly fashion, in turn, is what expedites the service. The last ones have scarcely been served when the column moves off once again, towards the canvas that serves us as a room. God alone knows how hungry we were and I think that not one man arrived under the tarpaulins with his plate full, because as we marched the spoons were marching too. No one could resist the temptation which was just too strong. With a hunger like that, seeing a plate of soup like that in front of you was too tempting. Also, when the sergeant gave the order to break ranks and to get on and enjoy our soup, many were like me, that's to say they were looking at the bottom of their bowl. This stew was excellent, well-seasoned, good and thick to your liking, it hit the spot in the stomach just where it was needed.

With that over, they left us in peace; there were a lot of the lads who would have emptied a second and even a third bowl of the soup that everyone had thought very good indeed. After a longish rest, with my mate Caplong, we left to have a wash because we really needed one. I could smell the shirt that was sticking to my skin. We went off to the lavatory and had a damn good wash. We wanted to shave, but we didn't have anything, either of us. He went off to the swap-shop which, as at Saint-Dizier, was open all day long in the huge yard of the camp and soon came back with a razor in quite bad shape and three razor blades rusted to the core, that he had exchanged for a tobacco pouch. I shaved with this instrument which was really difficult to use, especially as I had a beard several days old. The wash and brush-up refreshed us very well but even so we were still too much in need of a lot of sleep.

When we went back to the tents, the evening meal was being distributed, consisting of one-fifth of a loaf of German war bread and a lump of fake honey that they served up like bars of nougat. The bread was rye mixed with several other additives, the whole thing not bad at all. This modest meal was finished off with two metal cups of a quarter of a litre of a sort of brew, made from a mix of herbs, which tasted good. Yes indeed, the food was better than at Saint-Dizier.

When this meal was over, some of the lads suggested having a look round the camp, but in the end we went to sleep on our duckboards, rolled up in our overcoat and the blanket that had been given out to us. It was good to be able to stretch out to your full length, even on duckboards. With my wretched bag under my head for a pillow, I was happy at the thought that I could get a good night's sleep.

Conversation died out and, although it was still broad daylight, all noise soon quietened down in the huge circus tent, where it didn't take long for us to get to sleep. I slept until the following morning without waking, I didn't even hear the storm and the rain which apparently fell in squalls on the tarpaulin for half the night.

When I woke up, I was on good form, it had done me a lot of good, in spite of my ribs and backbone aching from the duckboards. Waking up in the early hours of the morning, too early really if you have nothing to do, but there are orders here that must be obeyed, it's not like at Saint-Dizier where everyone lived as they wanted. Parade and first roll-call, done quickly too because the company was split up into groups of 10, one corporal per group answering the roll-call for his men. Then it's coffee. We called it coffee out of habit because what they served up was a herb brew, very good as well and boiling hot. I drink two mugs of it before going for a wash. The morning goes by in conversation with one another, in the course of which we are left alone, while other companies exercise as if at their barracks.

Parade, another roll-call, the big sergeant at the head of the company, each man with his earthenware bowl following in good order and off towards the kitchens. We realise at once that we've happened upon a good company leader, one of the best and most resourceful in the camp, because by shouting and gesticulating he gets us in before our turn, in front of other companies who've been waiting on the kitchen forecourt for some while. He slips his way in all over the place, gets into a row with some of the other company leaders and finally gets us through. We line up like we did yesterday, but today they fill our bowls to the rim with boiled new potatoes on top of which a second cook pours a bit of clear gravy. On the march back, just like yesterday I eat three or four of my potatoes without taking the skins off. The ranks are broken and the potatoes wolfed down without their even being peeled, nor mixed in with the gravy which I drink up afterwards.

Two o'clock. Parade, roll-call with our staff. Leave for the showers, during which our clothes are steam-sterilised and fumigated. I have a decent shower, which does me a load of good, but we have to stay put for a long time to wait for our clothes which arrive after perhaps two hours in a very unpleasant state. Several of the bundles, having come undone, have been mixed with others, and it's a real bind to find your poor old rags all wet from the steam that has heated them up so much that they burn your skin.

We go back to the camp, but instead of going under the canvas, we are given a room, not very big though, to lodge 200 men. We sleep in sorts of crates with three tiers and on each tier, about one and a half metres wide, three men bed down. We are rather squashed but doesn't it matter, it doesn't stop me from sleeping right through the night.

The third day after our arrival at the camp which must be Friday 9 August, after reveille and the usual brew, there's a documentation

parade for entry to the camp. We are led to a huge building quite a
long way from our room at the far end of the camp. One by one, in
single file, we go from one table to the other. Some officers and some
soldiers are writing things down. A lot of them speak French very well.
Your name, that of your parents, address, religion, political persua-
sion,[4] everyone is questioned and everything is written down in
duplicate on large sheets of paper which make up our individual
dossier and which follow us progressively as we move on to the next
table. Your occupation, under that heading they fairly insist on knowing exactly what you do for a living. Now it's fingerprints that you have
to put covered in ink on a blank sheet of white paper. And last of all
they hang a badge on a string around your neck. Mine is engraved
with number 90969 in Stalag XI.A. My name is obliterated. I'm nothing any more but some sort of number amongst thousands who pass
through this camp. The procession continues, we had to take out
our knives which a soldier shortened with the help of a pair of shears.
I have a little penknife, a present from a hospital porter, very inof-
fensive but which had given me good service all the same. In spite of
its small blade it is nonetheless blunted, that's the rule. Then it's the
general search. I have almost nothing so it's quickly done. And to
finish off, before going out of the huge building, a soldier speaking
very good French checks your civilian papers and the content of the
folder. He lingers a long time over reading my notebook where the
summary of all that I'm telling you in my exercise books was written.
He readily gives it back to me, congratulating me on it.

   The investigation and matriculation session over, all the entry formalities were more or less finished. We return to our barrack and
straightaway to our meal, crossing other columns all the time which
were going or coming. I was looking carefully at all these prisoners
who came from France like us, hoping to find a familiar face in this
mob, but no, no one. I couldn't accept that in so many people, at that
time there were 50,000 of us Frenchmen at Altengrabow, that I
couldn't at least recognise a face of someone from home or the
nearby villages. That was to admit that I was alone. In the afternoon
of that day, the last formality was fulfilled. We passed one by one in
front of the photographer. A soldier made our respective number
with some enormous black figures that he hooked on to a piece of
white card. The whole thing was put on our chest and immediately
the photo was taken and then on to the next. The operation scarcely
lasted two minutes. I'd like to see that photo, it must look like a real
convict, with his number always on his chest.

   Snack time again, the piece of bread and a piece of sausage and the usual brew. At last after this meal we are free because, since we arrived, we hadn't had one minute, always being taken off for some formality. We were going to be able to look round the camp, which was, it happens, very well-equipped. Big trees on each side of the barracks spread a thick shade which we could do without because it was rather chilly in this part of the world. Here and there, baskets of flowers, patterns, roundels of flowers or bricks represented the insignia of the Third Reich all along the various paths of the camp. The eagle and the swastika, very well-designed too, alternated with the German soldiers' helmet or stars. All about, washhouses provided water to keep you clean. We walked down several paths, all carrying the name of a German general. We visited several barracks all much the same as ours. We saw the canteen, an enormous bandstand with the camp clock on top. In the end we came to the prisoners' huge sportsground. Some people were playing football, while thousands of spectators, all prisoners of course, were cheering on their respective teams. That day, there was a big match, pitting a Belgian team against a French one. These weren't just amateurs because on both sides there were several internationals who had played in the best teams of the two countries. This match had attracted not a bad crowd at the end of this August day. I got caught up in the match a bit but I was looking more at the spectators. Wouldn't I meet up with someone from my part of the world in this crowd of prisoners? I ended up thinking that I wouldn't.

When the match was over, we went back to the barracks round the edges of the camp and we realised that it was well-guarded. First a fence of barbed wire about five metres high. Behind that a tight barbed wire entanglement two metres high that in my opinion would be impassable. Then a second row of barbed-wire posts, five metres high like the first fence. That made three obstructions. I think it was just about sufficient to deter the most reckless man from escaping. What's more, at each corner and about every 200 metres along the straight lines a sort of sentry box was mounted on an observation tower, constantly guarded by a sentry and we could see through the openings the threatening barrel of the machine-gun which could be fired in any direction. What's more, between each of these guard towers that watched over us from a height of five or six metres, a sentry with his gun shouldered ready to fire, was patrolling the circular path that went right the way round. We were well-guarded, at least I was sure of that. We went back to go to bed even though it wasn't really night. Inside, on the tables in the centre of the room, a lot of people were passionately engaged in playing *belote*, some others were reading but the majority were hurrying to get to bed because at nine o'clock exactly the lights were put out. From then on absolute quiet was compulsory, there was nothing left to do but sleep.

The next day, apart from a few roll-calls from time to time, where we had to line up by numbers in four rows, they left us alone, while the other companies did physical exercise, watched over by their company commanders who didn't let them have a minute's peace. We talked for a long time, behaving like lizards, searching out the sun, because we were still rather cold, made worse by weakness. It's true too that the weather had been very dull since we arrived in Germany. It rained in intermittent downpours, you'd think it was the middle of March.

Once the midday meal was eaten, which we all looked forward to eagerly, I strolled along one of the paths, staring at the groups which were coming from and going to the meal, always hoping to meet someone I knew. So many of my comrades had already met lads from home that it seemed impossible for me not to find someone. A big company marched past me, still no one I knew, when suddenly the last one in this endless column caused me to shout out: 'Gazelle!' I shook his hand with pleasure because for quite a few months, I hadn't seen anyone from Aigues-Vives. We talked for a long time, I went with him to the meal because that was the main thing, you couldn't miss that and we didn't want to part without finding out our respective lodgings because maybe we wouldn't meet again in this mass of prisoners. We had so much to say to each other, unfortunately, he had scarcely more news of home than me. He really thought that I was dead because, on the evening of 15 May, he had heard on the German radio about the crushing defeat of my regiment in the area around Sedan. He had scarcely recognised me, so thin had I become in those few months. From then on we were hardly separated and we quickly formed a nucleus of lads from our part of the world. My mate Caplong from Montpellier had also found some pals. For his part, the Gazelle had made friends with a wine broker from Moulezan who worked a bit at Aigues-Vives, had married in the village of Clarensac and was related to the Ruas-Cabanis family. We were friends straightaway. He soon brought to the group someone who had lived before at Gallargues, related to the Gallargues Espazes. One of Gazelle's friends knew one of my best friends, being from the same place, from Millau (Aveyron). Every day, the group gained a new member and that involved long conversations that passed the time. It was in the evening especially, after the snack supper at three o'clock in the afternoon, that the whole group met up. Together we went up to the sports ground where there was always an exciting game being played, then we went to the market shop where the bloke from Gallargues had acquired a reputation in the group for being one of the best dealers. So it was that he changed a packet of tobacco for a cigarette lighter and exchanged that two minutes later for two packets of tobacco that he exchanged in turn for a watch. The watch was then changed for six packets of cigarettes and that wasn't the end of it. I didn't have anything much with me, all my possessions being left behind in the fighting, but I had a fair amount of money, which allowed me, too, to get involved in a bit of business, more to pass the time, because smoking didn't concern me much and it was that which particularly counted on the exchange market where tobacco was considered a commodity of prime necessity. So it was that one evening we saw a packet of tobacco pushed up to the fabulous sum of 1,800 francs, to a Parisian who didn't know what to do with his money.

Tobacco was the main concern of the majority of inmates. Next to me in bed I had an old colonial who had at least 15 years' service, having travelled all over Africa and a bit of Asia in various campaigns, which had brought him loads of medals, with which he decorated his whole chest on a horribly filthy jacket. He had pushed the craving for tobacco to such an extent that he had brought from France quite a large stock of fag-ends that he took apart on his pallet, chewing some of them from time to time and looking after the others meticulously. One day the main part of this stock disappeared during our absence and the furious old colonial accused everyone of having stolen them, even me, his neighbour who didn't smoke.

To get a light was another concern, because matches or all the other things for a light were strictly forbidden. Numerous cigarette lighters had escaped the search, but the virtually unavailable petrol would reach the price of a car on the exchange market. It was then that French ingenuity came back to the fore. A new type of cigarette lighter began to appear all over the place and was soon to invade the whole camp. It wasn't a complicated system. In a little closed box, the lads held in reserve bits of sock or sacking already burnt. A spark from a piece of flint on a bit of iron was enough to set light to the already half charred stuff and with that to light cigarettes or pipes. Another system had already caught on, but was only practicable in full sunlight, which was rather rare in this country. You needed the thick glass that covers electric lamps or the little rear lamps of bicycles which, placed in the sun and acting as a magnifying glass, lit up the cigarette, which got going quite quickly when of course, the sun chose to come out. The Belgians were very strong on the introduction of all these articles and I think that it was really they who were the toughest on the exchange market. There were a lot of Belgians, one regiment had been taken in its entirety without any fighting, and was there complete with its music. Every evening they gave a concert. They played very well indeed and often in the evening we went to spend a bit of time near them.

On Sunday 11 August, straight after roll-call and the morning coffee brew, our company commander collected together in a group those men who wanted to go to the service. I was going to mass with a few of my mates, we were taken to the stadium. In the centre of the huge football field, they'd put up an altar. Soon a German civilian priest came. Clad all in black, in civilian dress like the pastors that I'd already seen in American films. The priest went up to the altar, put his robe on top of his suit and started the service straight away. The camp commandant was there alone, on his knees at the foot of the altar, while several thousand Belgian, French or Polish prisoners made a circle round him. The German army was represented only by the commandant at the service, the region not being one of the most Catholic in Germany. (Maybe the commandant wasn't even from this region.) The service started while four prisoners, perhaps they were even priests, I don't know exactly, two Frenchmen and two Belgians, served the mass. A Belgian choir sang mass and alternated it with some French hymns, then the music started up again. The effect wasn't too bad and it sounded fairly grand in the middle of this huge field. I expected that someone would start to speak, but no. Unfortunately, the priest was much hampered by a strong westerly wind that got up and swept across the altar continually. At one time, it was blowing so strongly that the cross on top of the altar was blown over. The German commandant was the first to pick it up and put it back in its place. When the service was over, we got back to our barracks and Sunday passed like the other days, though quite cheerfully among friends.

Days passed like this, all much the same. We passed the time talking, while waiting for the midday meal or the evening snack. Some Belgians came to talk with us for a long time, telling us about what happened to them, and how they had seen the invasion before it reached our country. On Thursday 15 August, which isn't one of the days most celebrated in Germany, I expected a mass like the previous Sunday, but no, throughout the entire day nothing gave any indication that it was a holiday. The hours passed by normally as on other days.

A Modern Slave Market

In the afternoon, some of the companies went out to work in the neighbourhood. There was a rumour that our company's turn was for the following day, although no official announcement was made to us. On Friday 16th, a dreary, dark day, it rained at times in strong squalls which were driven forcefully by a violent west wind. We were assembled in the early hours. A superior officer was going to review some prisoners. Our German sergeant had a good go at making us parade, but couldn't manage it. Anyway, he didn't insist upon it. A French adjutant who was nearby took command and immediately things worked a bit better. After a few minutes it was perfect, and we marched in time towards the place where the inspection was to take place, but which no one came to take. There they told us that in the afternoon we were going to leave the camp to go to the kommandos, which meant that, divided into small groups, we were going out to work as chance dictated, either in towns, in factories, on big farms or maybe in villages with bigger or smaller landowners, one here, another there, sometimes two or even three on the same farm, which, if you were lucky, was more interesting. We were led in front of the huge camp stores which must have contained the equipment of the regiments that were formed when the German troops were mobilised. Some shirts and pants were given out to those who most needed them. We were even given some pairs of red trousers that dated from the stocks of the other war. After that the meal was served up rather early. Straightaway they made us pick up our meagre possessions and, in four ranks five metres apart, they made us put our poor old clothes on the ground, each man in front of his own pile. We were searched one last time, a sergeant and a soldier went by, taking out forbidden or extra things, a towel here, a handkerchief there, or the most unlikely objects that some people had collected.

The column formed again and, ranked by number and in good order, we went out of the camp where we had only stayed for about 10 days. I had shaken hands with friends who had to be left behind once again. I regretted leaving them, because I had taken quite a lot of pleasure in this little nucleus that we had formed. They were all lads from home and often the conversation was in local dialect which really brought back the area around Nîmes. That's war for you. How many friends I'd made since the start! We cared for each other, we did things for each other, we shared together the smallest bit of bread and the least thing, and then, after having lived together for days, weeks, sometimes several months, an order arrives, one is sent in one direction, the other in another, and off we go to start again.

Anyway, after we'd marched for a couple of hundred metres, they made us go into a vast courtyard where soon about 1,000 prisoners were drawn up in a square all along the buildings, company by company. We stayed there for quite a time, while a lot of civilians gathered in the centre of the square. At the far end, coaches, lorries, tractors were arriving, one or two pulling trailers. Some officers arrived, followed by military administrators carrying registers and papers. They set themselves up in a corner, sitting at tables, and work began straightaway. The companies filed past, number by number, because by now it was no longer a question of names. The civilians, too, came forward, one by one, nearly all of them dressed completely in hunting green, the German's favourite colour, to judge by how widespread it is, well-shod with boots right up to the knees, or nearly so, with the hat, also green, usually with one or two feathers in it, a lot of them with a baton in hand, doubtless to make them look good. I didn't understand the conversation but I was following it with my eyes. The civilian said a number and doubtless the name of the factory, village, town or enterprise for which he came to look for prisoners. Immediately a German soldier made the prisoners step forward one by one. As they went by, an officer counted them, while others recorded them and you could hear the number, in German of course: eight, nine, ten, *guéno*, which seemed to me to mean enough. Straightaway, according to the size of the group counted out, an officer called one or two or even three guards who were standing to one side. These came forward to the table and took delivery of the group. Immediately, in front of the group of officers and in front of the group of prisoners, they opened the breech of their guns and loaded the five rounds prescribed. Although we didn't speak a word of German, we knew what that meant and the group went off, followed by its keepers. On to the next, and the distribution continued like that, a sort of modern slave market, twentieth century style.

They were still counting, our turn arrived, there were still some of us from the 12th Zouaves whose numbers followed one another, five or six of us, the remains of the regiment and, according to the size of the group, we could be split up. We went by like sheep to market, just one after me and then they stopped. The group was big enough when 25 had gone by, but one of our mates, one alone was left behind, just one man from the Gard, from the Uzès area. We had been together from the beginning and abruptly, by a stroke of fate, we were separated. The three of us from the Gard, all three from the same company of Zouaves, followed each other by number. I went first, Astier from Alès followed me, but Allard stayed behind and, sadly, watched the group in front go off, followed by a guard who had carefully loaded his rifle.

The guards grouped us in a corner of the huge yard, then got into a parley with some civilians. We stayed there for some time, then they made us get up into one of the two trailers that were being pulled by a tractor, in which there were several groups of prisoners, which meant that we were very tightly packed in. The tractor started up at last, for a while skirting the barbed wire fence of the camp, inside which we could see our comrades pacing up and down their cage. At last the camp disappeared from view and we were going at a steady speed along the main road where lorries and coaches full of prisoners were all the time setting off to work also, but faster.

The weather was very bad, at times there were downpours of very heavy rain which more or less soaked us. It brightened up, we could see the sun for a few minutes and the showers started up again. To right and left, well-cultivated fields. From time to time little villages with rather rough cobbled streets, which made our vehicle bump uncomfortably along. In the fields, here and there, some Frenchmen waved to us with their tools. Deer herds watched the convoy pass without taking fright too much, while a number of hares were fleeing in the newly harvested fields. A river appeared in the distance and it wasn't long before we crossed, via a magnificent bridge, the great River Elbe which flowed by with gentle waves forged by the numerous barges. We crossed a superb autobahn and, a few kilometres further on, we entered a town that seemed quite big, Stendal.

The tractor parked near a pavement and they made us get down. Have we arrived? Are we going to be working here in some factory? Another mystery. Other groups come with their guards, others are getting into more lorries, a small team goes off in a car in which a mate from the hospital has a seat and he waves to me as they go off. We stay there on the pavement for a long time, while quite a few kids gather round us. Meanwhile a tractor is brought up and parked near us and straightaway we get into the trailers. Obviously, they want to make us do the whole journey by tractor. Other groups are taken with us also and we set off along the streets and boulevards of the town which is rather pleasant with its monuments and houses all in red brick. The town seems to be almost enclosed by ramparts, if that is the right word for some high walls and towers with many and various carvings, all of it in red brick. Like the old streets in the Middle Ages, the towers have their gates in the centre, by which the people go in and out. As night falls we finally get out of the town, quite slowly because the contraption doesn't go very fast. We are very cold in that trailer, all damp. The light cold breeze almost makes our teeth chatter. The countryside, monotonous in the dark, goes by in front of us, interrupted from time to time by going through a small town, the approach of which we feel through the large stone cobbles of the only street that goes through it. From time to time, groups leave the convoy. They have arrived but we are going further, always further. Again another group gets down and no more than 25 of us are left in one of the trailers, that's the whole group which must be going to work together. We halt for a long time in a village. At last we are off again up a nasty little path, you could even call it a dirt track, there are so many bumps and jolts. We make very slow progress, now through woods, now through fields. A sharp bend, and here we are in a village with a made-up road. Another hundred metres and the convoy stops.

We understand from the guards that we have arrived. We have to disembark. We are quite numb with cold. We are undoubtedly in the centre of the village because some people are grouped in the little square in front of the small establishment which must be the town's café. In spite of the late hour, kids, girls, a few men and women, have wanted to await our arrival and look curiously at us, being almost surprised to see people more or less like themselves. Meanwhile, we are taken to the far end of the village where they make us go into an old shed which is three-quarters ruined, if I am judging it right in the dark. I'm one of the first to go into the building which is nothing but a hovel. I have summed up the situation quickly in all this decay. In the two small rooms that make up the building were mattresses with their stuffing coming out, pallets, papers, sacks and all sorts of filth lying around anyhow, because the building has been evacuated that very morning by Polish prisoners. I straightaway spot three or four foul beds coupled together in twos with warped boards. I take possession of one of them immediately because I guess that there won't be enough for everyone and, my God, it's still war and it's the most resourceful people who get hold of things. My friend from

Montpellier has a bed too. The others sort themselves out as best they can on the straw and the sacks, packed together like anchovies. A German sergeant is also there, he sorts out the accommodation which is very precarious. He talks at length in a rather nice gentle voice, but no one can understand him. He seems to be excusing this chaos and to be saying that it's too late now, but that tomorrow they'll sort things out and everyone will have his own bed, anyway, if I understood his gesturing correctly. I shiver on my mattress, all damp, stomach unfortunately very empty, which doesn't help to warm us up again very quickly. The NCO who had gone off comes back a moment later bringing some sandwiches, one of which he gives to each person. Things turn out quite well for me: between two slices of buttered bread, there's a good piece of ham, whereas other comrades have paté or cheese. But we all of us have our sandwich and frankly it goes down so quickly that we don't even notice if we've eaten. After which the lights are put out, the door is closed, a sentry is on guard duty in front of the door and, somehow or other, still wet from the afternoon downpours, we try to sleep. It's daylight when a tremendous 'Aufstehen!' rings out in the midst of the room. We get up and go out into the yard. It's barely five o'clock and the sun's already coming up on the horizon. Everyone is ready in five minutes because we have slept in our clothes, and here come some of the village landowners into the yard. The new distribution of slaves is about to start. One of the landowners present comes forward. A little man with quite a belly on him, gaitered and with the inseparable green feathered hat on his head. I recognise him, it's the same one that I saw yesterday at Altengrabow. He looks round for a few moments, then decides to do the share out. The other landowners, slightly behind him, were waiting, without saying anything, for their leader's decision, because I found out later that the man who was doing the sharing out was the *Bauernführer*, that is the head man among village peasants. He didn't choose too many and progressively distributed the rest as they came. Anyway, how could he choose? He knew neither our ability nor our occupation. One man, big and strong, who seemed like he ought to get through everything, counted for nothing in farming, not even knowing how to pick up a fork handle, while the next man, skinny and weak-looking, could be an excellent worker. A big cheery fellow about 30 years old came forward and indicated that he wanted two of us, with large gestures, because we didn't understand a word. I step forward two or three paces, my mate Caplong follows me, and so it is without any further formalities, that he takes both of us away with him down the main street of the village.

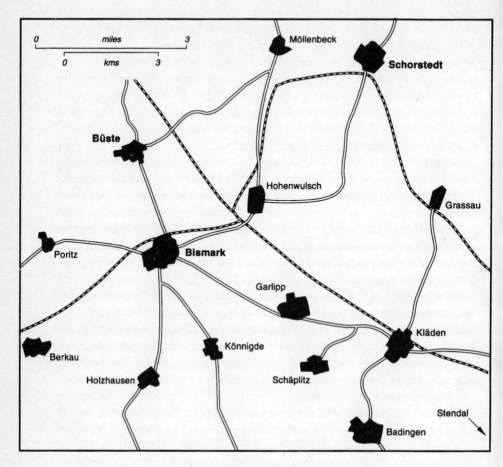

The Vicinity of Schorstedt

The Village of Schorstedt

We cover about 200 metres and our guide and boss takes us into his farm buildings. Pretty old buildings! To the left and right of the yard, stables and barns are on the edge of ruin. Half-wood, half-brick, the farmhouse at the bottom seems a little more solid. Using signs, because we don't understand a word, he invites us to go into the house through the door of the washhouse which also serves as a store for potatoes and meal used in the preparation of pigswill. From there we go up two steps into a cubby-hole where there's the bread oven and beside it a sort of unlit alcove. In this semblance of a dining room, the boss signed to us to take our places at the table on which there is a big plate of cakes. I have never had much of a sweet tooth, but all the same my eyes didn't leave that plate. It had been months since I'd seen a plate so full of things to eat. Without waiting to be asked we take a place on either side of the table. Sitting at a table to eat, something that seems very ordinary when you're at home, you can't have any idea of the joy we felt at sitting there. It was a very long time, in fact since 26 March when I'd left home, and now it was 17 August, since I'd had a meal at a table. But there we are with the boss coming from the next room carrying a big badly chipped jug full of the scalding liquid that they call coffee in this country, but which has nothing in common with real coffee. And we start to eat. To our great joy, the boss leaves us alone in the little room, because we didn't want to make gluttons of ourselves in front of him, when, before a feast like that, our stomachs were really rumbling with hunger. We worked our way through the cakes, the pile getting visibly smaller. It was good. These cakes, four centimetres wide by twenty long, made the day before, with cornflour, kneaded with milk and eggs added to the mixture, a layer of butter on top and lots of sugar, I had to admit that they weren't bad, especially coming after fasting for so long. Only four were left on the plate, so we decided to leave them, mostly out of politeness, and with some regret, because we could have filled our bellies with I don't know how many dozens of them.

The boss comes in and finds us quite pleased with the meal and immediately takes us into the yard, gives both of us a fork and takes us into the cowshed. Nearly a metre of manure covers the floor in this hole which contains nothing modern at all. I start to chuck the dung outside while my colleague piles it into a heap. Not being a novice in how to muck out a stable, I manage quite well, but I am extremely weak and it's such a long time since I've worked, that the first loads with the pitchfork make me sweat freely, even though it's not too warm. My mate Caplong hadn't touched a fork in his entire life. I did my best to show him how to get.hold of the manure, but the poor bloke is killing himself to get not very much done. At last, somehow or other, after a lot of effort, we finish this task to start straightaway on another one. Under the eye of the boss who is doing the weighing, we fill sacks of grain that must be carried to the mill to make into meal for the pigs.

When this job's done, still using gesture because we don't understand a word, the boss takes us into the living quarters again. In the little room where we'd eaten in the morning, the table is laid with our second breakfast. On a plate, four pieces of bread and butter are waiting for us as well as a piece of bacon each. We wolf down this modest meal and we are back to the job again. This time, we're going to be working on the threshing machine, we're going to thresh oats. Seeing our uncertainty, the boss smiles all the same because he realises that neither my mate nor I know very much about this kind of work. In the end, somehow or other, we just about manage.

At midday, a good hearty cabbage and bacon soup, thickened with lots of potatoes. My God, it's such a change from the usual camp food that everything seems good. Three full plates each are devoured at a gulp. The meal ends with dessert, apples in a saucer steeped in juice, really quite good. Nothing to drink, we think this is an oversight. Then an old woman that we hadn't yet seen arrives and chatters on for a long time, doubtless asking us if we want more to eat. The boss's wife then shows up. A woman of about 25, for it's difficult to put an age to her hair, which isn't blond but quite white like the old woman. She is immediately christened Snow White. We are obliged to make up a whole new vocabulary for ourselves to get our bearings in this country that's so new to us. So it is that later on, at the Camp which is the shed where we're shut up at night, we come to identify the whole village through the nicknames that we give to the inhabitants.

In the afternoon, we work in the barn because it's raining slightly, which doesn't stop a farm labourer, a young lad of 18 who was the only employee of the household before we came, from going ploughing.

At four o'clock in the afternoon a snack of two slices of bread and butter, then supper, the day's work finishes at eight o'clock. We are served a huge dish of boiled potatoes that we peel and once on the plate we baste them with a thickish sauce made with water, flour and a little bit of bacon mixed together. It delays our return to the camp where some of our comrades have already arrived, and straightaway we swap our numerous impressions of this first day of direct contact with the German civilian population. Each person tells about his work, describes the establishment where he works, above all talks about the menu served up which is almost the same for everyone, then tells about the family of the house and the other workers who make up the staff. Everyone sorts his bed out better. Everyone has a bed now, if you could so call the two wooden boxes on top of each other which are arranged in the little rooms of the barrack block. We go to sleep early, because we are all tired out by starting work again.

The following day, it's Sunday, the day of rest. Nevertheless, we muck out the cattle on the farm, then sweep the yard. At the second breakfast, they serve us a big plate of cakes with the usual coffee, but we don't get dinner on the days we don't work. We go out to inspect the village where all the houses are very old, some more so, some less. All built with a frame of horizontal and vertical timbers, which form squares of about one metre that are filled in with bricks. Windows glazed with little diamond panes and put in flush with the walls almost flush with the outside, with no shutters against the wind, which surprises me in this country where, considering its position quite far north, it can't be one of the warmest places. Two rows of linden trees line each side of the street, which makes the village seem quite pleasant. In the centre of the village, a small square shaded by some big oaks seems to be the meeting place for all the farmers. A memorial, made out of a big stone, marking a centenary, placed on a pedestal of smaller pebbles, marks the centre of the square. We carry on with our tour. First, we come to the café painted green, with the sign above the door 'Gasthof, Von Rudolf Wernike', which attracts our attention, pleasant enough with its nice clean dining-room that we can see through the windows overlooking the street. We keep on going, pass by the house of the only craftsman in the village, the blacksmith, who is one of the most important residents of the district, then, at the end of the village – which is very small – there's the Church surrounded by its cemetery. We go inside but an old woman makes us leave, ranting on about I don't know what. A bit further to the side, a big farm, opposite the village flour mill, ends the built-up area on this side. On the south side is the station for there is a station in this little village. A small branch line winds through woods and fields to link the little scattered villages to the main town which is Stendal. Around the station are some farms and the co-operative dairy, making up a modest group that straddles the minor road which is the only important and well maintained one in the district. This road is a north-south link between Osterburg and Bismark. Bismark is the capital town of the district that is part of the *Kreis* of Stendal, which is one of the several *Kreis* that make up the little province of the Altmark, which makes me think of that affair of the boat boarded by the English off the Norwegian coast at the start of the war, which the French newspapers had covered at great length at the time, the boat taking its name from this little province of the Altmark, which itself forms part of the large province of Saxony.

Let's get back to the life of a prisoner in the village, where he spends his monotonous days looking endlessly at the horizon and never seeing anything come along which has anything to do with him. Now we are lifting potatoes. Every day, a patch of something like five hectares confronts us and, since we've never seen so much in our whole lives, we think we'll never see the end of this punishing work that's quite new to most of us. Yet, at the *Kommando* which is the barracks where we sleep, life is quite organised and each person tells his story, what he's been able to glean during the day. Any news, most of it wrong, is discussed at length in the evening around the fire where we warm ourselves because October is very cold. Towards the middle of the month it even snows quite heavily, which doesn't prevent us from carrying on with the work because whatever the weather the sugar beet, which is often lifted from frozen ground, must be pulled, carted and loaded up at the station.

By now some of us understand and speak German quite well, which is a great help. We start to talk things over with the civilians and because of this we get to know them better, they're not shy in front of us either, they're even pleasant and it's almost an honour for them to have a Frenchman on the farm who, in general, because there are some special cases, is better treated and dealt with much more leniently than the numerous Poles who are in the area.

On 1 November 1940, my mate Caplong leaves me for another farm and as a result I am the only Frenchman left on the farm; the days seem much longer to me, because with him around we were always talking away, which made the time go much faster. Moreover, on 15 December, not happy with his farm, he managed to get into hospital and even to be evacuated back to France.

Then the winter is very cold, a thick layer of snow falls which stays for nearly three long months. We are badly dressed, most of us don't have pullovers, others like me don't have jackets, very few have suitable shoes, no one has socks. We wrap bits of sacking around our feet which we stuff into nasty big clogs into which the snow drives like into a ravine. The long winter is very painful, two or three friends only just escape death. Brought down with bad bronchitis, these poor blokes who are coughing enough to tear their chests open day and night are left to themselves, without care, without medicine. Their bosses content themselves with bringing meals to them according to the regulations, midday soups and sandwich snacks, and we have nothing, absolutely nothing to bring them. The doctor is 12 kilometres away in Bismark and will come out only to desperate cases because, completely over-worked, as he's the only one in a vast area, you have to get over there to be seen, which is totally impossible for these poor lads. In the end, after going through many formalities, the one who is most ill was hospitalised.

It was nearly eight months since we heard anything from home when the first letters arrived. With what joy we read and re-read those letters, the first link between us and our families after so long without news. We spend Christmas and New Year very sadly in our meagre barrack-room, luckily quite warm because we were allocated some coal, but outside it's appalling weather, it freezes, it snows endlessly, nearly every morning we have to clear the snow away from the road opposite our own farms to let the truck through picking up the milk churns, then yet more falls again during the night. I suffer very badly from the cold, I haven't got a shirt, the boss's wife gave me one but on the second day it ripped in two. Since we have no money, I work all day in my sweater, which is nothing but holes held together with threads, and my overcoat. We cut up my blanket into strips to make mufflers and to be able to cover our ears. And, in spite of our hard lot, still we laugh about it all in the evening around the fire.

IV

FARMING FOR THE REICH

1941

1941 has begun. The first newspapers published in Berlin in French reach us. Some of the articles give us hope that we will shortly see the end of this captivity which has lasted so long when we suddenly discover that everything has been broken off between the two governments as a result of a sort of coup having taken place in Paris. Because of this, large numbers of prisoners that were still in France are taken to Germany, which leaves us little hope of getting away soon. Some of them come to our spot and bring us news of France.

Towards the middle of January 1941, the first parcels sent from France reach us and they are very welcome. I get some overshoes for the clogs, some woollen socks, mufflers, a jumper and several other bits and pieces which are a great help to me. My friends get things too, those who have too much giving things to those who haven't yet received anything, and little by little things get better.

February is very cold; unfortunately we finished the job of threshing in the barn and in spite of the snow and the bad weather we go out to work in the woods, we pull down pine trees all covered with snow and flounder around in there all day long. On the road, from time to time a sleigh goes trotting by, pulled by two horses which jingle the bells on their harnesses. The drivers, fat farmers making for the neighbouring town, wrapped up in their blankets and warm furs, smoke big cigars. Seen through the trees and sliding over the frozen snow, it reminds me of scenes in Russian films or even novels about the banks of the Volga.

March is much better. Although it's still cold, it's more bearable. Relations are renewed between the two governments. There's talk of freeing certain prisoners, which gives us great hope and, as they say, fortunately hope keeps you alive, because without it . . . Now it's Easter. Last year I was at home on leave. Good Friday is a holiday in Germany, which gives us a bit more time off.

Whitsun comes and goes too. It was a year ago that day that the big

battle near Sedan started. Now it is really nice weather and the main
work has begun. We have sown great patches of potatoes, fodder beet
and sugar beet, and we have begun the different cultivation of each.
The civil population doesn't hide its joy in what is in fact an immense
triumph for Germany. Her latest big successes are mulled over at
length, the taking of the Balkans in so short a time, crowned by the
masterly capture of Crete, is an immense triumph for the German
people. Some of the farmers with whom we chat foresee huge
conquests. After the taking of Africa, for the German armies are
advancing in Africa too, it will be the turn of the East and then
America will see its time come. Germany is showing itself now to be a
formidably powerful force. All the time formations of aircraft are
flying over the fields where we are working and we lift our heads to see
these tremendous machines which made us tremble in May and June
1940. To nark us some of the German farmers ask us if they aren't
English, and then split their sides laughing to see our mortification.

In June 1941, on a beautiful Sunday when I'd gone to rake up
some alfalfa, the news broke like a thunderbolt: Germany has
declared war on the Soviets. Immediately the usual chatterboxes
give the Russians a fortnight, some of them three weeks, while those
who see Russia as a great power give them one or two months at the
most. At any rate the German armies are advancing very quickly
into the Ukraine, taking numerous prisoners and accruing military
hardware in colossal quantities.

Yet time goes by, and here we are once again at the harvest. First
it's the corn harvest which this year is extremely good, but which
takes place in appalling weather: it rains nearly every day. We take
advantage of the slightest break in the weather to use the reaper, the
sheaves are stooked, all soaked with water, and it's with great difficulty
that we manage to gather in the harvest, very late too, because the
potato season begins straight after.

September has arrived, the mornings are fresh now. For several
days things haven't been going too well with my bosses. For some
months now, the head of the family has no longer been back on
leave, being in the north of France. With the women, who didn't
seem to understand, there's much too much work for our very
reduced numbers. The youngster is going to leave to be a soldier one
of these days. I'm going to be left all alone at the house, while at the
same time last year there were four of us men. About mid-September,
relations broke down completely with the old woman and I managed
to change places on 21st September. In the same village, but two
farms lower down, going towards the Camp, I went into the service

of Frau Willy Bitkau. Things are better here. A man, neither old nor young, injured in the other war and not liable for call-up as a result, is in charge of the work which does not, as at the last place, always fly in the face of good sense. The workforce consists of a Pole, about 20 years old from Posen, with whom I quickly become firm friends. What's more, he has a few words of French and, being very intelligent, he is quickly able to speak as well as me, which is a great help. A Polish woman from the Lublin area, about 30 years old, rather ugly, with the complexion of a gypsy and not at all sociable, works as a general help. Working especially in the fields and milking the cows, like most of the maids around here, I often work with her, but I can't manage to get on with her, an impossible character. A 70-year-old woman runs the whole show, even though the son is there; she's the one who gives the orders and everyone's under her thumb. She only goes out of the house very rarely, once or twice a year to go to see the crops. She sees to the numerous poultry and prepares the food for the whole household. Although it is more or less the same in all the houses, the food here however would seem to be a bit better than at my old place, but on the other hand it is less hygienically prepared. There is too much work for this old woman, who readily serves you up a piece of meat with her fingers which she then sucks, when she has just been squelching around in the pigsty for half an hour, or almost always serving you with the spoon that she takes out of her mouth, wiping a cup or a plate with the bottom of her often very filthy petticoat. I'd heard the meticulous cleanliness of the Germans boasted about but I notice that compared with the country areas of the South of France they have to concede a lot to us. For example, I'm not talking about us the prisoners, but them. On a Sunday, in spite of changing into their beautiful green outfits, in spite of the guard and even visitors from the town, often coming to this household, they dine here all in their Sunday best, but no napkins are brought out. I have seen several households, even quite rich ones, where the head and his family were eating, but in none of them have I seen napkins, the customary thing in the poorest cottage in France. Besides, since I'm talking about eating, I learnt that the pleasures of the table were unknown here, even for the biggest celebration, Christmas or Easter for example, whereas in France every household suitably celebrates the holidays by meeting together around the table for a meal which, on those days, is always more lavish and much longer than usual, where every housewife prepares a dish worthy of the day. Here it's not like that, all the meals seem equal. Always the same, and as is customary nothing to drink, glasses don't clutter up on the table. While in France the poorest household brings out a good bottle for these celebrations, at the very least a bottle of table wine. They know nothing about all that here; I know very well that they can't drink wine as much as they like, like we do at home, but all the same, to eat without drinking is a bit much! The only thing that marks festivals in this region is an abundance, you might say a colossal abundance, of the cakes that they make and serve up on the table in large amounts on special days. I certainly wouldn't say that they're bad, they're good, especially for us prisoners, although the cakes at home are not made at all in the same way, by housewives who each have their very own recipes and specialities, and are better in a different way. But that's what marks the celebration, a large amount of cakes more or less the same in every household, that are eaten at all times of the day, to the point that after the Christmas and New Year holidays we were sick of them. The actual meals were over in five minutes. Cakes were made in profusion for all occasions, marriages, births, baptisms, deaths and especially for birthdays, which are never forgotten, the *guebousta*, as they say here. When a member of the family has a birthday, everyone gets together and, on that day, you should see the beating the cakes take. Each region has its own ways and customs, quite different here from at home: it's true that almost 2,000 kilometres separate us.

The beginning of October, we finish bringing in the potatoes. A very big harvest. On this farm, which is one of the most important, we have also prepared a lot of silos. Straightaway, we get on with the beet crops, the forage ones first that are put in silos for the cows in winter. At the moment, they're given leaves to eat, a wagonload every day, which causes a veritable flood of urine in a shed not equipped to drain it away. Mid-October, a thick blanket of snow covers the ground when we alone start to dig up the sugar beet, a huge patch of it. It's cold, very cold for October, which really promises well for the winter. The snow stays on the ground about 10 days then lingers on, but the ground freezes and defrosts every day and we have to finish the sugar beet harvest, which isn't over until about 15 December, either in cement or in a real mud-bath.

The German armies have advanced once again a good way into Russia, being within firing range of Moscow, whose fall a lot of civilians predict before next Christmas.

Leningrad is also very much under threat, being more or less surrounded according to the civilians. And here comes Christmas, it's cold, very cold. Three days of that we spend in our meagre shed around the fire, looking out of the window at this low grey sky from which the snow falls without a break. It's sad, sad enough to die from, on these Christmas and New Year holidays. How many memories are building up in my mind. Having to spend these holidays in a situation like this so far from the family, so far from those I'm born to live with, so far from those who make life seem sweet.

1942

1st January 1942. The new year started this morning. What hope it brings! Will the wishes that we all made when we woke up come true? Will we see our own roof, our own bell-tower this year? Will this captivity, already 18 long months of it, finish? It'll soon be two years since I've seen my family, my land, my village. Are such trials necessary to bring home how much I'm attached to, how much I love, my village? How little is this vast plain, this great River Elbe, all in comparison to our vineyard at home. The tiny Razil is much more beautiful than the Elbe, even though it's dry for half the year. The winter is very very cold, the third we've spent since mobilisation, very very far from our homes. The snow reaches a tremendous depth. We go on a snow-clearing detail. The road for the postman must be cleared for several kilometres.

The beginning of March is the worst bit of it, in places the piles of snow are twice as high as me by the time we reach the stones on the roadway. A relentless east wind moves the snow, filling up the trench we've opened up behind us as soon as it's done, and the next day we have to start again. Icicles hang from whiskers and noses are purple. Nevertheless, there's less suffering than last winter, as we're better clothed and better shod than at the same period last year. On the Eastern Front, the soldiers who are bogged down suffer cruelly from the atrocious winter, with many frostbitten limbs.

April, the thaw arrived with the first beautiful sunny days that we had seen for several months. And life starts afresh. Fresh sowings, spuds, turnips, swedes and carrots come back to the top of our list of main things to be done. And here we are again at Easter, weary in this land where there's still nothing pushing up under the weak sun. The days are rather cold, whereas at home Easter marks the renewal of everything. Here not a flower, not a leaf, not even the grass which is beaten down with patches of winter frost, marks the changing seasons.

May, it's quite nice now, although the nights are still cold. Work continues in the same rhythm. Letters from home which are really good to have are still arriving quite regularly, as well as parcels. Always the same thing in the letters: chin up, it will soon be over, the end predicted for a date that's always pushed back. It's the last year of the war, it's always the same phrases that come up again and again. In the meantime, the German armies are advancing vigorously into Russia. In the Crimea, the German offensive advances with giant steps. It's the same on the central front where the Russian army seems not to exist at all.

July 1942, we begin the harvest at the end of the month, poor in rye, very good in oats and barley.

September, the potatoes hit their peak, it's the biggest crop that I've seen. This enormous field, seeing as there are six hectares in one holding alone, is glutted with potatoes. For 45 days we pick, carry to the station, fill silos with these huge potatoes. The bosses are quite happy because they've never had so enormous a crop of potatoes, but it's also a very, very hard job that we have to do to finish before the big frosts, because it's freezing already in the mornings and the ground is covered with white frost again. We hardly stop for half an hour to eat the meal that we're served straight up at the place where we've stopped work. The earth is cold and I become achingly cold in the legs and especially in the stomach that I suffer from for a long time. The beets follow the potatoes, a very good crop of sugar beet this year too that must be lifted in the snow. It's not until Christmas Eve that we get to finish everything. These last four months have been the hardest since our arrival in Germany.

At the *Kommando* life is little by little a bit more organised. We now have a cooking pot, plates and, with our parcels, we make meals, and often chocolate, coffee or a brew of tea. Almost every evening, a hot drink of one sort or another is concocted. Not many of the original arrivals at the camp are left. Some go away, others come back, it's never really the same people. Apart from a small kernel of us who remain caught up in this village, all the others have changed.

On 13 December, we go to Stendal for a shower and to have our clothes steamed free of lice. We come back via Rochau to call at the post office to collect the parcels that the postman either can't or won't bring to the village. For my part, I've got two enormous parcels which smell wonderfully of Aigues-Vives because they're bursting out on all sides with tins and delicacies. I would never be able to carry them to Schorstedt if less fortunate friends hadn't helped me. There were 25 of us, there were 28 parcels, everyone carried his own, even the guard carried one on the end of his weapon, because he knew that there would be a little something to be salvaged from this terrific avalanche. We covered the seven or eight kilometres that separated the villages singing and laughing, the parcels had infused the band of prisoners with joy. We entered the village, each man holding his package high, and all the women, who had heard us, were on their doorsteps looking at these enormous boxes that they knew would contain chocolate which for them is something supernatural, an invaluable commodity which we actually paid scarcely any attention to.

In spite of the violent cold, Christmas 1942 was celebrated as it should be, several large meals marked the holiday for which the parcels provided the means. We drank and we ate amply. Naturally some beer of inferior quality stood in for wine and the dishes we put together weren't all perfect, but in the end, helped by the little bit of happiness, this Christmas was spent better than the two previous ones. A Christmas tree was put up with its candles and decorations in a corner of the barrack-room, but instead of making us forget home that only made the heartache worse. Home, how much this long exile can make you love home. Anyone who has not been separated from it for so long a time can never have any idea. December drew to a close while we rested in the barn from our enormous fatigue watching the snow fall. The year 1942 came to its end.

Changes in 1943

1st January 1943 finds us still prisoners. The same good wishes that we had exchanged twice already since our capture are made again that morning. The same desires which come up all the time and which are thought about all day long. Will this captivity, already as long as 30 whole months, end in the course of this year? We hope so but we are not too sure. In the end, the day passes well enough in the dormitory where, to celebrate the holiday, we have a decent meal. And the New Year gets under way with work. We are at the threshing-machine until mid-February. Rye, wheat, barley and oats, are all put through it, and then we go into the woods to cut down pine trees, either for the mines, or for heating. The winter isn't very cold, much better than the two previous ones, very little snow, and we are happy enough.

The German armies are pulling back a bit in Africa, holding up under strong pressure at Stalingrad, which people are talking about a lot, and forced to fall back from the banks of the Volga. They are also beating a retreat in the Caucasus; the Russians seem to be wanting to wake up, after so long and painful a set-back. Although none of us would have given much for their skins, here they are in the depths of winter seeming to take the initiative with some very powerful offensives. The German civilians don't seem very disturbed by these small set-backs which are really very small compared to their great conquests and terrific successes. Yet the American army, having landed in Africa, seems to be tipping the balance. Here, the civilians think that with the first nice weather the German armies will take the offensive again and get ahead, and everything will be quickly put back in order. As for us, we don't know what to think, but it seems to us that the German army has reached the height of its glory. Certain indicators suggest that now things will no longer be the same, the trump cards seemed to be on the verge of changing hands and it appears to us that it will be very, very hard for the Germans to maintain their positions on every front.

In the course of the first months of the year, night bombing starts, quite spaced out at first, then more frequently as the year advances, but these raids are always at night. First we hear the sirens which hurl their sinister moans into the dark night, others farther off answer them, then it's round the village to give the alert. The night-watchman goes through the few streets to the sound of his hooter, the same one that used to round up the pigs in the morning to bring them to the grazing ground. Then the Bismark siren, the nearest one to us, sends out the most desperate cries, and depending on the wind, the sirens of Stendal, Rochau or Osterburg can sometimes be heard, with other village hooters, and immediately you can make out a terrific throbbing which rapidly gets nearer, sounding off in the dark of night for half an hour, an hour and often even more. Far off, the anti-aircraft guns fire, but without it seems much hindering the planes which are making either for Berlin, Leipzig, Magdeburg or elsewhere. Sometimes you can hear bombs falling far off, or quite near, which makes the barrack-room shake and brings down the rough cast on the walls that isn't very well held on. I get up, not because of the alert, because they almost never let us out, but to look at the sky, or the little bit I can see of it through the bars of the south-facing window. The searchlights rake the sky while the planes mark their passage with numerous flares of varying colours, red, green, white. Sometimes a corner of the sky resembles the entrance of a huge station with its multi-coloured lights in the night. Fighter planes skim the roofs or circle above the village, making the inhabitants shudder.

Life goes on, always the same for us prisoners. We talk a lot about this question of a changeover which, having wet our lips, appears to us a cruel deception. We have the impression that the French government is only groping its way in this business. Announced at the start with a great to-do by the scanty newspapers that reach us, on the previous basis that one prisoner would be released for every one worker coming to Germany, that quickly changes to two workers for one prisoner, then to three, then to five and even to ten. In the end, no one, or very few prisoners, gets away. Some rich kids who could not be kept at home in June 1940 before the rapid German offensive, are repatriated, some footballers, racing cyclists, runners, and even Rigoulot, champion weight-lifter, those were the ones repatriated. You can add to this list well-known film people and actors, some friends of important doctors who manage to get their sons home as hospital orderlies, while qualified nurses wait behind barbed wire. Those were almost the only winners from this relief scheme. Bringing back heads of families, country people, what's the good of that? France may be dying of hunger but it has more need of sportsmen, going to the cinema – that'll fill up your stomach. As for the farm worker, he will be left to the end, having no importance in terms of his age, or his work, or his family. The Pétain–Laval government which, I must admit, had behind it the vast majority of prisoners, who had full confidence in the Marshal, has lost every bit of its prestige with this release scheme that's nothing more than a real fiasco. Some lads of 22, 24 or 25 years of age are sent back while men who are fathers of families of 40, 42 and even some who are more than 43 years old, very much aged by the ordeal, are there behind bars. No, the prisoners as a whole will never forgive Laval for that. We asked nothing of the government. Why spin us such yarns when they can't deliver what they promise? On the other hand, from the German point of view it seems to be working well. Trains arrive from all sides, with a great fuss made in the newspapers, but very few go back in the opposite direction. The scheme continues, the civilians come but the prisoners stay put. So, once again, the German government has really got the better of these gentlemen.

The whole party of prisoners is discontented, when yet another new system is brought out for us born of the war. We will have seen everything in the course of this war. Now, with wider coverage, as always when they need to drive something home into the prisoners' thick heads, the newspapers are talking about transforming us into free civilian workers. Here's yet another story! We French soldiers, taken on the field of battle, weapons in hand, who for almost 40 months have been watched over by a guard with bayonet fixed, who would not have hesitated, and anyway they are under orders, to fire on us like rabbits (unfortunately, it's what has happened to some people) at the slightest provocation, at the least infringement of the rules, there we are suddenly considered to be like anyone else, having the right to go to the café, to Church, to the cinema like all the good German citizens, to walk in the street, to go and visit this town, that museum or the other monument. No, really, you'd never have thought it. What advantage can Germany be wanting to gain from it? Because it's sure the advantage can't be with us. Germany suggests something, it's surely in her interest. The nature of the interest escapes us but it surely exists. But me and my mates smell a trap. The relief scheme has disappointed us too much, but it has woken us up.

Disgusting to read, the newspapers divided their pages between the continuing story of this famous transformation and politics, or anti-English and anti-American articles. Nothing is working for them, everything is going from bad to worse; some of the papers are almost counting the days until America will be invaded in its turn. Poor Americans, poor Englishmen, according to our newspapers you haven't got much longer to count your dollars!

However time passes, the offensive in Africa has spread widely, and they're fighting now in Tunisia. In Russia too, things seem to be deteriorating for the Germans who have to make retreat after retreat. What's more names that we haven't seen for a good few months are reappearing in the communiqués: the Don, the Donetz are once again in our conversations. Even though the newspapers preach to us every day about the German offensive recommencing, we are all still waiting to see this enormous undertaking which is always being put back. While waiting, news reaches us of the end of operations in Africa. The newspapers report the affair as a great Italo-German defensive victory. July, August, landings take place on several Mediterranean islands, Lampedusa . . . then finally in Sicily where fierce fighting takes place. The newspapers talk of Italo-German victories in Sicily where the Anglo-Americans, aided by the Gaullist troops, are strangely deployed, which in the end doesn't stop the Allied troops from sweeping right through the island. Corsica, Sardinia also see their turn come, this is all getting very close to my part of the world now. What will happen down there next?

September 1943. On the 21st of this month, we are summoned to Stendal for the signing of the civil contract. In the kommando, opinions are divided, for and against signing. There is quite a number of us, other kommandos have joined up with us, we are drawn up in front of a little barracks lodge. Several German officers are there. An interpreter reads a short speech before the contract signing. First of all, the advantages are numbered: leave, earnings, freedom, and other things as well. Next they go on for a long time about the great favour that the German government is according us and that we must show ourselves worthy of it by our conduct once we are civilians. The signing process follows immediately afterwards. We are called one after the other into the lodge where several officers are seated. Already several people are coming out who haven't signed. The officers can't get over it. What? You are refusing the freedom that's on offer, we've never seen anything like it, they seem to be saying! I am one of the last of the kommando to go in. Just seeing me come in told the officer that I was not for freedom and he dismisses me without even questioning me. In the end, out of the 25 who made up the kommando, only five have signed and they are immediately set free. As for the other 20, we go back to being prisoners, in a column of threes, followed by the sentry, with his gun on his shoulder, after being reminded quite sharply that it would be a long time before we had the favour we are refusing today offered to us again and that we would bitterly regret it later. It doesn't matter, not one of the 20 budged, we wanted to stay prisoners, even if everything is lost. Are we doing right or wrong? The future will tell us. While waiting, the comrades who had signed were looking forward with the greatest delight to the time of their longed-for home leaves. Shut-up in our barrack-room, we were thinking: if they are getting away, then we would be really caught out.

September, potato time. Not too big a harvest this year, quite good for the sugar beet that we start to pull in October in not always very warm weather and then take to the station. This is quite hard work and is considered one of the most arduous tasks of the year.

The beginning of December, some comrades are designated to leave for work elsewhere, in a factory or else in the forests with the woodcutters. One of my best friends is leaving to go into a factory near Magdeburg, Georges Garrier from Paris, a good mate, delightful, talking quite late into the evening, which I quite liked because a good number of the lads go to sleep very early. He talked to me about life in Paris, its peculiarities and its customs, and then was always on about organising little camp diversions and rustling up our little Sunday dinners. His departure is very hard for me to take for the first days, then life takes its course once again and the coming events make me forget those of the day before.

The Great Hare-Beat

12 December 1943. Today the village is *en fête*, it's the day of the great hunt for hares all over the parish. The biggest beat of the year. For the first time since our arrival in the district we were invited to go to act as beaters. That's to say, last year we had been invited but we were at Stendal for disinfection and showers. The first year, they hadn't wanted us: only having been there four months, we had not yet gained the confidence of the hunters.

The day itself is a holiday for virtually everyone. From first thing in the morning the domestic servants and bosses do the indispensable work on the farm, that's to say looking after the livestock. Then, very early, we prepare for departure. Breakfast was two hours before its normal time, and at 11 o'clock the hunters and beaters were put in groups where the village ended, on the west side. All the great hunters of the area are present, although there are very few of them for – unlike France – in Germany the working man does not hunt. Its only the biggest farmers who hunt, six in this village of 300 people (in normal times), and that's very little. Still, each one of them has invited two or three colleagues, big farmers and hunters from the neighbouring villages, which brings up the complement to 18 or 20 guns. There are nearly 80 of us beaters for these few guns. The Poles and Ukrainians, even some Italians, are there, mixed up with the French. Some German farmers who have not been mobilised also serve as beaters. Some Russians who have brought their bosses in carts, and two Serbs, have also come to beat. In other words, this is an international hunt! Unhappily we have no gun. It's all the same to me, as one who has never hunted, but for a good number of my colleagues, inveterate hunters, it hurt to carry a stick in the guise of a gun.

However the most important farmer in the village, Milord Beckman, very splendid in his rig-out and his yellow, highly-polished leathers, his traditional hat topped by the no-less traditional feather – a stage-hunter, as the enthusiasts back home, running through the undergrowth on the moors after some elusive rabbit would say – is running the hunt, giving orders to right and left. The hunt begins, but it is nothing like what I have seen at home on similar beats. Each hunter, flanked by three or four beaters, two to the right and two to the left, goes to get his place, that is to the place which he has been assigned. A vast circle is thus formed and when everyone is ready, that is when the circle has been fully closed, the hunt begins by everyone walking forward. We have only gone twenty metres when already some hares have sprung up and the first shots are heard, on the right and on the left. There is also firing on the other side of the circle and the march forward continues. Gradually the circle tightens. Other hares are flushed out little by little by the advance and the noise. They run hither and thither in the circle which is pitilessly tightening around them. And there are two more which jump up frightened by the fusillade which is now raging. The centre of the circle is on a small hog's back and you can see at the crest of the little hill, among the rye or in the ploughed fields these poor beasts criss-crossing each other, no longer knowing how or which way to turn. Five, six, eight or ten run in every direction and the firing redoubles in force. The circle tightens even more, this is the moment when the hares are going to try to get out of the vast ring. Suddenly three or four charge straight out at us, who, batons raised, try to beat them back onto our hunter. He fires and repeats, and his nearest neighbour does the same. Often the hare survives four, five or even six shots and still doesn't seem to be hit. Just as often the first shot hits it; it's then you see the beautiful pirouette that immediately precedes the beast's death. Others are mortally wounded and let out plaintive and distressing cries like small children. Many run away on three legs, still much too fast for us to be able to catch them. Many of them will die far off, undisturbed by anyone.

Now however the circle is too tight for us to continue to walk forward; a hunter could fill his opposite number on the other side of the ring with lead. There's a blast of the whistle and all the hunters stay in their positions while the beaters alone go forward to flush out the few hares still remaining inside the circle. That's quickly done, and one last volley puts an end to the first round-up. The bag produced by the hunt starts to be assessed. Each beater brings his load onto the nearest road. The hares are lined up, one by one on the edge of the road and facing the same way. A man counts them. At every 10, a hare is slightly pulled out to help the counting. There are 36 from this first beat and it is scarcely an hour since the hunt began. The hares are secured onto some poles by their hind paws and in lines of

10 on each pole. Then the poles are mounted on a cart with the ends placed on the sides so that the nicely lined up hares are hanging into the body of the wagon.

And then the second round-up takes place on another piece of land, right next to the first. The same manoeuvre is used, and when the collection is finished, after some intense firing, 46 new hares are laid out next to the first group.

After this second beat there is a halt for a snack. All the participants in the hunt went to the flour mill a little outside the village, on the Osterburg road, just at the point where the second stage finished. At the miller's, the hunters and their guests sit down around tables laid for the purpose in the barn and drink beer while eating their snack, and discussing boisterously the various shots, successful or botched, which each had had in the first two hours of the hunt. As for us beaters, we stamp our feet in the mill courtyard while eating bread and butter, for it is not warm. A freezing east wind, carrying a little snow, chills you right through. However we have not been forgotten and a generous distribution of beer takes place. Everyone can drink as much as they want, but the weather does not make you thirsty, far from it. One small glass is enough to wash down the bread. Some mates, taking advantage of the windfall, for it is rare enough that they give us anything, drink six or seven of them, some even manage eight or ten, but in time, with the cold, that has some unfortunate effects.

Here we are, the picnic is at an end, it is two in the afternoon and the hunt restarts. This time the round-up will take place in the great plain and we have to scour it three times, one after the other, right to its furthest extent. This plain is only hunted on one day a year, today. It's then that all its game can be seen. Oh! What I would give at this moment to have the Aigues-Vives hunters around me, they who run for whole days through the brush of our *garrigues*[1] or striding along through the vines just so as to put up one poor hare or one questionable rabbit, which nine times out of ten bolts back into the ground as soon as it is fired at . . . No, I will never be able to hunt back home, I have seen too much game during the war years to have the patience to run for whole days without putting anything up, as often happens to our hunters in Aigues-Vives, while here I have never yet gone out into the fields, whether with horses or on manual work, without flushing out game. It is not unusual, working in a field and going up and down the furrows, to raise three or four hares or even a covey of those beautiful grey partridges, almost not frightened of you because they are so little hunted here. Often, and above all to the south of the village, large numbers of pheasants will come up almost under your feet. In the autumn the lapwings spend a good two months in the harvested fields. And I have not mentioned the graceful flocks of deer which graze on the plain and to which no harm comes. At the very most, every possessor of a hunting permit might kill one young male during the course of the summer, sometimes two but no more, which is nothing given the total number. One sees through the year these pretty does living in families of 8, 10 and even sometimes as many as 16 or 18 keeping you company in the fields, quite unafraid and scarcely lifting themselves up so as to slowly move off before you as you approach. But the really beautiful sight is when the rye or the corn reaches a height of between 80 centimetres and one metre. You can see these nice creatures a few metres in front, lifting their heads and looking at you, following your movements over the tops of their walls of straw. We must add to this list of game quite a few ducks which nest and frolic in all the waterholes or streams which in the summer serve as drinking-places for the cows, but the ducks are not bothered by them.

Also in the summer, flocks of starlings frolic by the hundred, even by the thousand, in the cattle-pens, looking for food, and unlike back home where this bird is startled by the approach of man at a great distance, here it comes up virtually from beneath your feet. Even better, all the farms and houses place wooden chests, like little closed footwarmers, against the walls of the cowsheds, the barn and even the house, and cut in them a round hole rather like the bung in a barrel where the starlings come to nest and return every year, just like the swallows do at home. And so we have some real concerts whistled from the roofs of the houses or the nearby trees in the garden. Here none of these little birds is hunted. The crested larks, all grey and pretty in the morning, the blackbirds and thrushes, even if less common, the mass of sparrows, none of these little beasts is killed. It happens often that, in pointing them out to my boss, I tell him that we eat these things in France. The people here laugh in our face to hear us say so. But damn it, that's a lot better than the boiled potatoes in a quick sauce called '*pel kartofel*'[2] that is invariably served up to us in the evenings here. A thrush or even a skylark, properly basted on a piece of fried bread . . . I stop myself for I won't be able to eat for a week if I think of that while looking at a plate of boiled *kartofels*. No, for them that wouldn't be good, eating such little things. They think we are queer, we French, to eat them. But God knows how good they are! Even the partridge is in the same boat and is not shot round here. They prefer proper meat, and above all pork, a piece of which is boiled for a long time after soaking for two days in cold water, like all the meat that they cook, boiled of course, for they do not know any other way of preparation.

We must add to all this some storks going round and round the meadows in search of frogs or holding themselves up on one leg for hours at a time, while occasionally having something to eat and twisting their neck in every direction round the chimneys of the houses where they build their nests. There are some rabbits, but not very many, which stay in the woods on the fringe of the fields. And that is virtually the sum total of the game in the district where I'm living for these long months. It's not bad, and it would be just a dream for the hunters back in Aigues-Vives, who come back empty-handed from a day fruitlessly scouring the countryside.

But let us return to the beat, that I abandoned to say something of the hunting hereabouts. The third round-up takes place, similar to the two before, and it brings in another 30 hares. And we start on another great circle. Groups of hinds, does, find themselves caught in the circle and run, poor things, in every direction, frightened by us all raising our sticks at them, to the great annoyance of the hunters who shout to us to let them pass through quietly. But these poor little beasts do not run, they are almost flying they go so quickly, pursued by the dogs. It's good to see them go by so close, within reach of one's stick, and to stretch out in indian file, with their white backsides. Quite a few coveys of partridge are also flushed out, but no-one bothers them despite their being well within range of the guns. It is half past four when the hunt ends on a last beat that only nets about 15 hares. The total is then reckoned and they are laid out on the side of the road. A total of 142 hares are there, lined up or hung in groups of 10 from the poles across the wagon. It's a good hunt, the spread before us is really quite impressive. And the return to the village takes place in small groups behind the cart full of the hanging hares. The entrance into the village is triumphal, for all the housewives come out to see us arrive. In the years before the war, it seems, everyone went together to a great banquet. Hunters and beaters were together at the celebration, which finished late into the night and which was to conclude, this the great hunt of the year. But now times have changed. Besides, the beaters are little more than strangers. The hunters and their guests booze on alone.

The Fourth Christmas

Here we are at the end of the year, while in these last few months the bombing has redoubled in intensity. It is unusual to pass a night without several overflights from planes making for Berlin or Magdeburg. One evening, towards eight o'clock, at the end of October, a major alert took place. A large number of planes circled endlessly in the immediate area of the village. Some bombs fall quite near, making the hut shake dangerously so that the window-panes and the rendering fall out. I was preparing some soup in a pot, but I left it to go out to see what was happening. Some flares had just been dropped and had rapidly dispelled the shadows, for it was very dark that night, cloudy with a fine, freezing cold rain. A plane skimmed the rooftops and sent a shiver of fear through us. There are problems now, and so all the prisoners have also come out of the hut, and several have even put some distance between themselves and the houses, going into the neighbouring fields. We can hear the civilians talking, and they have also got into the shelters or into the fields. Another group of planes skims the ground, lighting up the village and its neighbourhood brilliantly with their flares. Some bombs are again dropped onto the south of the village, a few kilometres away from us, and suddenly a huge fire breaks out making a vast circle in the sky while at the same moment you can smell phosphorus right up your nose, brought to us by the westerly wind. Some planes, with a terrible throbbing, pass over again and turn at rooftop height in our direction. Are they going to bomb the village?

With some friends, we quickly get to the bottom of the meadow where there is a pretty deep trench half-full of water, but which can serve as a shelter if needs must. Another scattering of mines and bombs occurs, after a dramatic illumination of the sky towards the east. The earth trembles violently, then everything returns to calm, the planes go further away, while the fire rages on. The next day the news of what had happened arrived, and it was rather sad so far as we were concerned. The village of Walasted, three kilometres away, had really copped it. The kommando of the French workers had collapsed, trapping several prisoners under the rubble. Two had been got out badly wounded and taken immediately to hospital. Several others had been hit, more or less badly. Another Frenchman, who was with a Polish woman in a part of the house next to the billet, had been killed, like the Pole, the both of them frightfully mutilated as the house had received a direct hit from a mine. The milk co-operative had been almost completely demolished, several houses had had their roofs carried away by the blast of air, others were either half or completely demolished. The village had taken a heavy blow. The fire had been put right out after the complete destruction of five farms of some considerable importance. One man from the village who had been seriously wounded had been taken to hospital.

Christmas 1943. Here we are again at this great holiday which finds us still here, in our hovel. The fifth to be spent away from home, the fourth in Germany. In previous years we spent the festival cheerfully enough, if cheerful is the right word, but now the length of our captivity, whose end we can neither see nor predict, is affecting even the toughest of us. To be sure, like last year we have planned – and will carry out – a good midnight supper for Christmas Eve, but it's not the same. We have put up our Christmas tree in the hut, but all that only makes you more nostalgic for the celebration at home. These festivals are particularly hard for me, and also Sundays, when without your mind absorbed in work, you think over and over again about home. This year most especially, despite the hearty midnight meal which hardly lacks anything apart from a few bottles, the holiday is a sad one. You feel that despite the talking everyone is thinking of his family, of his home.

What is more, the room is emptier. Last year, we were 15 at midnight. Now, after the departure of those who became civilians, and two others gone off into the factory, there are no more than seven for the feast. The servings are certainly bigger and the feast better as a result, but there is no atmosphere. Last year the banquet had lasted almost right through the night. This year it is a quiet meal and at eleven o'clock everyone turns in for a good night's sleep. The day after the hunt I found a superb hare of nine or ten pounds, a beautiful beast which contributed a lot to our menu and did everyone good, besides the Christmas parcels which we had received in considerable abundance. As for the bosses, their Christmas was marked, as in previous years, by an abundance of cake and the traditional hare eaten at a midday meal, the only one of the year.

And so the year 1943 is coming to an end without bringing any great change in our situation. We expected a lot of the year that is ending, during which we have been counting on the war ending and our return home. True, the Russians have advanced a good deal, they are nearly back at their frontiers almost everywhere, having almost thrown the formidable German armies completely out of their country. In Italy the Allies have been marking time outside Rome for quite a while already, after the great effort of the previous summer.

1 January 1944. Once more it is New Year's Day. What will this year hold for us? We do not even dare any longer to form plans for the future, when we have been so disappointed. Our New Year wishes are no less fervent than before, but we have so often been disillusioned in the year which has just gone that we can no longer make predictions. We have moments when we doubt the future completely and seriously wonder whether we shall ever see France again, our towns, our villages. The villages of which we think night and day. This long captivity where there is no way of seeing the end, after 42 long months of life as prisoners, affects the most determined, above all because there is nothing, absolutely nothing on the horizon to make us think that it might all end one day. There are times when we are seized by despair and when we seriously ask ourselves if we are to finish our days in this miserable life, in the midst of this great forest, in a strange land.

We can't complain physically, to be sure. The work, although sometimes very hard, isn't beyond us. Most of us are peasants, used to working on the land all our lives. Naturally some of the blokes tire much more from the work, it not being their line, and they take the more credit for it. For example, Simon a teacher from near Agen, and some others, Parisians or men from the North, employed in banks, offices or small factories, had to work harder than us, but all things considered they come out of it pretty well. Of course when we first arrived some of them talked about arranging sport, in the summer evenings after work at the Camp, football and other things. But they quickly came to understand that after turning over manure with a pitchfork or labouring behind a horse for 10 or 12 hours, or having loaded heavy logs for the whole day, or kneeling for days on end harvesting potatoes, or moving tons of sugar beet, they understood for themselves that sport, however enjoyable, was not too sensible for arms and legs which had just been on the go for 12 hours at a time.

The food was always the same. The same things appeared on the table every day from 1 January to New Year's Eve, and there were times when frankly it became nauseating. But it was at least sufficient to keep us in more or less normal health. No one, it should be pointed out, suffered from hunger, far from it. If anything it was thirst we suffered from, but it was not really thirst because there was plenty of water to drink, even if it was not particularly good in this area. But most prisoners are lads from the South, and being good southerners they adored their wine, something precious that we have seen nothing of for coming up four years. Four long years without seeing the colour of wine, which is only present here in our endless discussions on winter evenings around the stove. There were amongst us some great experts on the most celebrated vineyards and interminable discussions took place on all the colours and tastes of the great wines of France. Sometimes minor quarrels even broke out on the subject of wine, which was thoroughly debated. But it all stopped there, for there was never any tasting, all that we had from time to time was a few small glasses of a beer which was low in alcohol and poor in taste, a real cow's piss which provoked no discussion on the subject of beer. I thought that in Germany, such a big consuming country, the beer would be better than the French. I was terribly disappointed when I drank that trash. For all that it seems that the regions bordering on France drink much better beers than here. In the Rhineland, in the Saar or in the Ruhr basin beer is drunk in large quantities in the brasseries and cafés, and even in private houses, in every farm, and at meals or any time of the day, but here that isn't the case at all, the habit hasn't spread this far (more's the pity), where everyone eats without anything at all to drink. Glasses do not weigh down the tables in this part of the world where meals are quickly dispatched. However on the few occasions that I have had to go to Stendal or Bismark I observed that the beer was much better in the towns than in these villages lost in the Saxon bush.

But I am wandering off the subject of New Year's day that we spent pretty sadly in our meagre hut, all the time watching the snow fall. Some play at cards, while others patch their old clothes , but you sense that even if we are not suffering physically everyone has some sort of crisis of morale. Each one in turn has his dark, even black days. The blues hit even the hardest at times. Then it passes, a friend tells some stories – more or less true – and some subjects are endlessly debated, which passes time on these interminable winter evenings. The war is one of them, it's a daily concern. In the evening everyone tells what he learnt during the day. The news is more often false than true, and most of it is improbable, but it runs from one kommando to another, often at record speed. A mate, seeing a Frenchman from a neighbouring village, brings his news which by afternoon has already spread to another village, in completely the opposite direction. It is one of our means of information, the most widespread and the quickest the prisoners have.

We do however have some papers which come every week, some French and even some German, but they are often very old, two, three or even four weeks old, which undermines the news they bring, particularly about the war. In our hut it is not like in the other kommandos, where the dedicated blokes, to amuse or relax their friends, organise some entertainment. Some plays, proper comedies were organised, shows such as I saw at Bismark are beyond criticism; on the contrary, sincere congratulations are due to those who put their amateur talents in this way at the disposal of their mates. But at our place it wasn't at all like that. It is true that the small number of us in our kommando barely allowed us to put anything on. We have never been more than 25, and we are no more than 18 at present[3] but despite the low number Sundays and holidays are full enough. Above all, and it's this which really takes precedence over everything else, there is *belote* which takes up the tedious hours of the day, and often enough goes far into the night, most prisoners being addicted to cards. Then there is draughts which also passes a good few hours. But there are few who have the great patience needed to play this game. I have a few matches, it's in fact the only game I play. When the weather is good the boules come out. Everyone has made for himself a pair of boules in wood, more or less well crafted, and as some of the keen players train the others, there are real, interminable games organised in the courtyard of the Camp.

Gastronomy in the Camp

1 January 1944. It has snowed all day, which keeps all the prisoners shut up in our miserable hut. To break the sadness which is enveloping everyone, we organise the famous *belote* competition which is always a great success. These card competitions pop up on every holiday. On good days we also have the hotly-contested boules matches, but the main thing among all our distractions in the Camp is still the little meals taken together, that join the useful to the enjoyable. In this, no abstentions are tolerated among the group of mates.

Above all it's on Sundays that we have a nice little meal. The kommando is divided into various rooms that form an equivalent number of groups for these small binges. In my room, having been 15 we are no longer any more than seven to share the meal, and since we understand each other very well, we are the better for it. These menus, prepared in great detail during the course of the week, are focused on properly during Sunday and eaten with all due respect at the evening meal. What are these menus? They are changed as much as possible to avoid monotony and above all we try as hard as we can to give them the taste and aroma of the French dishes which we have been deprived of for so many months.

To begin with, the parcels received from home are all put into the pot, apart from a few trinkets, tobacco and underwear; all the rest is for the group to build up our reserves. Coming from various parts of France as we did, we had a great variety of dishes on our table. At nearly every meal, and rare was the exception to the rule, we started with an onion salad, which in the general view is the best treat of all. The onions were mixed with some tins of sardines, tuna and often salmon, which is better. At the end of the summer and in autumn, we mix in a few poor tomatoes, which does not spoil in any way this authentic and much appreciated Russian salad. Then the second course arrives, also varied a good deal. First there is paté which goes down very well. Some friends from round Agen,[4] notably the teacher Simon, get a goose paté de foie gras which is heavenly. Then come

200

the rillettes[5] which a mate from the Vendée gets in abundance and which are really delicious. The sausage, often from the Lozère, and sent to a friend who comes from Mende, is also something we have as an hors-d'oeuvre. To the three 'musts' of hors d'oeuvres[6] we often add a variety of tinned food.

Then the main feature starts, the one that can fill the biggest stomachs. First of all it's beans, a *cassoulet* as they say in Toulouse. In fact it is Laval, the gardener from the outskirts of Toulouse who is in charge of this dish. What is more he works at it nearly all Sunday, then puts a huge spread on the table which everyone agrees is succulent and unbeatable. How does he do it? I don't know, but I do know that a great deal goes into its preparation. Leeks, carrots, celery, even some potatoes. A good bit of fat and rind, a lot of margarine and of butter. Then two or three tins of bully, corned-beef, complete a course which is worthy of the best cooks. This dish is often replaced by macaroni, noodles prepared in different ways, with cheese, butter or meat, but here our cook changes, because every one specialises in a single dish and continually improves in his own branch of cuisine.

However we have a principal chef who does the extras and supervises the apprentices, which does a lot to keep down the number of gaffes, which would otherwise be irreparable. The macaroni and bean dishes are replaced by local produce when the harvest comes in, that is to say by petit pois, new carrots or green beans or even new potatoes, all of them cooked, of course, in the French style.

But the principal dish, surpassing all the others by popular acclaim is the huge plates of mushrooms. There the head chef himself takes over personal control of the cooking and will not tolerate any apprentice getting near the pots. We go out on Sunday, immediately after the midday meal. Some crazy hunters have already been out all morning, like the market gardener Blaise for example, and we come back with great loads of mushrooms. There's a specialist here following the teams, for very few of the gatherers are experts. Yet not many of them are poisonous in this district, where the locals cannot be bothered to pick them. But some of them, seeing that none amongst us is on the verge of death and that on the contrary we are in very good health, also begin to pick them. In the meadows, to begin with, are loads of pink mushrooms of which we can pick as many as we like. Then there is a form of mushroom which comes up in the shape of a chinese umbrella, also in quite large numbers, along the hedgerows and in poor soil, that we call '*gouloumelle*'. I don't know if that is its real name, but it really makes a succulent dish. In the woods of oak and silver birch, and even a little in the pinewoods, we pick the king of mushrooms, the *cèpes*, the big and delicious *cèpes*, also found in abundance. There are some Sundays when we bring back so many different kinds of mushroom that it takes a few days to eat them. And so some supplementary meals are put on the programme: Monday supper, Tuesday, sometimes they last until Thursday, that's to say until the complete exhaustion of our stocks, and again sometimes during the week someone working in a good spot will come back with a bagful.

In the Spring, there are salads to flesh out the menu. Dandelions can be collected in colossal quantities, really white and tender. All the lads, like me, love salad, and it fell to me to prepare them in such a way as to keep them all happy, in a great cauldron used for heating the water for washing clothes. Salad is more or less my speciality, the cooking being easy to manage! We also get to eat some lettuces, the peasants sow them in quantities in the fields to give them to the geese and chickens in summer. For they don't think of salad as something to eat, even if for dessert they eat a few leaves in a saucer. Their seasonings are completely simple and not at all complicated: three or four leaves soaking in a lot of sugared water and that's it. That's not at all to my liking, as someone who is used to eating big plates of salad at home. The peasants, seeing us prepare these big dishes of dandelions, ask us if it is to feed the cows with.

For the holidays, the meals are doubled and improved further, and some real hotel-style menus are drawn up for such days. Here is the latest one:

Midnight Supper, Christmas 1943

Saumon sauce provençale (salmon)
Tranches de porc glacé (slices of cold pork)
Paté américain
Poulet de Bresse en fricassée (chicken)
Lièvre en gibelotte (hare fricassée)
Fromage américain (cheese)
Confiture, Gelée de fruits (jam; fruit jelly)
Fruits de saison. Pommes et Poires (fruit of the season; apples and pears).
Biscuits. Pain d'épices (biscuits; gingerbread)
Bière à volonté. Café. Cigares (beer on demand; coffee; cigars).

This menu speaks for itself, particularly since it is one for prisoners. Meals of this kind happened often enough. Of course they weren't as copious every Sunday, but every Sunday there was all the same a dessert, often proving too much even for us since, coming at the end of the meal, people didn't have the appetite to eat it. Those who had got parcels during the week stood a round of cigarettes, as was our rule. Up to now we have had beer virtually on tap, not very good but all the same better than water. It happens quite often that we bring to the Camp a barrel of 30 litres for Sunday and then, my word you can drink as you like all day. But now beer is getting scarcer and it's pretty hard to have only a few small glasses to wash down our big meals.

Naturally, thus far the individual food parcels, which have been very large and comprehensive, have helped us a lot in making these meals. In recent weeks everyone has received his 'Pétain' parcel which has rapidly inflated our reserves. And now there are these American parcels which have made a serious contribution to our programme. Naturally we don't lack fats for cooking all our dishes either. A lad from Brittany and another from Normandy get big pots of butter. Some others get nice big bits of lard, all that helps a lot. But what almost burst the reserve chest was the arrival of the American parcels, the first that we had had anything to do with. A batch of preserves unimaginable for prisoners had just now arrived: margarine, butter, powdered milk, tins of ham, paté, meat, salmon, chocolate, packets of raisins or prunes, sugar, and then five packets of luxury cigarettes and, I forgot something which for us is of the greatest importance, and that's the packet of coffee that is in all the American parcels we get. This coffee, with an aroma strong enough to awaken a dead man and which we have not smelt for such a long time, is the delight of all of us. But it is too strong and it stops some of us from sleeping; nevertheless everyone drinks it with almost adoration and it finishes off our meals nicely. All these American preserves, coming from Chicago, New York or other cities, are presented in an impeccable manner. Superbly wrapped in packets of strong cardboard, you could almost take them for a feast, so much does it please the eye to see all these luxury products arranged in a special way, really lovely. If you add to that the gifts, quite small but still good to have, from the French Red Cross, we really can't say that we are badly off in the physical sense. In fact, as we receive these parcels, almost too luxurious for prisoners, we think of our families back home. What are they doing down there? Surely they don't have so many things available, and surely many French families plunged into terrible misery have a lot more to complain about than us. We have had some dark days as well. When, standing before this avalanche of tinned food and other things, we think of the days and weeks spent in the Saint-Dizier camp of such sad memory, for all those who did time there, when for weeks they forgot to feed us, we weep to think of how hard it all was, of the terrible times for all those who lived them.

I will finish this already long account by saying something about our little evening feasts. That's to say, about the drinks prepared every evening when we came back into the Camp, especially in winter when it was very nice, on cold days, to have a hot drink. The man of the day, that was the one in charge of the upkeep and cleanliness of the room for the day, lights the stove and keeps it roaring away all evening, and is charged to prepare the drink of the day. It's often coffee; if there is none, then it's milk. Pretty often we make a light meal, Kub broth, Maggi soup, tiny pasta, vermicelli, and regularly, every Saturday, a compulsory hot chocolate. Up to now we haven't missed a single evening, since we have had all the supplies. Coffee and chocolate are often accompanied by a snack, biscuits and gingerbread. The American parcels have now given us a precious helping hand with the coffee and milk, the packets of fruit, raisins and prunes, and also provide some dessert. We make infusions sometimes, when most people in the kommando are down with 'flu, lime-blossom, mint, vervain, orange-flower, tea all take turns, tea with milk is actually very good with sugar and even laced with a little honey that one of our room-mates gets. That's really nice, especially in winter, in the long evenings when you don't always come back very warm.[7]

V

THE DISINTEGRATION
OF NAZISM

The Prisoners, Spectators at the German Defeat

And now the year starts up again. The wheel keeps on turning. The threshing-machine keeps us busy now during the cold days of January. However the winter has not been too bad so far, there's been a little snow but not too much and the cold is much less sharp than in the first two years we spent here. The first days of the new year are notable for the heavy bombing, really close, but always at night. On 31 January we are brought together at Stendal once again to put our signature on the contract to become a civilian. There are a lot of us at Stendal. When we arrive some people have already signed the contract making them free civilians, while others have refused and stay prisoners. We line up opposite the buildings where the signing operation is taking place. An order is given us. Those who want to become civilians are asked to step forward from the ranks, but no one moves. Believing that we haven't understood, the order is repeated but we all stay where we are. The few officers there look on shaking their heads. They can't understand our attitude. The situation is difficult, we are anxious that it should end. Finally an NCO puts a stop to the proceedings, and gives the order for a half-turn and forward march in the direction of the station. For the second time we have just rejected civilian life. We don't want the freedom that they are offering us. Are we doing right, or wrong? The future will tell. For the moment we think we are doing the right thing, for our comrades who have been civilians since September last no longer seem so enchanted by the business, as the promised leaves have been long in coming, and other advantages promised do not seem to have been forthcoming either. And while waiting they are no longer receiving anything, or anyway not much. Not from the Red Cross and nothing, or nearly nothing by way of parcels from home. In these last few days we have all had our individual American parcel, but they have been forgotten in the share-out. And there is a point of honour, as far as I am concerned, and most of my mates are the same, we make it a firm point of principle to be treated as prisoners. Made prisoners on the

German front, we want to be treated as such, we do not know what to make of civilian life in Germany. Of course we want to enjoy normal life again, in fact we hanker for it desperately, but not here, it's back home that we pine to be back in civilian life. Now we return to our kommando, prisoners as before. The peasants look at us without understanding too much the reasons which might make us reject what they see as the favour which they are doing us.

February 1944. We have finished work in the barn, the thresher is still until the next harvest. Now we are going into the woods every day, cutting wood for heating and preparing some to take to the station for the mines. The air raids are now constant and ever more frequent – but still always at night. Some bombs fall near us but for the most part the planes are dropping their loads on Berlin.

The winter draws to a close, not too cold, without too much snow. We have got off pretty lightly this winter too. The post and the parcels continue to come fairly regularly from France. On the various fronts there is nothing important happening, which leads us to think an end to our captivity is in sight. The newspapers are putting out stronger and stronger propaganda in favour of collaboration, which it is as well to acknowledge did not find many followers amongst us, despite the anti-English and anti-American articles in the daily press. Rather than alienating us from the allies it does the opposite. In March the articles start to comment on a supposed landing on the coast of France by an Anglo-American force. Could such a thing be possible, given the way the newspapers are so concerned about it? And yet, according to the newspapers which we get, if the hazardous undertaking is attempted, it is doomed to a resounding defeat. All the papers are now discussing the possibility. They talk about the Atlantic Wall being impregnable and the inspections made by the German army's top brass are commented upon at length. The Atlantic fortress can't be broken and the same is true of the Mediterranean. If the attempt is made it will be real suicide for the invading army. The attempts which have been made at Dieppe, Saint-Nazaire attest to it, and the press harps on the same note – if in different keys – every day.

While we wait the bombing redoubles in violence. On Monday 6 March, towards one in the afternoon, a formidable attack takes place. For the first time we see the British and American bombers in German skies during broad daylight. It's a huge demonstration of force which makes a huge impression. We all saw the German bombers at the time of their attack on France in May–June 1940, we were all strongly affected by the Stukas which dive-bombed us with their screaming bombs which shook you right through to your guts.

One afternoon I counted 85 of their attacks on Sedan. We found that terrible. But how those attacks, which seemed to us so awesome at the time, now seem insignificant in comparison to this uninterrupted fly-past for more than an hour in a deafening roar overhead, and what is more at high altitude. For more than an hour, squadron after squadron with only small gaps, three lots of three groups, each group containing about 20 aircraft, in an impeccable formation like a parade, while in every direction innumerable small fighter planes manoeuvre, protecting the immense column, tracing in the sky a whole network of vapour trails, clouding up to the heavens in all the turns and twists of their high speed course. How many of them pass over? Opinion is divided: between 1,200 and 1,500 bombers alone, without counting the fighters. In any case, the population and us are strongly affected by this formidable deployment which says a lot about the capabilities of the Allies. The immense wave still seems to be targeted on Berlin.

Recently, some of the villages have been badly hit. You sense that the outlook of the population has changed a little, we are now far from the days when everyone bowed their head before the invincible German machine. When they experience similar forms of war and despite their formidable army, the German civilian population starts to tire of war. Every family, every farmer has in these last few days constructed his 'bounka' as they say here[1], that's to say an underground shelter made with tree-trunks and timbers and then covered with earth, either at the bottom of the garden or in the nearest hedge. The people no longer have any confidence in their cellars, which are not proving strong enough. They are down in the mouth. And with reason, it has to be said, for nearly all families are affected and it is rare to find one which has not had one death in the house as a result of the war, and in many houses there have been several. We are far distant from the enthusiasm which was apparent at the time of our arrival here. Far distant from the days when, watching German bombers circling overhead, we would be asked in mocking tones whether they weren't English. Now it really is the English and even the Americans who are circling overhead, and derision has become reality.

What is more, quite recently several families have arrived in the village, from Hamburg for the most part but some also from Berlin or Magdeburg, with stories of dreadful things, above all in Hamburg, which has the effect of sowing dread and fear among the population, which however stands up admirably to the shock. A fact, an advance, a heavy bombing overwhelms them, while a trifle, a piece of gross propaganda, a well-timed speech, a well-phrased promise pumps them up again for a time towards the prospect of final victory. In the meantime the refugees are well enough received by the villagers even if they do not like townspeople in general. Often these small *rentiers*[2] or civil servants will come to the farms from the town, asking to buy eggs, a chicken or a duck, but the peasants are tight-fisted over these prohibited dealings. They prefer those who can exchange some material or clothing which is very difficult to find in the country. It seems that in the cities you really must eke things out to survive.

April 1944. Work restarts in the fields. It's the time for sowing and for preparing the ground for beetroot and potatoes. The bombing continues, day and night. Always there are these formidable over-flights, sometimes several days running, and often right in the middle of the day. Sometimes the wave of bombers runs into German fighters and then we watch some bitter scraps, usually short-lived, but which nearly always finish with one or other aircraft crashing, sometimes both. Far away the bombs fall, smoke rising into the sky. Now and then there are great black columns which climb to hide the sun for hours at a time, while a bitter stench fills the nose.

The propaganda redoubles, there is more and more talk of this famous landing. Will they land, won't they land? We laugh about it to begin with for it seems to us to be yet another of the tall stories they use to fill the columns of the newspapers. But now there is too much talk of it, it seems serious. A notice has just been put up on the walls of the Camp which seems to throw out a challenge to the Allies. The coasts of France are set out on the poster, all lined with guns, and at the centre there is a German infantryman with a fixed bayonet who is defying the British and American soldiers with the slogan 'Will they land? Let them come!' In a corner of the notice are photos of Saint-Nazaire and Dieppe with the caption 'They have already been, and we have welcomed them'.

And now it is the month of May. We are sowing the potatoes, hiding the horses in the nearest thickets at the time of full alert for in some villages the ploughing teams have been machine-gunned in the open fields. It happens that we see two or three American fight-ers pass in a flash with a frightful roar, skimming across the plain at ground level as if they were on home territory. Sometimes, in the far distance, there is a violent crackling of machine-guns lasting for sev-eral minutes: it's a train which is just being hit or even the aerodrome at Bostel, which is about 15 kilometres from us and which, for some days now has served as a target for the allied bombers and fighters and where they have wreaked a good deal of havoc.

On Saturday 29 April, while we were coming back from the fields for our midday meal, the alert sounded in the village and the sirens in the neighbouring small towns moaned at full volume. The huge wave comes on. One of the strongest forces we have seen so far flies overhead. I was with the boss outside the barn door, looking at this impressive sight, which today was at quite a low altitude. One group was coming right over the village. I was looking at it when I started to hear the noise that I had heard so often at the front and that I shall never forget as long as I live: the descent of a bomb. Even as it left the aircraft I had distinguished its noise from that of the powerful engines. I was the first to shout 'a bomb' while rushing straight into the cellar which was already open. But the boss, hearing me, had understood straightaway and had overtaken me followed by two of the maids and by the Polish worker. Only the poor old woman Gandoule remained outside in the courtyard. We were scarcely in the cellar when the bomb went off, the whole thing had lasted hardly a second. We came out and the fire bell was already sounding the alarm, while even more planes droned overhead. In the street the terror-struck people were running hither and thither, some out of the village but most of them towards the shelters. I left the village as well. It was not too reassuring and certainly not too prudent to stay because the procession of planes was longer than ever. All the same I wanted to see where the bomb had fallen for I could see a plume of smoke climbing up from the area of the flour-mill. Some people, especially the women were shouting that the mill was on fire. I stayed for quite a while in one of the boss's meadows butting onto the village, close to a ditch which served as a watering-place and which, could if need be, serve me as a shelter. The fly-over went on for a while longer and immediately afterwards I went to the place where the smoke was rising from. Many men, not to say everyone, had done the same as me, that is sheltering until the end of the raid and coming out now, running towards the fire. They were more afraid than hurt. About 50 small incendiary bombs had only just missed the village, nearly flattening several big farms and falling here and there in the gardens behind the barns. Some had set fire to a haystack. This was the total damage, pretty insignificant. A French mate had however only just missed being killed. One of the bombs had fallen right at his feet but had failed to knock him over. These incendiaries are not very big but despite that they weigh a good five kilos and falling from such a height can easily kill a man. But it wasn't these little bombs which had produced that terrible whistling. A few minutes later we had the explanation, for some people coming back from

work brought the news that a large bomb had fallen behind the little
hill which overlooked the village to the north. With some mates we
immediately went over there and soon found where the bomb had
come down. A huge crater had appeared, right in the middle of a
field of rape. A vast hole, six to seven metres deep and around 20
metres across showed the violence of the explosion. I would compare
this hole to one of the old quarries where they got the stone at Mus.[3]
A flange of earth more than two metres high surrounded the hole.
Some big stones had been torn out of the ground and thrown a fair
distance from the hole. One among them, weighing more than a
ton[4] had been thrown nearly 100 metres from the point of impact.
That shows the violence of the explosion. Two of my mates, prisoners
like me, who were ploughing, one on the right of the field of rape
and one on the left, had been terrified. The bomb must have been
enormous and it had fallen in the open field. You couldn't see exactly
what they might have been aiming at with such a huge bomb.
Looking at the direction in which the aircraft were going, the bomb
had been dropped exactly on the line between two villages, but too
late for ours and slightly too soon for the next. The flour-mill could
well have been the target, as it wasn't too far away and could well have
been taken for a big transformer. However that may be, if the bomb
had fallen in the middle of the village there is a good chance that it
would have been completely buried in the rubble.

At the end of May the propaganda reaches its height over the
question of an invasion. In Italy the Allies have advanced a good
deal. Rome has been taken and the troops continue to make ground.
But this front does not really seem to interest the public here which
has its gaze fixed on the coasts of France for you sense that something
is going to happen there.

June 1944. On the 6th, at midday, as we were going back to our
meal, the news breaks: the landing has taken place that night on the
coasts of France, and it is continuing. Some names are bandied
about, but there is nothing definite yet. There's talk of Cherbourg, of
Le Havre, but the details are pretty hazy for the moment. In the
evening the news is discussed long and late. Will they dig in or will
they be thrown back into the sea? We are nervous in those early days.
the news has also brought the locals to life. They are sure that the first
allied divisions are going to be quickly repelled. In the camp, it seems
to us that after having established themselves on French soil for a few
days, being reinforced a little more all the while, the invading troops
cannot be driven back.

The days pass. The invading troops seem to have been reinforced, but the front is stabilising around the line Caen/Saint-Lo. The civilians here have got their confidence back after the first dazed moments and they smilingly tell us that the German armies are allowing the biggest mass of troops possible to gather in Normandy so as to drive the lot back into the ocean. The month of June passes, and so does that of July. We are anxious, we should so much like to know what is happening in France, but there is no or nearly no news. The newspapers we get are often very old and are recovering their confidence in the German armies, declaring that the Anglo-American force will be thrown back when the German High Command sees fit. In the meantime the front seems to have settled down in the same sector which is no laughing matter for us, seeing such a huge front in the centre of France.

August 1944. It's warm, very warm for the harvest. This year an awful drought has ruined the countryside. Cows are dying of starvation in meadows burnt by drought. This part of the country with its sandy soil like a seaside beach, is very bad when it goes two weeks without rain. There is even a water shortage in many places. The harvest is pretty good in rye but very bad in oats, corn and barley which just cannot grow in such dry conditions. The harvest in potatoes, sugar beet and beet fodder will also be very bad.

At the end of August some good news arrives: the allied armies have broken through at Avranches and are reaching the banks of the Loire. From this day on news follows news with incredible speed. The names of various towns in France march every day across the newspapers and radiowaves. Between times a landing has taken place near Toulon. Now at last, all the southerners, and especially those from nearest the Rhône are eager for every nugget of information. For my part, I am in a desperate hurry to know. What is happening back home? I look at the newspapers, even the German ones which I don't understand much of, and I see the names of towns, I listen to the radio. They talk of Cannes, of Toulon, then a little about Marseille, they talk of Durance, then suddenly they talk only of Montélimar. For those not from the area that might be alright. But for my part I can't begin to understand why they have not talked about all the towns and settlements bordering the Rhône from Marseille to Montélimar. Not a word is said about the right bank of the Rhône. I conclude from that that there can't have been heavy fighting round our part, which calms me down a bit.

On Sunday 27 August we learn that Paris has fallen to the Allies. The prisoners are as joyful as the civilians are disgruntled. Another few days and the names of Reims, Sedan, Givet, Brussels, Verdun

parade past at a record speed. At the beginning of September I go to
Stendal to get the Red Cross monthly parcel. I find down there the
leading men of the district, people in whom you can trust, together
with some friends. All of us think that the war cannot last long now.
Some dates are even mentioned: mid-October, end of October, but it
is mid-November which gets most votes among the prisoners present,
who are all in a pretty cheerful mood. There's good reason for it and
I think it's our right, for we have been in Germany nearly four and a
half years, and heavens it really will be good to see our homes again.

However the month of September ends without any great change
in the position of the Anglo-American armies which seem, after their
record offensive across France to be stuck on the German frontier
and in Holland.[5] In the Vosges the battle seems at a standstill.
However Aix-la-Chapelle is taken and the armies are even advancing
a little beyond it, which gives us new hope for the end of the war this
autumn.

On Tuesday 28 September at one o'clock in the afternoon there is
a violent alert. Several waves of aircraft are crossing through the light
cloud and you can see planes in the gaps. Suddenly one of them lets
out a strange noise, you would think there was something not quite
right on board. Then it starts to come down gently and it is properly
visible through the thin layers of cloud. It goes further away then
turns and comes back again over the village but now a long trail of
flames is following the plane which seems huge. It turns again and I
follow it from the top of an eight-metre long ladder from which I am
gathering the pears. Suddenly between two clouds I see the monster
on fire and seeming to dive straight down onto me. In less time than
it takes to write I am at the bottom of the ladder just as a loud explosion occurs and for about a minute I see a horrible vision. From
everywhere debris is coming down, while the main part with the four
engines which continues to go forward in a cloud of flames, is
detached from the rest of the machine, which is coming down in
pieces. The four engines go by not far from me and crash 300 metres
further down the field, where the same morning, my friends had
been in the midst of harvesting potatoes. A vast sheet of flame rises
up followed by thick blackish smoke which forms an impenetrable
screen from which little jets of multi-coloured fire spurt out produced by the melting of various metals. The debris is now coming
down from everywhere. Near me the plane's gun has just crashed in
a plume of fire and the ammunition is exploding in a series of small
detonations. A little further down two twin machine-guns have also
crashed. Once the minute of fear has passed, all the people in the

village run towards the thick smoke which the block of engines has produced. Some fighters are circling again overhead but that does not stop the stream of curious people who are hurrying towards the machine. I am one of the first to get there, with some friends, but I cannot get too close because of the intense heat and because of the smoke which hinders any approach. It's an American four-engined bomber, we see from some nearby debris. We think of the poor lads who might be inside that inferno. While the crowd of people from various villages is quickly gathering around the wreckage the police also arrive and evacuate the place at speed, while the fire now seems to be decreasing in intensity. I return to my pear tree and from up there I watch events. Several fighters are prowling around the vicinity, but without doing any damage.

The following Sunday we were requisitioned to gather up all the wreckage which had to be transported onto the platform at the station. The whole area was strewn with all kinds of debris spread over a vast space several kilometres in diameter. Here there was a wing in a potato field, while in a wood the other wing was held caught in the trees and we had to get it out of there. Some fuel tanks and parts of the wireless, many varied instruments whose use no one understood, were scattered over several fields. The vast cockpit had fallen a good kilometre from the tail, from which it had become detached, and still further on, the immense rudder. We got it out with the two biggest horses in the village which dragged it with great difficulty, stopping often for breath. There were innumerable bottles of oxygen, no doubt serving to help the crew breathe at high altitudes, spread everywhere. Many people searched the woods and fields, finding here some trousers, here a jacket, gloves, shoes, helmets, first aid kits, rations, American cigarettes, and even chocolate, a product which the Germans really like. We took the whole thing onto the station platform on rubber-wheeled horse-drawn waggons, and several journeys were necessary to do it. You could not imagine the mass of ironmongery that produced. No, you have to see it to believe that there are machines of that size which fly. Everything was there except the engines which were too embedded in the earth to get out. There is no trace of the occupants of the machine who must have jumped far from the scene for we never heard exactly whether parachutists had been seen in the vicinity and if the plane had continued its circling empty before finally crashing near us.

The following week a team of specialists equipped with pullies and the necessary equipment lifted the engines and the forward fuselage mixed with the melted and twisted metal of wing spars which were surrounded with miles of wires of all kinds. Several twin machine-guns were also collected from around the district, and numerous cartridges were found almost everywhere. Funny things the bullets fired by these gentlemen! No less than three 20-ton wagons were needed to load up all the wreckage at the station. That can give you an idea of the flying arsenal that one of these machines is, and I am still not counting all the debris that for one reason or another the local people have made off with. Some days later, in a wood, I found a silver medal, struck in England, which also came from the aircraft.

October 1944. We expected a lot of this month, but it still passed without any great change in the situation. The Anglo-American armies have been stopped on the German frontiers. Aix-la-Chapelle was taken a few days ago, and even some small towns beyond it, but it doesn't seem to be the final offensive. The Russians seem to have penetrated a fair amount into Prussia but they too seem stopped along a vast line. The Germans are putting up strong resistance on all the fronts, they are fighting with desperation. The Balkans have been nearly completely retaken by the Russians who now seem to be virtually in Hungary. In Italy, since the big push of last spring, nothing definite seems to be in preparation. And November changes nothing either, despite the great hopes that we had invested in that month.

In December there is some movement, first through heavy bombing then by the offensive which, towards the middle of the month, the German armies launch on a level with Luxembourg. The newspapers publicise it for all its worth, and talk of the irresistible offensive on the western front where the Allies have been rapidly routed. The locals, who had been pretty knocked back by the events of recent times, regained confidence, become talkative again, and are even cheerful up to a point. Some of them are clear that Paris will be retaken by German troops by the New Year and then France will be completely cleared. The peasants are happy at the prospect and talk already of the return to their homes of the refugees from west Germany in a short time. For in these last few months many refugees have arrived. After those from Hamburg and Berlin, quite a few have come from Magdeburg. This November special trains turn up full from Westphalia in the central regions of Germany. There is a big new batch in the village from Essen. The village starts to seem small, the houses are crowded for the population has more than doubled. Some farmers are lodging 8, 10, 12 and even 15 refugees in their houses. And this influx, although unforeseen, is an affliction. At least if there were more workers then that would only be half bad, for someone who can work is well enough regarded. But those who have arrived don't seem to want to do much work. These city women, as they are for the most part, are not countryfolk and do not help at all in the work of the farm – but don't sit any lower down the table by virtue of it. There are many children and some old people, which puts the owners in a really bad mood. Thus they view the offensive which could take all these people back home with pleasure.

Christmas 1944. Is it our last? This time we really think so. We celebrate as best we can this holy night which is so popular in France and so sad here. We make the same effort to have a good midnight meal, and some friends who became civilians also came. A good little menu is prepared from the means at hand, for our reserve, which has not been resupplied for several months now, is exhausted. Still our midnight feast goes off in good spirits and it finishes late into the night, marking our determination to continue French traditions come what may. We want to mark this fifth and last Christmas here just like the others. The celebrations are marked by heavy bombing. Despite the stinging cold of these days, the heavy raids follow one after the other, endlessly. During these two days of holiday the areas round Magdeburg and Hanover are badly hit and several aircraft are brought down in both places.

The Inferno at Stendal Station

1 January 1945. This time there's no joking in the good wishes that we exchange, for it is not possible that this year starting now shouldn't be the last. No, it can't be otherwise, it must really finish, damn it, one day or another, if we are not to die here. But we have had so many disappointments in these long years that sometimes we ask ourselves if it can ever finish. This first day of the year, like all the Christmas holiday is marked by the most violent bombing. Towards the middle of the afternoon there are some fierce aerial battles, machine-guns crackle ceaselessly. Several planes, both fighters and bombers, come down near us. It seems that there are pretty heavy losses on both sides.

It's very cold during January, it snows quite heavily and seems to want to stay. We're getting nothing, or almost nothing, these days. For Christmas I received a message through the Red Cross bringing me good tidings it's true, but four months old. For a message marked urgent that's not too bad, four months, especially since I note from the stamps that it was held up for two months in the camp; that shows how the administration which deals with our correspondence works. On New Year's Day some letters and cards also arrive, but all very old, dating from September–October. The most recent are from the first ten days of November. I get two letters, one from my home, the other from Gilette,[6] bringing me some pretty bad news. They have been bombed at home, causing many deaths and heavy damage. As for the parcels, we haven't seen them for many months. Even the American parcels are not arriving regularly at the moment.

In the first days of January, impressed by the offensive the Germans have launched in the West, the locals remain very confident, even joyful. The papers tell us in big headlines that the worst days are past, the Germans have got back the upper hand, aerial supremacy is once again German etc. But here we are in mid-January, without warning in the worst days of winter, in a severe cold spell, the Russians make a big push forward. Immediately the names of several

218

big Polish towns are heard on the radio and at a record speed the Russians reach the German border – even, in some places, the Oder. At the same time Prussia is surrounded, Silesia is nearly completely occupied, while on the other side, Stettin is taken. Now at last the population takes fright. The most extraordinary rumours take hold, such as the Russians entering Berlin. The news is false but it is none the less true that the Oder has been crossed in various places and that the Russian vanguard is at the gates of Berlin. The locals are cast down and are quite humbled by comparison with recent months, above all because now the British and Americans are redoubling their air onslaught. Magdeburg is taken to account and for several days is the target for huge waves of British and American bombers. The town is virtually annihilated and some thousands of Germans and foreigners from all countries pay with their lives.

On Saturday 5 February, on a day of thick, low cloud a massive air attack takes place, the worst so far, just as we are making sausages with the pork butcher, who came that day to the house to kill the pig. The planes keep coming with their terrible throbbing for more than two hours, some wending their way back, others seeming to head for Berlin, which that day was receiving the heaviest attack of all. And then the first waves of refugees from the east are turning up on every road. Column on interminable column of peasants coming from Prussia, Poland, Silesia, even Lithuania, in four-wheeled carts, with tarpaulins, drawn by small horses, thin and emaciated, at the end of their tether. Women, children, old people, for the most part as black as coalminers through having travelled for days through snow during very low temperatures.

All these hordes that you could easily take for real Romanies, real nomads, stream westwards towards Hanover. Germany in its turn is getting to know the horrors of having to leave hearth and home. It's nearly the same picture that I described in June 1940 when we were close to Sedan. These people tell the worst things to the Germans, which ends up by demoralising them, and they start packing their trunks and cases in terror, for we are no more than 130 or 150 kilometres from the eastern front and it could be that on one of these fine days they will need to follow and swell the columns on the roads to the West, which does not at all seem to fill our bosses with joy.

The month of February saw some terrible days of bombing, now it is all the railway lines which are for it, morning, evening, night, dawn, twilight, every second fighters and bombers are streaking across the German sky. On Thursday 22 February, at midday, there is a most violent attack, a wave of 40 bombers escorted by countless fighters, apparently heavily-loaded, aim right for Stendal, describe a huge circle over the town and then in three minutes empty their frightful cargoes on the main station where huge damage results. On Saturday 24 February we are called to Stendal to give assistance to the clearing of the station. We left the village at four in the morning and do eight kilometres in a cart and the rest, 15 more, in a tractor-drawn vehicle. At seven o'clock we are at the main station square which is strewn with debris of all kinds. The big buildings surrounding it, despite being badly hit, are still proudly upright. But when we get into the huge station it's totally different. How can I describe the spectacle which confronts us? I give up for I cannot do it and I am not capable of finding the words necessary for such a description, so far has what we call the inferno of Stendal station gone beyond my comprehension. Human imagination could never have come up with such a cataclysm. First of all we go onto the platforms for travellers. All kinds of rubble is lying on the various platforms. But, continuing on to the vast marshalling yard and the big locomotive depot we see something other than debris. The first thing, which at first sight affects you most, is the signal bridge which stretches right across the station. The poor bridge, or rather what is left of it, all blackened by fire, has collapsed in various places, leaving a scene of tangled and twisted beams, wires, signals and rubble of all kinds. One part of the bridge has collapsed onto an engine which was immediately underneath. Right after the bridge comes the real disaster. The chaos of equipment mixed up with earth is unimaginable, all twitching, upside down in the most incredible positions among the vast, huge craters that adjoin each other and even in certain places form real ravines where trucks disembowelled of their contents are lying higgledy-piggledy, engines overturned, wheels in the air, wooden debris, sleepers, twisted and intertwined rails. No, what I'm writing does no justice to what I've seen. Of the tracks, there's nothing to be said for nothing of what's left could lead one to suppose that there were in that vast space, 25 or 30 lines of shunting track. Nothing is left except a horrible vision. Some beautiful locomotives, the latest models made for speed, streamlined, these mastodons of the track of 80 tons, have been thrown aside like mere playthings. Fifty engines are there in the station, ripped open, on their sides, overturned in the strangest positions. One of them has even mounted a group of wagons which have themselves been smashed open.

We are 6,000 men confronting this spectacle. How are we to organise the work? Where can you start on such an enterprise? How can it be that there is no discipline in the face of such a disaster? No police, and we can see no officers, no one at all in command. We were used here to seeing all the work in Germany, like everything else, minutely organised, supervised very closely by a swarm of zealous officials! Here, there's nothing, not an order, nothing happens. Of the 6,000 there are a full 5,000 foreigners with no one in charge. And that for the huge station which is nearly the same in size and layout as the Courbesac station at Nîmes,[8] is quickly transformed into a vast museum which everyone visits but no one works. We discuss things a good deal, we meet a lot of friends we have not seen for a long time, and the visit continues among the volcanic landscape with its unimaginable and fantastic sights. This lack of organisation completely astonishes us, the general disorder shows us that right now Germany is being overcome by events which begin to be beyond its powers.

However, here and there some teams, all on their own initiative, are putting themselves cautiously to work, in fact very cautiously. In small spadefuls we throw earth into the vast craters. Further on some flame-cutters are being used to cut up the trucks and locomotives that are taken away in pieces so as to try to put at least one line back in action, for Stendal is a very important railway junction. It's there that some important lines meet, from Magdeburg, Hamburg, Hanover and Berlin to cite only the most important, for a mass of other lines have their termini here, less essential lines than the others, but which all the same have a great importance and since the day before yesterday no train has been able to travel on them.

One engine shed has only suffered a little, another is completely destroyed, while the repair workshop has not been touched at all. On the left side of the station the scene is even more frightful than in the station itself. Here, next to the station is a large sawmill which makes sleepers for the railway. Two to three acres of land are covered with piles of sleepers and it is there that most of the bombs have fallen. A train was coming into the station just at the moment when the wave of bombers turned up. Troops were cramming the trucks. The soldiers, seeing the danger, all ran to take shelter under the piles of sleepers which, two minutes later, became their tombs. Vast craters were left everywhere and the wood depot was transformed into a scenic railway of the strangest kind. The bombs cut through to the water which has squirted out everywhere, and the sticky, clayey soil has turned this cemetery into a huge mud-pit. How many soldiers were dug out of this hellish cataclysm? No one knows exactly yet. The only survivors of this inferno are 40 fairly badly-wounded men. Up to now several hundred dead have been pulled out. How many still remain under the avalanche of sleepers? Nobody

knows the exact figure. There are many that we will never get out for
it is impossible to find them in there. But the damage doesn't stop
there for, in front of the sawmill, a little to the left, a suburb of the
town has been almost entirely flattened. It's frightening to see it
because it's ordinary houses which have bought it. Some down at the
bottom, where the frame of a wall remains standing, are still burning
and the firemen are soaking the smoking remains with their powerful hoses. But most houses are completely razed to the ground, not
even one stone remains on top of another. We go close by the ruins
of what was once a farm. Cows, pigs, horses are all there, stretched
out, while in the midst of the rubble they are trying to get out the
bodies of those who, not 48 hours before, had been the owners of a
profitable estate.

It seems that 200 dead have been brought out of this rubbish.
Further away, some big properties have not been brought down,
although they are roofless, but you can see on the joists and the rafters
which remain the straw and the hay from farms, thrown up to the fifth
or sixth storeys by the displacement of air, while from chimneys, still
upright despite the absence of a roof and of window-panes, you can
see a thin thread of smoke which shows that despite everything life is
beginning again in this dreadful furnace.

We work for a little throwing earth into the bottom of a huge
crater where already a little water has collected, but now at midday
the '*vor-Alarm*'[9] is sounding. The siren, with its lugubrious sound,
warns of planes in the area, and without waiting for the alarm itself
the whole mass of 6,000 men dashes out towards the fields and nothing, not even the machine-guns, could have kept them in that
far-too-dangerous square. Through gardens broken up by the bombs
we quickly reach the vast plain where it seems to us that we must be
safer. But the aircraft pass by far off and two hours after the end of
the alert we go back to the works via a more extensive visit to the
suburb which has been destroyed and to the nearby gardens – all of
them in a really frightful state.

As we arrive we collect our voucher for a meal, then go to the canteen where we stay another two hours without getting anything other
than our vouchers. But we see there some really miserable things,
some poor prisoners much worse off than us, in rags and tatters,
unshod or barely so, starving and scraping the pots which have contained the meal, miserable hordes, above all the Russian prisoners
and more especially those from the big factory kommandos. And in
seeing these poor lads our own sufferings in the camps came back
into my mind. Some poor Polish and Ukrainian girls, also in rags, are

there, starved. What suffering and what a disgrace to make people suffer so! It's over, we leave this hell by skirting the engine depot on the right side of the station where a factory chimney has come down, causing serious damage to the next-door properties, where some bombs have fallen too, notably on the post-office which is partially destroyed. We return deeply affected by what we have seen in the course of this sad day.

The American Offensive Runs
Past Schorstedt

The month of March arrives and the bombing continues worse than ever, alert after alert almost throughout the day, and continuing in the night. We are only half-reassured in our miserable hut during the night where, locked in from nine o'clock they only open the door to wake us at six o'clock, and nearly every night – sometimes several times, formidable flights of allied aircraft pass over for what seems a very long time. We know well enough that the villages are not the target for these great armadas but it only takes one and after what we saw at Stendal, well that's enough to make the bravest tremble. On Friday 8 March at nine o'clock in the evening there's an alert as a small group passes right over the village. An incendiary bomb is dropped and falls right slap in the middle of the barn of the head peasant, the *Bauernführer* as they say here. In less time than it takes to write it, the farm is nothing more than an immense blazing mass. The horn sounded the alert again, but it immediately becomes a call for help to the fire brigade. In the first few moments there's a general panic, huge flames climb very high into the sky and light up the village as if in broad daylight. The aircraft, droning away all the time, increase the level of fear, and everyone gets away from the village as far as possible into the fields, thinking of their own safety first and foremost, because they are afraid that the fire will draw more bombing. But the planes pass over without doing more damage and everyone hurries to run to the fire. They hasten to set up the village's motorised pump, but it takes a long time, the unions are leaking from everywhere. The firemen, or rather the firewomen, for since all the men have been conscripted there are only some crippled and very old men left, they are young girls, and despite daily training it seems to me that it isn't work for them, they are doing nothing well and the fire burns even worse as the barn is constructed for the most part of wood and being full of straw it provides good fuel for the fire. Some help arrives from neighbouring villages, some other pumps are set up, but soon the water runs out. Furthermore the

224

motorised pump stops, there's no more petrol. It's a pity as, for a small village like Schorstedt, they have some very good fire-fighting equipment which plenty of the bigger villages back home would envy, with their poor, old-fashioned hand-pumps. The roof, the walls, whether of wood or brick, cave in. The only thing left to do is to protect the next-door properties. The fire is dying down now but everything has been burnt, the thresher with all the equipment being in the barn, and the next day as usual it was the prisoners who were required to clear up the debris. This fire has made a real impression on the population in the village, now very large since it has nearly quadrupled with the arrival *en masse* of refugees who are quartered in the farms like rabbits one on top of another, piled up in the rooms, and at each alert everyone runs to the shelters.

1 April 1945. Easter. The last one we shall spend here, of that at least we are convinced. The events of recent weeks no longer leave any doubt on the outcome of the war and we hope it will come soon. In these last few days the bombing has been even harder than usual. The siren at Bismark, the nearest to us, moos its lugubrious sound at all hours of day and night. Yesterday, 31 March, Stendal was again badly hit. The big sugar refinery was entirely destroyed, and we heard that the station was blitzed again.

Unfortunately, four of us were also killed there. And the list gets ever longer. The other day, while working, a French prisoner was mown down by a bullet which hit him right in the chest. A few weeks ago in the fields near Stendal another was the victim of a direct hit on the head from a small bomb. The bomb did not go off but the poor lad was pulverised. Again, in the area round here several men have died through lack of rapid medical attention, most of them being saveable. Poor lads not to see France again! And yet that's the only hope which keeps this destitute mass going, who have waited nearly five years for this longed-for moment: to set foot again in France. Five years, 60 long months in which most of us have not seen our village, our town, our land. As for me, I had leave for Easter Day 1940; it was, if I remember right, 24 March. What things have happened since then! How will I find Aigues-Vives now, where I will not even recognise more than a quarter of the people? Many people that I wanted to meet will have disappeared, others will have aged a lot, while the kids that I liked to tease will have become men. How am I going to find my acre of land, my garden, and all my folks who I have heard nearly nothing of for what will soon be a year? Life will have really gone on. I'm truly pining to see the sky in my own parts, and yet in another way I'm afraid of going back. It's bizarre, but that's how it is,

I think of it throughout the day, and I even think about it for a good part of the night, I think all the time of that new life that I'm going to have to start. I would so much like just a quiet little life without worries of any kind, but what I should like is surely not practicable. When I go back I shall certainly get married for here more than anywhere else you feel the need of someone, of a human being to share the anxieties, the troubles, and also the joys.

To be sure there's friendship amongst us all. There were no big disputes in our room, everyone sought to help out his mates within the bounds of possibility. Here there were represented nearly all the political opinions of pre-war France, and quite a diversity of views on religious issues. Despite it, no conversation on these various subjects became stormy, everyone respecting his colleague's view. But even if we all kept each other going, brought together by our misery, there are, it's inevitable, moments when each man thinks of himself. It's the law of war that everyone must look out for his own neck. And life, even if it has its brief moments of joy, becomes more and more difficult to endure as the months go by. The lads, while staying good friends, become peevish, irritable, we all become soured and the nearer the moment of liberation seems to approach, the more edginess gets the upper hand.

This evening, to celebrate Easter, a nice meal is in preparation with the means to hand, for we have not received any more supplies for many months. This meal, although good, will be pretty sad to begin with there will be nothing to drink, then there isn't any longer the previous gaiety, everyone has become introverted. Despite the formidable advance of the American armies which in the last few days have reached Kassel, that is barely 150 kilometres from us, time seems to drag, more especially as it gets closer and liberation seems interminable.

12 April. And there it is, it's finally happened. Phew! what a relief, and despite the very confusing times that we are living just now we see with a smile and spot on the horizon that so longed-for day, of deliverance. But it would be better to begin at the beginning, for these last few days have been so fertile in events that it's a struggle for me to remember everything. The week that followed Easter saw some very heavy bombing in the area, but it was last Sunday in particular when the real fun began.

And so on Sunday 8 April three officers in a car brought the order at midday to put up anti-tank barriers right at the entrances to the village. I had wind of all this and once the meal was eaten I went with some friends to hide in the woods from where, after a good nap, we gathered up a salad from the fields. Straight after leaving the village the alert sounded, all the sirens went off and immediately in the clearest of clear skies the first long-nosed fighters – as we call them – made their appearance. The first waves of bombers, many of them, streak across the sky. The ack-ack, which was withdrawn from northern Germany, is all over the place and there follows one of the most violent duels that we have seen. The fighters fly at ground-level and strafe the anti-aircraft batteries savagely, knocking some out, but the others redouble their fire. None the less the first waves pass and the others follow. The airfield of Bostel is heavily bombed while, on two occasions two groups of 50 bombers drop their loads onto the town of Stendal. The ground trembles underfoot. A bomber comes down in flames behind the woods, while three or four launch a heavy attack on the banks of the Elbe. Three more groups turn up and empty another three loads onto the town. You could say the end of the world is coming, that's how it feels. The ack-ack fires furiously, two more big four-engined planes come down, again in an appalling din.

Monday, 9 April. The town of Stendal, once so nice and cheerful, has been nearly razed by yesterday's bombing. There are some thousands of dead under the rubble, wounded and buried alive that cannot be rescued. Above all it is the centre of the town that has suffered most. The beautiful central cathedral is completely collapsed, only one of its bell towers which is listing dangerously is still miraculously upright. All around the vast perimeter there are only fields of ruins. Today we make anti-tank barriers at the exits from the village with huge tree trunks. That really gives an impression of danger. The Germans are feverish and the French are jubilant, with all the same a touch of anxiety. Is it possible that the battle might come here? Are we going to see the Front now on these Saxon plains 1,000 kilometres from France? How is it going to turn out? Are we going to catch it in the neck after five years of captivity, in this brawl which looks like being serious?

Tuesday, 10 April 1945. After heavy night-bombing the day looks like being one of the most cloudless. The morning is calm, but at two o'clock in the afternoon there's an alert once again. This, which is to be the last, is by far the most savage. For nearly three hours, the waves of bombers follow one after the other without pause. All the strategic points, but not the villages, are bombed. The ack-ack fires back fiercely. Flying at roof-top level, 1,000 fighters knock them all out, plus the gun batteries, in a very short time, and once again it is Stendal which is hard hit. The main station is reduced to ashes, and

some roads still intact the day before yesterday are flattened. On the
airfield, the fighters are now diving, taking turns, and with their
cannon and machine-guns they set fire to and demolish almost everything which remains standing. From behind the big tree where I
have taken refuge flat on my face, I see them turning in all directions,
as I see banking over the town, groups of four-engined bombers
dropping their loads. On my right Stendal, on my left Osterburg, are
in flames. Great clouds of smoke completely hide the sun. Behind, in
front, to the side, they're bombing everywhere, everywhere is ablaze.
You feel shocked. Your stomach, your lungs, all feel bad even after
calm has returned. The fight lasted three long hours during which I
didn't move a foot from behind my big tree. There's no reaction on
the part of the Germans, but right at the beginning a big four-
engined bomber, fatally hit, came down with all its bombs in a street
of the town that it has completely wiped out. Yesterday evening
Hanover was still holding on. For the last four or five days, the
German resistance has seemed to be strengthening in this sector.
That makes us nervous and in a bad temper.

Wednesday 11 April, at daybreak, despite the great risk, as I often
do, I can listen to the English radio at the house of a kindly woman.
Without that we would know nothing for the German radio and the
Germans themselves are not at all talkative, above all now that things
are deteriorating, but they believe firmly in the miracle and
Hanover's resistance gives them hope again. They even announced
yesterday evening a slight withdrawal of 20 km by the Allies before
Hanover. This news knocks us back, and without hesitation, I decide
to get to the bottom of it. I go there with my bit of chocolate, which
gives me the right to be there for a little more than an hour. At daybreak I bring my friends the news. They're all awake, anxious. They
listen to me: 'It's okay, lads, Hanover has capitulated. Braunschweig
is surrounded. The tank divisions are in front of the small town of
Celle.' Straightaway the point is made on the huge and very detailed
map which, for more than three years, has been stowed at the bottom
of my mattress. '130 km from Bismark, lads, scarcely 140 from us
now. Three days, my friends, and we will see the Americans.' There's
joy, there's delirium in the room, in the poky little house which in all
the bombing raids threatens to entomb us.

From 5 April we had heard the guns, above all in the evening
when night fell, but today it becomes even clearer. We plough for
potatoes with the Pole. Hour by hour it seems to us that the noise is
becoming ever stronger. At each new burst, the Pole says to me: 'One
more little town has fallen.' The boss, who is breaking up the ground

at our side, often stops his donkeys. He listens anxiously. I guess his thoughts: 'Is this possible?' At 9 o'clock, at snack time, he asked me if I think that that is the sound of guns. I do not want to commit myself on it positively to him, but finally I tell him that it's just what I had heard at the front. He, who had been in the war of 1914, had fully understood as well.

10 o'clock. Suddenly, in the woods, not very far away, a first broadside is fired. Pou, pou, poum. Once the surprise has passed, I explain to my Polish friend that it's a German gun battery which has just taken position there and the sound is of their firing and not of shells arriving.

Midday, the noise is worse than ever.

One o'clock in the afternoon, the German gun batteries go quiet and then fire from behind us. They are falling back at speed. Is it possible that everything is approaching so quickly? 140 km this morning, all the same!

Two o'clock. On our small road all kinds of vehicles are retreating endlessly towards the Elbe, and there are more and more of them in proportion as evening falls. We are ecstatic and yet we feel that the shells are soon going to be for us.

Six o'clock. We return to the village where there's only one cry: The tanks, the American tanks are at Gardelegen which has just fallen at the end of a 15-minute resistance, which was enough to reduce the little town to ashes and to rout the 25,000 men of the garrison. The town resists, the tanks stop, the bombers turn up, drop their loads, the tanks go off again and it's all up with the town. It's unbelievable and yet it's true.

Nine o'clock. It's a rout, it's a débâcle. The tattered army that we see withdrawing has nothing in common with that which I saw on the Meuse and the Marne.

Ten o'clock. The population of the village is raving. 'The tanks, the tanks!' That's all we hear from all these panic-stricken mouths. Bismark has just fallen in its turn, without a gun being fired, for there was no resistance, as the small town would have been reduced to dust in three minutes. Only two Germans were killed; they really were brave enough to try to stop an onslaught of this kind with revolvers.

Half past ten. The great station at Hohenwulsch, scarcely 5 km from our village, has been taken. And that's where these monsters of modern war stop for the night. The guns fall silent, while across the fields, meadows, woods, streams, and marshes soldiers emerge, in the exceptionally clear night. It's a collapse of the most dramatic kind. All the soldiers, or nearly all, are without any weapons, without a pack, without a helmet, keeping off all paths or roads where they could find themselves face to face with one of these machines that they don't seem to like very much. In the camp, that the warder has forgotten to come to shut up, his fear must be so great, there's joy and delirium. 140 km, and there they are right on the borders of the commune, stretched out on the main road which goes from Hanover to Berlin via Stendal where it crosses the Elbe. No one goes to sleep in the hut where, nevertheless, we stay fairly quiet, for the overexcited people and the passing troops do not look on us too kindly, and you never know.

Thursday, 12 April. Hardly had we made out the dawn when the rumbling of engines can be heard. Once again there's a great flight before them. Immediately the guns fire and machine-guns crackle. The woods are full of German troops who are trying to flee and it's in the great woods of the commune that, moving all the time, the guns send off their salvoes. The boss sends us off to size the potatoes in the sorting machine. We go off with the two horses, the Pole, myself and the two maids. Our silos are right on the edge of the big wood scarcely 4 km from the main road where there's a huge column of men filing past in a frightful din. We hesitate to go to work. Some German soldiers, SS and some others, are passing by everywhere. The reconnaissance aircraft overflying the huge column are patrolling over the woods and at various intervals they see the coffee mill going when they spot some German soldiers in a clearing. Doubtless they are signalling to the tanks where the biggest group of Germans are, for after an aircraft has gone over it is nearly always followed by a cluster of shells, coming no doubt from a tank that doesn't even have to slacken its pace as it advances towards victory, towards the Elbe, towards Berlin.

We start up our work, but after scarcely five minutes a machine-gun is firing in the middle of the thick woods. An artillery gun replies. Some shells fall not too far away from us. The maids start to cry and wail. Immediately we turn the horses, abandon all the equipment, and get back to the village at full gallop. Everyone across the big plain is doing the same. In the village the whole population is in complete disarray. There is firing from everywhere. I have a quick snack and with some friends go off on to a little mound near the village, where in a small copse we had dug a trench kitted out as a shelter to keep us safe in case of need. One moment the firing goes further away, at another it's very close, while in the distance, on the main road, the file-past of motorised columns continues without interruption, rolling by in this incredible din.

At midday things seem to calm down a little. The firing has gone off further away towards the south-east in the direction of Magdeburg. Stendal, town and aerodrome, is burning in the distance. We learn that the town, or rather the ruins of the town, have been taken without resistance at daybreak. They have already gone more than 60 km beyond us, when yesterday morning they were near Hanover, 140 km from us. We have not yet seen any Americans, for it is the American army which is operating in this sector of the front. There are no Englishmen among them. We haven't yet quite realised what has happened to us and we are wide-eyed, and yet we are free, entirely free.

The beginning of the afternoon is fairly quiet. A mate from the outskirts of Bismark comes to warn us that the reserve stores of the German army are open to pillage. The order has just been given to take out or to destroy everything, for the American armoured divisions have gone by. The infantry and the regular divisions can't follow at this mad speed which means that the war is in front of us, and behind us, but for more than 100 km there is nobody else other than the German troops trying to flee, in this the greatest of all the débâcles that we have ever seen. With some friends, we go off towards a big farm, right behind the big woods, where we know that in some large premises there are thousands and thousands of pairs of shoes, the reserve of the German army that had been evacuated there from Berlin in anticipation of heavy bombing. Moreover, all these large farms are, with the small villages, the dispersed warehouses of the German reserves evacuated from Magdeburg, Berlin and even from Hanover. Here there are only shoes, but two kilometres further on in a very small village, are thousands of military uniforms which were piled up in a large barn fitted up for that purpose. Nearer to where we are, there is also an enormous stock of lorry and car tyres, most of them stolen in France like nearly all their stocks. While crossing the great woods, near to a small road, we fall on a large convoy of lorries and German cars, about 200 of them, all abandoned for lack of petrol. All the vehicles are loaded chock full of various kinds of equipment and all completely new. Already the pillagers are arriving from the nearby villages and they will soon be at their work. We hear that we have the right to prevent all pillaging, but how are we to do it? We don't have any weapons and there are many German soldiers, well-armed for the most part, wandering around all these woods. Most of these cars, perhaps even the large majority, were just delivered to Hamburg scarcely two weeks ago and they are still being run in. On the other hand, looting has already started, packing chests emptied out, cardboard boxes opened, bags emptied onto the ground. The great looting is beginning. It's not only of war equipment, or rations, but also of the equipment most likely to be useful on the farm. Whole lorries are filled with nice toolkits, tools of all kinds for large and small-scale mechanical engineering, for the forge, for woodwork, for the locksmith, tinwork and a whole variety of trades, and all this equipment is new, packed up at the exit to the factory in entire lorry loads. The Red Cross is here. Some lorries full of medical kits and bandages discharge their contents which greedy hands start to loot. People are running now from all the villages around, many on bicycles but most of them go back to get wagons. I would really like to choose some small tools which would be most useful in the house, but how to take them away, that's the big question, how to hump them 2,000 km away from here. We leave the wood, where now there is general looting, without taking anything away.

No sooner are we on the road than we come across some people who are returning from the big farm at Friedrichsfleiss with piles of shoes. The group of prisoners from my kommando is already returning with 10 or 12 pairs each of really nice new shoes. We hurry on as the stock is diminishing before our eyes. The room, open to the public from yesterday evening, is beginning to empty out. Poles, Russians, Italians, Ukrainians are lugging round their piles of shoes on handcarts. Some Germans are digging in the gardens and burying everything they can. We arrive too late. The stock is exhausted, and it's with great difficulty that we can even get one pair each. However I find a pair which suits me pretty well.

Now it's the clothes shop at Hohenwulsch which is under siege by the whole population, German and foreign, and there are many of them. Some people come back home loaded up with coats, jackets, trousers from the German army. On the way we learn that there are no more trousers but there is still a big stock of coats and tunics left. We press on since we don't want to end up in the same situation as with the shoes! We arrive at the small village where we bump into people loaded up with clothes. Entry into the room is free, also choice and delivery, there is looting of everything and people are taking away as much as they can. We choose, we try things on, throwing out higgledy-piggledy what doesn't appeal to us, all the time unpacking, like all the people who are there, new packs of clothes which, at least yesterday, were set out in perfect order. We have come from a long way off and so we can't load ourselves down too much. Nonetheless everyone takes three or four tunics and the same number of coats. We go to the kommando in the little village where we find seven of our mates. There we learn that the French have possession of the keys for the large stores at the small station at Hohenwulsch. We go off with three other mates from the area who have hitched up a cart to a mare. On the roads, the people who were all panicky in the morning are fairly calm. Nonetheless, there are white flags flying everywhere as a sign of surrender, for the Americans are giving no quarter. A village which doesn't surrender is razed to the ground in a very few minutes. Once arrived at the station, which nobody is guarding, we open the warehouse where, among other things, there are 8–10,000 hundred-kilo bags of sugar. It's the sugar warehouse of the army and of the city of Berlin. Immediately we load up ten bags on the cart and shut the door again meticulously. This is a waste of time for several hours later the doors were forced open and throughout the whole night and the morning of the next day there was a general battle of all the people from the area who had run to this sugar paradise. We returned to the village as night fell, loaded up like mules and we decide that tomorrow, at daybreak, we will hitch up two strong horses to a cart with rubber wheels and six of us will go off to clean the place out.

The war? But here we are hardly talking of it any more. It's gone, this morning, like a big storm. You can just hear in the distance, fairly weak, the noise of it towards the south-east in the direction of Magdeburg, of the bombardment in a continuous rumble. We can't see any soldiers, any Americans. There are Germans who are withdrawing, but most of the German troops had not yet fallen back to us, for the Boche army has been completely overrun in this headlong rush of the racing vehicles of modern war which have charged, breached and gone through the lines in only a few hours, annihilating everything that was in the way of these monsters.

The night is fairly quiet. In the distance we see a ring of flares which marks out the ends of the front for, towards midnight, the usual big wave of bombers turns up.

The Prisoners Take Prisoners

Friday, 13 April 1945. As dawn breaks we can still see German troops, who are withdrawing in groups without being bothered by anyone. American tanks seem to have reached the Elbe and are not yet looking to cross, following it in the direction of Magdeburg. Another advance party has reached the Elbe, but much further down the river than us, so that we must now be inside a vast ring where the surrounded German troops are milling about.

Today is a big day for looting, one could almost say the big day out for cut-price looting. These reserve stocks have everything, but it is sugar which is the most popular. There were some customers for flour, but none for the potatoes which are also there. Throughout the night, from all the neighbouring villages, large numbers of peasants have come to take away sugar, and yet the inhabitants of the little town of Bismark could not come to join them and profit from the windfall, for, at Bismark, as the American tanks passed by they left a French officer who immediately armed the prisoners with guns, rifles, revolvers, and under the direction of this officer the French prisoners quickly became soldiers again, occupying the town and holding it under martial law. No one was permitted to leave their house under any pretext, under pain of death, and it is a formal order that the numerous prisoners from Bismark make sure is respected. The Americans continued with their headlong dash while leaving the responsibility of the town in the hands of the French, a really big responsibility, for the population, frightened yesterday, was fairly easy to bring to heel, but seeing no more tanks or American soldiers, they started to want to get the upper hand again, and if the infantry delays its arrival any longer the hours to come could be tough for us since they take a pretty dim view of us. However we load our huge truck up to the brim with equipment and the most varied kind of supplies. In particular, 30 sacks and three tons of sugar are piled up on the wagon. What will we do with all that? At midday a brawl breaks out, a Belgian fires in the air and tries to get the German

234

civilians to leave the stores. The latter react, for they sense they are stronger in numbers, and we could have a very nasty quarter of an hour for they feel themselves on home ground, and we, we are trying to throw them out. We sense that a battle is close at hand between the Boche and us, when a gang of German communists arrive, I don't know where from, armed to the teeth, and they soon restored order. The civilians are thrown out, the loaded wagons are emptied into the station square, there is a general scuffle among the Boche. Nobody bothers us and we take advantage to leave with our big load.

At Schorstedt the sea is also getting choppier. The Bürgermeister comes on several occasions to implore us to re-establish order. People are arguing amongst themselves, they are stealing from each other the various bits of swag coming from this great looting. Some of them come to blows. But we laugh about it, for there's no great harm done if they're going to kill each other, these bloody Boche. However, we decide, as in the villages roundabout, to disarm the civilians, as much for our own security as for theirs. A note is taken to the Bürgermeister: in the next hour, all arms have to be deposited at the town hall. Apart from some of them that we know already, for in the five years that we have been here we have come to know where most of the weapons are, all the farmers bring in arms and ammunition. We do our best, labelling the weapons, quoting the number, make, type and the name of the owner of the weapon. It all goes fairly well, there are many magnificent hunting guns, rifles for deer hunting, quite a large number of revolvers, and then the military rifles from the Grenadier section of the village people who, despite having had a big exercise last Sunday, took good care to leave the evening of the day before yesterday and yesterday morning, at the moment when fighting began. In fact they were the first to put out the white flags on the anti-tank barricades which had been left open. But that was the only thing they could do. All the equipment was arranged in the kommando in a locked cupboard, apart from a soldier's rifle for each of us, loaded and ready for all eventualities. We do all this without any orders. It's a great responsibility, and if the Americans were to withdraw, if we didn't quickly disappear we would get it in the neck.

The hours pass and the American infantry still doesn't come. Four of our men, armed, leave to get information in Bismark. And there they still can't tell when the American troops will arrive. They manage to hold on nevertheless and take great credit, as for 48 hours now everyone has been on duty without a break, there not being enough for any relief, and this handful of about 60 Frenchmen, holds in check 30,000 German civilians, which is the population of the town now with all its refugees. In the evening the situation in the village gets worse. Some brawls break out among the Poles, the Ukrainians and the Germans. The latter come to us to complain and are convinced that it is we who ought to protect them. On the other hand the village is surrounded by thick, extensive woods and it's that which makes us most fearful. Some entire sections, some companies of the SS and other German infantry are hiding everywhere in the woods. As night falls, they come into the village where the civilians give them refuge, letting them sleep in the barns and giving them supplies. Most of them are armed with machine-pistols. Our duty will be to disarm them and take them prisoners, but there are hundreds of them all around the village and if we take them on, it can only be to our disadvantage. We are only 80 without even one machine-gun. The best thing for the moment is to keep a lookout and to mind our Ps and Qs. We stay on guard all night, which is calm enough despite the endless movement of soldiers on the roads, and in the farms and the woods all around.

Saturday, 14 April. When day comes there is a lot of firing on the banks of the Elbe and the gunfire seems to be getting closer. The rumour is even running around that the Americans are withdrawing. The civilians who had all put out their white flags, hurry to bring them back in. They even give us unpleasant looks and some start to get their courage back and cross-question us pretty sharply. For the moment we are holding the village armoury; there isn't too much to fear in the daytime, but as the hours pass the civilians react by degrees and the situation gets worse. This evening the situation will no longer be tenable, we will surely get attacked by the German troops who are in the woods, in order to get back their weapons. At the camp we discussed the situation at great length. Some of us, and their view is pretty sensible, propose that when night falls we should bring back all the weapons to Bismark where we would give assistance to our friends while all being in less danger than here, for you feel that the night to come will lead to us being attacked by the civilians, who will make sure they are helped by the groups of armed soldiers that they resupply during the night. Some others, and I am among them, find their reasoning sound, but we can't consider abandoning the village for one night, for that would be proof of our weakness that these Boche would then exploit thoroughly. In the end, by a majority, we decide to stay, come what may. That night everyone is on guard, entrenched behind the hut, each with his own gun, and we will sell our lives dearly even if we are weaker. It's adopted unanimously.

One o'clock. A Pole runs up. He comes from Bismark and has seen some American patrols in the little villages roundabout, which spurs us on considerably. At last they are finally going to arrive, and it's not a moment too soon given it is three days since the tanks went by. A few minutes afterwards, we hear their engines, and we get ourselves into the village square at the double at the very moment when a half-track emerges followed by three other well-armed smaller vehicles. They stop. We give them an ovation. They grasp our hands. I climb up onto the automatic gun and try to fire off a few rounds in the air to bring the civilians to reason and to make them understand that if they make a move we will now have what it takes to subdue them. None of these Americans know either a word of French or a word of German. It's very difficult to get them to understand all that we have to say to them. Then they seem in a hurry, they seem pretty happy that we should have taken over the weapons and they let us know that they are patrolling from one village to another and they do not have time to listen to us. They turn around and go away in a cloud of dust. Then the civilians come back out. And they are curious and want to know what they said to us. We hadn't understood anything, but immediately we let the rumour run that a company will be coming to be billeted in the village in the evening or the course of the night and that anyone who revolts against us will be immediately executed on the spot by the American soldiers. The move succeeded beyond our hopes. Many families who even now had not wanted to put out the white flag, and others who put it out in the daytime for fear of our reprisals and brought it back at night for fear of the German soldiers who were prowling around the woods, they all now showed a huge white sheet on the front or the roof of their house. At our hut in the camp, a large French flag is hoisted to the top of a pole 25 metres high, in such a way as to be seen by the whole village, it climbs and waves in the breeze while our little orchestra plays the Marseillaise while the French, the Poles and the Russians, all bare-headed, watch it go up.

Saturday, 14 April 1945. Three o'clock in the afternoon. An American recce party comes into the village, around 30 vehicles. We shake innumerable hands. The first man that I come across is a Canadian speaking French quite fluently. Three or four others are there jabbering away well enough in broken French. They act as interpreters besides the officers, who you cannot distinguish from the men. We inform the officers of what we have done, they listen and content themselves from time to time with replying '*Oh quet*',[10] or something approaching it, which seems to mean 'that's alright'.

They ask first of all to see the weapons that we have removed. We take them to the hut, while explaining to them that we have been in this village for five years waiting for someone to come to liberate us. I tell them that the Boche (I don't know if they learned this word in France but they use it frequently) would have kept us captive until we collected our pension, that's to say a long long time. They laugh at the thought. The hut doesn't appeal to them too much and they consider it really uncomfortable. All the weapons are brought out into the yard at the edge of the road. Fifteen military rifles, the best, stay with the French, with a lot of ammunition. As for the others, they show us what we have to do, that's to say they take them by the barrel and break them into pieces on a big block of wood, the butts fly into splinters while, with a great sledgehammer, the barrel and the firing mechanism are smashed. What a pity! Some superb hunting guns go the same way, five-shot carbines for deer hunting. The nobleman Bekman, one of the richest men in the village, delivered his five guns, superb weapons all tied and wrapped together, well-greased in their leather cases. Everything's emptied onto the ground. I pick up a beautiful gun with carved wood, three barrels, two for normal bullets, and a smaller one in the middle of the other two, and below, for wild boar bullets. I hesitate for a moment: such a beautiful weapon, which right now must be very valuable, but in the blink of an eye an American, who must be an officer gives me an order and chucks it on the block of wood. Now it's our turn and five or six of us go hammer and tongs at the guns. Right at that moment the café owner of the village passes by, he's a great hunter as well. I look at him, and I see him blanch in front of this pile of scrap metal that now represents the weapons of Schorstedt.

We return to the vehicles. The detachment has grown still bigger. Some large lorries carrying troops and equipment, some machine-guns on armoured caterpillar tracks, and all of a sudden the big tanks emerge from the rue de Wolenrade. One of these mastodons comes into the square. Frightened by the appearance of such monsters the population quickly returns to their houses, as the caterpillar tracks make the paved roads vibrate. They're quite some machines, must be 80–100 tons,[11] for they're surely more than the 40 tons of those that went with us to the front, and quite a lot bigger than the German 60-tonners that I've seen. Ten of these motors line up along the main road. The officer explains to us that these are mopping-up troops who are going to operate in the area and to scour the woods to crush the scattered islands of resistance.

Right now one company is designated to search the houses while the others rest. Machine-pistol in hand, teams of five or six men scrupulously searched the houses. Some more arms are gathered up, mostly from people that we knew hadn't handed them in. All the apartments are visited, right down to cellars and up to attics, closed doors are broken down, locks are smashed, nothing stands in the way of the search. Several house owners are threatened and they are happy that we intervene on their side so that they are not taken away. However, the Poles get the teacher taken off to jail, the real leader of the Boche, the area head of the Nazi party, a Hitlerite to the marrow, whose speciality was to create as much misery as possible for foreigners in the village. At our insistence, the Americans tell the Bürgermeister that any revolt against the troops keeping order, that's to say the French who for now are charged with the occupation of the village, will be severely stamped on. They tell the mayor, what is more, that if there is any trouble we have *carte blanche* to kill the sowers of rebellion.

And the convoy departs, but this time the civilians have understood. Heads lowered, they obey our orders without any more discussion and do our least desires. Our authority has really grown since this morning. We give the order that the materials that have served to make anti-tank barriers should be immediately taken away from all routes into the village, as they could get in the way of the convoys of American troops. And then we see these gentlemen who, last Monday, cane in hand and cigar in the mouth, watched closely over us while we made the barricades, lending a hand themselves to the job and sweating to lift the big bits of wood under the mocking eye of the Poles and the Russians, while the French, rifles on their shoulders, patrol up and down the road. We would never have believed, coming here as prisoners, that we would one day be the occupying troops. We will have seen everything in this war.

The day comes to a calm end, everyone retiring early at curfew into their own houses where they are formally forbidden under pain of death to give refuge to German troops who are wandering around in the woods.

Saturday, 14 April 1945. Midnight. Tired after these few days of troubles, and the village seeming quite quiet at 10 o'clock in the evening, everyone was sleeping in the hut, even the sentry, when we were suddenly woken up with a jump. The swineherd, the ordinary village policeman, was knocking violently. We had lain down fully-dressed. Immediately everyone takes up his weapon, which was ready to be fired in case of a surprise. The Bürgermeister had sent him to tell us that 30 German SS soldiers had come back into the barn to sleep, and having understood from the arrest of the teacher that the Americans were not messing around with their orders, he wanted to deliver them up to us so as to discharge himself from any blame. *My* first question is to ask if they're armed. Yes, no, he didn't exactly know. We decide that here we have to be prudent and not, on this dark night, fall into an ambush where we could be killed. 'You say to the Bürgermeister that we will take them tomorrow morning at first light.' That's our reply. We couldn't, in the black of night, nab people who, perhaps hidden, were waiting for us to come with their machine-guns. Half of us go back to bed, the other half stays up ready for any eventuality. But only ten minutes have gone by before the Bürgermeister himself arrives at the barracks. He only just missed being shot himself. He doesn't want to keep these men at his place at any price, the responsibility is too great. If the Americans turn up at his house from one minute to the next and find these soldiers, he will immediately be shot, the orders are categorical.

Alright, we decide to go there, let's see what's going on. Eight of us go off, each one with his rifle. The Mayor swears that they are all disarmed. We go into the farm round the back, in case somebody might be waiting for us round the front, for in the five years that we've been there, I have got to know all the nooks and crannies just as well as if I was patrolling in Aigues-Vives. In the farmyard, some soldiers are wandering round. We give our formal warnings in the darkness. They immediately lift their hands. Two of us search them. Two heavy revolvers and a pistol are collected in. Other soldiers were lying down in the straw, all fall in well enough with our orders and come out into the yard where they are searched in their turn. We put them into another barn since they could have hidden weapons under the straw during the night. We closed the door, wished them goodnight and three men stay outside to guard them.

The officers, for there are also three officers, a captain and two lieutenants, are in a room in the Bürgermeister's house. Five of us go into the Mayor's house, and immediately we go into the living-room, all three of them get up, take off their hats, raise their hands and, in very military fashion, stand to attention. We surround the room, our rifle barrels touching their chests. One man searches them and takes out a very nice revolver, and some maps from the general staff. We put down our weapons and stand back a little. 'Your papers'. All three are from around Hanover. Now they talk. They're not soldiers, they say, they're specialists, a kind of airforce technician. They will leave the soldiers to us, as they are infantrymen, and they themselves would like to go back and rejoin their families. 'Why, since you are not soldiers, are you dressed as officers of the German army? It's not for us to judge, you'll be kept here tonight and tomorrow the Americans will decide what to do with you.' Two men, arms at the ready, and I am one of the two, guard the exit from the living-room while the others return to the shed where, in two hours, the new guard will arrive. This little episode makes us all rejoice. We shall have some fun tomorrow: the Schorstedt prisoners who have taken 30 prisoners themselves including three officers, that's going to be a real laugh.

After my two hours spent in the living-room I stay for another two hours with another friend behind the barn, for there is a rickety door there and you never know, now that we're holding them, it's important that they don't escape. The night is cold, in fact very cold. We shiver despite the greatcoat, but it's of no matter, we're happy all the same and night comes to an end without bringing anything new other than the obligatory comic note: a friend stops on the road, ten metres in front of him, our old warder who was really afraid when he heard the rifle's breech bolt go. He had just been staying up with a mare who had just had a foal, and the poor man was completely disoriented, to the point that he asked us if it was the American prisoners that we were guarding there. We had no quarrel with him, in fact the contrary. It was he who had been charged with looking after us, to shut us up in the evening and to get us up in the morning, which he always did without upbraiding anyone with anything. Last night, we hadn't wanted to be shut in, a simple formality for over the last two years we had possessed all the false keys necessary to help us open up after his departure. He was worried, the poor man, he hadn't received anything from the officer in charge and he had no order and was completely penitent when we told him that the officer, just like the sentries at Bismark, had been prisoner of the prisoners since morning. At first light we stopped another two adjutants and two soldiers who wanted to escape on bicycles. Immediately searched and disarmed, they were going to swell the consignment in the farm that we were now holding under very tight supervision.

Sunday, 15 April. Two mates went off at dawn to Bismark to inform the American command post of our prize so that they could come to take delivery of them. As for me, I stood guard on the road where I had the luck to nab yet another soldier and then a captain of the SS who has the really evil face of the true Boche. It was there that I took my revenge as prisoner, not very spitefully, but absolutely according to the book. Two friends came to my aid, and while they held him in check, a gun 10 cm from his chest, I searched him. There were no

weapons, only some bullets and a grenade. The French prisoners, for
a grenade, used to get a good beating. My boss was there, among the
civilians, to whom I gave the order, under the threat of my gun, to
move to one side. I opened the captain's enormous Tyrolean bag,
100 packets of cigarettes fall out on the road: three-quarters of them
are confiscated for our benefit. A friend filled up our cardboard box.
I took out a bottle of alcohol, of rum, with a French label. He
insisted, saying he wanted to drink it with his friends who he saw in
the yard. I accused him of being a thief in front of all the civilians,
since the bottle was French, and now it was ours. He still kept on
about keeping his bottle but, far from making us intimidated, we
gave him the order to shut up and to put his hands up. The threatening guns butted up against his chest, the civilians were amazed and
silently looked on at the spectacle. The captain, and even one or two
of the civilians, protested saying that what we were doing wasn't in
order. And this left a bitter taste in my mouth, thinking of my bottle
of Carthagène[12] sent from my folks which had never arrived, I replied
vigorously that in the five years that we'd been prisoners, we had
come to know the rules. And a sharp '*Schnapps verboten*' put an end to
the affair. The bottle was confiscated. Three boxes of nice Gold Label
cigars, also *verboten*. Equally confiscated were his nice electric lamp
and its batteries. Chummy took it bad, but we on the other hand had
had to put up with much worse things than that when we were
searched. He went into the Bürgermeister's living-room to keep the
other officers company. An American patrol, passing at daybreak,
told us not to allow the soldiers to chat to the officers.

At half past nine a vehicle arriving like a tornado came to take
delivery of them and what a joy for us too to ascertain that the occupants, dressed as American soldiers, were French officers from De
Gaulle's army. We present arms fairly amateurishly, but immediately
they come to shake our hands and give us warm congratulations. I
accompany a lieutenant who goes in behind me into the house of the
Bürgermeister with a revolver in his hand. In my presence he questions the Boche officers in the most perfect German. In the yard, the
other officers and my mates have made the Boche soldiers line up in
columns of threes. When I asked the lieutenant whether a lorry is
going to come to get them, he replies to me: 'And how did they
bring you here? On foot. They'll do the same as far as Bismark'. We
take advantage of the presence of the French officers to carry out a
proper patrol in the village, which intimidates the civilians a good
deal. The presence of these officers is precious to us and considerably
heightens our authority.

We use the opportunity to disarm the Poles and Ukrainians who are spreading terror throughout the village, nearly always drunk like Poles are, there's no mistake about that. They only talk of killing and burning everything and, what a joke, the Germans, (who nonetheless we don't humour), demand protection from us. Complaints arrive from everywhere. All the time they come to us to re-establish order. There's a Pole who wants to cut the throat of his boss or a Ukrainian woman who is giving a systematic beating to her boss's wife. Two Russians have got one of the biggest landowners of the area down on the ground and, while one of them extracts his watch, the other relieves him of his shoes. And I could fill three or four notebooks with stories like that.

We have to be everywhere. There are hundreds of thefts. The refugees, who arrive *en masse* from the banks of the Elbe where the battle is raging, flushing them out down to us who are 30 km on the north side of the Elbe, stay in large groups in the barns, stealing each other's bundles, linen, provisions. Yesterday evening, three of us sorted out a comical affair, again with our guns. We never let go of them. Two families have been thieving from each other. It was impossible to know who was the robbed and who the robber, both of them making a complaint. I climb up on to a wagon and take out one after the other the possessions in the bundles of the two families. Linen, rations, women's underwear. A pair of knickers, two women lay claim to them at the same time. I am supposed to adjudicate. They can't hear me and I quickly cut the thing short. I use my two hands to tear with all my strength on the fine lingerie, which splits and divides down the middle. One leg to each one, judged and sold. We who came here prisoners, what we have to do! And what yet are we to witness before the end of this war!

Judging Nazi Germany

In the Camp, we laugh at all these stories. The Poles, the Ukrainians, the Russians make the Boche shake in their boots. The French, however hard towards them, have their complete confidence. We are compelled to let things go a little for the Boche are only getting what they deserve. For five years they have been building up hate in the breasts of these half-wild people, giving them a frequent thrashing with blows of their sticks or truncheons for the least misdemeanour, getting them thrown in prison, men and women for minor offences, and what men, what women, little boys, little girls of 15, 16 years old. What shame on Germany for having deported in their millions these children who are thousands of kilometres from their homes, with no help for these little girls for whom they have no respect.[13] At 16 or 17 years of age, they are easy prey, without anyone to advise them, they sink into debauchery, most of them getting pregnant, many having abortions on the advice of the Boche, so as to be free a fortnight later to get back on the job. All the doctors in the hospital at Stendal do abortions openly.

As for the Poles, they do not forget their miseries. They were the ones who were treated worst. I'm going to tell two stories, one quite recent since it dates from the first days of December 1944. One man having slept with a German woman who had lured him back to her place, although he had not been caught and he had never been willing to admit it, they had kicked him around for more than four hours. He was bleeding all over. They left him, passed out and near his end, half-dead, and it was there that returning from work I found him lying on the ground. It was the Pole who had been working with me for four years. I lay him down on his bed and I had the greatest difficulty in reviving him. They, the bosses, would have left him there to die. He crawled around for more than a month recovering from this beating. There you have them, Boche tactics.

The second story, that goes back two years. It was again a Pole who risked his life. A young German girl was thrown from an express train along the Hanover line which passes at the far end of the district of Schorstedt. She wasn't killed and wasn't too badly hurt. The police, however, decided that it could only have been a Pole who had done it. The next day, out in the country, a poor devil of a Pole who, at loggerheads with his boss, was wandering down the edge of the woods, was captured. He was 100 per cent ignorant of this business of the young girl. Without any further form of trial, in the afternoon, he was hung from an oak beside the line, in the presence of all the Poles from the neighbouring villages, guarded by police with machine-guns. Two Poles who were found to be his friends were chosen, under threat from a revolver, to act as hangmen. After the execution, the Poles filed by, one by one, in front of the warm body still hanging there and, as they went by, they received, from four German athletes, their ration of blows from a stick. A little boy who wasn't even 15 years old, and who, trembling all over and crying, didn't want to look at the hanged man as he went by, was condemned to cut him down and to take off the rope from around his neck. Four of his friends had to bury him. The Poles from the village came back from this display shaking all over. The one who was working with me didn't eat anything for more than eight days so much had it affected him and stricken his heart. This was Boche tactics! And this was no gossip, this happened here in the village where I am, there's no room for any doubt.

If I didn't write that at the time, it's because such writings, if they had been seen, could have cost me my own life. Many other stories of this kind took place in the neighbouring villages, notably at a factory where a Pole was left, to serve as an example to the others, eight days hung at the end of a rope, dangling in the void above the main entrance to the factory. And the Jews, what hard things they experienced! They were executed by their thousands, men, women and children, by the most barbaric means that I can't bring myself to write down.[14]

I must come back to my prisoners from whom I've strayed a long way, through telling my stories. In columns of three, impeccably to attention, they wait for us in the courtyard. A lieutenant asks for eight volunteers to help him take them as far as the exit from the big woods, where they could try to escape. Immediately we all come forward, which seems to make him happy. I am chosen to be part of the procession and I put myself, gun at the ready, at the head of a column, level with the first prisoner and to his left. Forward, march, not in step, and the small column gets under way, two officers behind with a machine-pistol in their hand, ready to fire. Thus we cross the village. The women are crying on the doorsteps. The same scenes, but in reverse, that I had seen across the Department of the Meuse are reproduced here. The men lower their heads, thinking of their sons who, in some corner of Greater Germany are being led away like these men.

In this column there are some oldsters, but the majority are youngish, idolising Hitler, and they slept in the uniform of the Hitler Youth, little bayonets at their side, before becoming soldiers, and only dreamed of even greater conquests, promised by their God Adolf. I talked with some of them this morning. Many were hardly more than 15 years old, others 16 or 17. They had been soldiers for three or four weeks. Two told me their stories, they were crying. Four weeks ago they were at home, near to their Mum, and now they're far from seeing her again. That affects me, I'm touched, but we can't be doing with sentiment, it's war. I asked them why they hadn't revolted instead of adoring their great Adolf right up to the last minute. They are funny people, it has to be admitted. Although Germany is more or less half overrun at the moment, they don't want to give in and they continue to resist. I can hear, as I write, the guns booming, seemingly northwards towards Hamburg. They will resist right up to the last man, they will never give in. Hitler has said it many a time and I'm convinced that's what they will do. Everything will be smashed, destroyed, but they will not surrender. After every débâcle, like this one here, they pull themselves together, they regroup, and hold on for yet more days. It's tremendous, even unbelievable, that after what we have seen they find the means to hold on to the other side of the Elbe. It's true the river has been crossed by the Americans towards Magdeburg, but here 30 kilometres from us, between Arneburg and Wittenberg, they are holding on grimly, very grimly, in this sweep of the Elbe. And yet they are taking a pounding. The artillery is now firing relentlessly, reinforced several times a day by masses of bombers, and you should see what these bombers have done as well! In spite of everything they hold on, almost without air support and without artillery. It's unimaginable and yet it's true.

On their side the Russians are attacking on the Oder. Between the Oder and the Elbe, isn't such a great distance, but the Germans will hold on to this band of territory having Berlin on one side and Hamburg on the other as points of support, until the last man, until the last village. In all that they sense that the situation is really critical. An old man more than 45 years old asked me this morning if they would take him prisoner. 'But of course, since you're a soldier!'. I even told him that he was surely going to be put into the convoy which is going to leave for Australia. They've buggered about us often enough with jokes, now it's our turn to have a little fun. He complains, and we get our answer in, '*Nych gout géfang! Oia ich fünf iaré géfang dise dorf!*'[15] Meanwhile we march down the road, keeping in step all the time. We go into the woods right at the moment when we pass a motorised advance guard of an American regiment which is going up the line. It's an artillery regiment which is going up and there's an interminable file-past of these monstrous vehicles. Each one gives us an ovation. They're happy to see this little group of Frenchmen supervising the prisoners. They shout down from their enormous caterpillar tractors dragging huge guns on trailers at high speed. Lorries, cars and yet more tractored vehicles, and more guns, equipment of all kinds, and all these men, many of them black, who stand up to applaud us. From nearly all the vehicles come these words: 'Boche, kaput.' The prisoners are not so haughty now, and I see the SS captain biting his lip. They are furious but they don't seem to want to escape even if we are in the middle of the woods, since the reinforcement is really too strong, especially given that from time to time, with a fantastic din a huge tank turns up, and from the top of the turret they train down their machine-guns, while shouting I do not know what to the prisoners who keep their heads down. Many of them take photos of our little column from their vehicles. Others, and there are many of them, throw us whole handfuls of chocolate and cigarettes. It's really the best day of our captivity. On leaving the woods, we take a break and a group of Frenchmen from the neighbouring village, who have got wind of the affair, come to relieve us. We shake hands with some French officers who thank us warmly. I ask them not to forget us deep in the woods and the fact that, just like our mates from the towns, we are also pining to see France again. They make a promise and go off, and we, in a hurry since it's late, go back to the village to eat.

Sunday 15 April. In the afternoon we go for a walk along the roads of the village, an ordinary patrol. The village is calm, apart from a few scuffles always coming from the Poles and above all from the savage Ukrainians of whom the Germans are terribly afraid. Towards three o'clock a violent fire breaks out in the Bürgermeister's machine shed, situated on the edge of the wood, and where, foreseeing the bombing of the village, he had piled up all his equipment. Threshers, two beautiful reaper-binders, one of which is completely new, grain seeders, fertilizer, harrows of various kinds, and many other machines, everything's the victim of the flames which in a few minutes have destroyed everything. Whether this is revenge or an accident nobody quite knows. In any case you can see fires everywhere obscuring the sky right now. The depots of the German army are burnt by the Americans who have no need of any spoils of war, everything's burnt. At Bismark, after having made the prisoners get into a huge circle, before taking them further back from the line, they have even got them to pile up everything from their packs and then burn it. Tobacco, cigarettes, personal effects, everything goes in, telling them that prisoners don't need anything, they will give them everything they need in the camp.

Around the villages the Americans are actively patrolling in the woods, machine-guns mounted on the front of their small but nippy jeeps, they circle the whole region, always coming out of the woods with some more prisoners sat behind on the wing of their vehicle or on the armour plating of their half-tracks.

Monday 16 April. The night was calm. This time the Germans have really understood that their resistance was in vain and would rebound on them. The whole day patrols were scouring the woods and the village, searching in the houses. The American soldiers are really very businesslike. At Bismark six small planes have even landed in a field of rye and they are constantly patrolling all around. I saw one of them come down in a meadow and the two occupants get out, machine-pistols in hand, to explore a copse which must have seemed to them suspect. The day however passes quietly. The inhabitants, watching the many American vehicles going through the village all the time in one direction or another, going up to or coming down from the front, have understood and they stay quiet. Many of the surrounding villages are occupied by American troops. Here there are no troops billeted and it continues to be us who maintain order, but without too much trouble, the Americans being happy to patrol from time to time and to make searches of the houses quite frequently. Life isn't too bad, we're no longer working, we go regularly to have our meals at the bosses' houses, who have to supply us without objecting, which they do while all the time looking across at us, but without daring to raise their voices too much.

Wednesday 18 April. I go to Bismark for we have to keep checking up with the central control, with whom we must be constantly in contact. There's nothing to report today, but on the main road to Berlin I can see a huge amount of equipment going by. Tanks, refuelling vehicles, transports of every kind, not stopping but travelling up and down the main road all the time. Some tanks are coming back from the front, the front smashed in, the gun hanging down, without caterpillars. They had been hit hard down there on the front. They are transported on strong load-carriers. The troops occupy the town completely and the inhabitants had to leave it to them, themselves sleeping in the barns for a few days.

Ah! The Germans understand this time and they haven't yet seen it all. If in 1918 we'd given them the same kind of lesson, they would have thought twice before launching such an adventure. The wife of my old boss complains, the Americans have taken away several dozen eggs from her and have forgotten to pay, which drives her mad. For a long time I said to her that she didn't know what war was and when they come to take the cows and the horses from you that's when you'll see it! She was so surprised when I said to her that the Germans had done worse in France, she didn't want to believe it when I told her that they had robbed the shops, emptied the houses, that they didn't stand on ceremony about making a woman or a girl get down from their bike on the road, to steal it and many other things besides, to throw out the owners from a cottage, to occupy it themselves, to cart away furniture or machines, tools of many different kinds which were sent away in lorry loads towards Germany. It's the truth, because I saw that at Saint-Dizier on the Paris–Strasbourg road. They're really getting paid back with their own medicine, but however it might be done, you could never give them back what they had done across the whole of Europe. It's true, they're dying in millions, but it's not yet enough, they ought to be all exterminated right to the last one, because they have thick skulls and can't accept being beaten, for they all believe firmly in their slogan: '*Deutschland Über Alles*'.[16]

At that moment I learned that at Gardelegen, around 30 kilometres from here, they have just found 1,500 dead foreigners or German political prisoners, who after being slashed with razor blades and half crushed with blows had been sprayed with petrol and set on fire. This is the work of those famous SS, Hitler's supporters. The same thing is said to have happened near to Magdeburg and, it seems, after the last news, an English team will be coming to verify it.

Friday, 20 April 1945. For some days I haven't been writing, for nothing really interesting has happened after the momentous days through which we have just lived. Now, in our neck of the woods, far away from anywhere, everything is returning to calm. Apart from the occasional American patrol, which is increasingly rare, there is nothing to show of the great drama which has just been played. The bulk of the American forces has moved on, either going down the Elbe in the direction of Hamburg or otherwise going back up it towards Magdeburg, Dessau and even further off Dresden. We can still hear guns in the distance, pretty faint during the day, but stronger once night comes. It's very infrequent – one could even say never – that American troops are billeted in our vicinity. At Bismark, and at Stendal, some detachments, staying close to the American command post, are enough to assure order in the region. There are also a few American police and that is more than enough to keep the Germans respectful.

Today is Hitler's birthday and God knows how this *Guébousta*[17] was celebrated in Germany in previous years. Then, at daybreak in all the towns, and even in our poor villages, the roads were decked in Hitlerian colours. Everywhere, on all the houses, flags, banners. Swastikas everywhere. This year the holiday unfolds under the sign of the white flag which floats in front of all the houses. Alone at the end of its long pole, more than 20 metres high, waves the French flag which, fully unfurled, provides the only gay note in the village.

During these few days, following on the American soldiers making their searches, and even sometimes alone, I visited quite a few dwellings. Nowhere is there any longer a trace of Hitler's supporters. It's true that we know, we who've had enough occasion to see it, that every house possesses a big picture of the celebrated painter. Many even have several. There's no living-room, dining-room, without exception which isn't decorated with a bust or a big picture, often both, representing in different poses the man responsible for all this killing.

All that has disappeared as if by magic and American soldiers, asking the civilians if they're not Nazis, receive invariably this reply; 'We're decent people us, we didn't want the war, we didn't know that man, we certainly heard talk of a certain Adolf, but his politics didn't reach us here, we were all against Hitler and his policies.' They are very careful not to tell how on the smallest festival, of the kind that happened several times a year, they brought out their red flags with the swastika on. They didn't tell the soldiers that their children of 18 months or two years old, instead of teaching them as their first words like in every other country of the world, those which I think must be universal, that's to say 'dada, mama' and all the parents in the whole world are proud to hear their children jabber out, it wasn't like that here. How many times have I heard kids who weren't even walking yet, lift up their little hand and cry '*Heil Hitla!*'. That's what, right up to these last few days, the mothers here were teaching children at their breast.

A bit older, when they were eight, already enrolled with their sergeants, their regular uniforms, their little bayonets at their side, they started exercises, and that was nothing like the scouts or other similar groups back home. No, they were training these children as army reserves. Older again, when they were 14, they went two or three times a week on special courses given by army NCOs, grouping four or five villages together at the same time, forming companies. At 16 years old, as well as these courses, they went several times a year to have periods in uniform. They were nearly real soldiers. That's how Germany teaches its children to become soldiers from the cradle. Of course this is far from the French way, but how much better is the method of sending children to school. For here, at least in the villages, they're not too bothered about that. The essential thing is that their children should become soldiers and good soldiers, sergeants at least if it's possible. Education is of secondary importance, for there is not much school, two or three times a week, from 10 'til midday and that's all that I saw in the time I've been here. Here the teacher wasn't called up, like the kids he didn't seem to know what scholastic overwork was. And anyway, the few hours at school only served to provide lessons in patriotism, for the teacher was one of the purest among all the pure Nazis. He taught them hate for other peoples, the French like the others, the Jews and above all the Poles.

The men have even more of a Nazi stamp on them than the little boys. Have we ever seen anything like it in France? Certainly from 1937 to 1940 we went through some very difficult political periods where each party praised to the skies its best men. But whatever you might see the royalists, the communists, socialists or the radicals, or even some others, doing you never saw men meet each other in the street, go into a café, into a tabac, or the hairdresser or in a restaurant, and instead of hello or good evening say to each other 'long live so and so' or 'long live someone else'. Well that's what you see here every day: '*Heil Hitla*' here, '*Heil Hitla*' there, it doesn't matter where, where you're going into, where you're coming out from, it doesn't matter who you might meet, evening or morning, it's always these '*Heil Hitlas*'.

That's as far as the men are concerned, but the women aren't any better, for it's really they who are the craziest for their bad painter Adolf. They banged away with their '*Heil Hitla*' much more strongly and without a break. Ah! what a shambles he's getting them into now, their painter! Even the rest of us, the French prisoners, were greeted like that. That made me sick at heart and if they had only been able to understand the kind of greeting I gave them back in dialect, they wouldn't have smiled so much. I'd taught it to my friends who were not from the Midi and even in the end the Poles and Ukrainians said it, they had learnt it themselves and invariably you heard it on the streets: '*Heil Hitla*' and immediately the response: '*Que crébé*' (let him die).

Little girls did not avoid this formidable military preparation and, from the age of 12 years they were also indoctrinated into the organisation. In regulation kit, dark blue skirts and khaki jacket, with the swastika in a diamond on the sleeve, they went off several times a week for exercises and took courses; they also had their sergeants, each group had its *Führer* or its *Führerin* and its NCOs. It was oddly organised and it went forward with a truly prodigious discipline. What could we do, we poor Frenchmen, against such methods of fighting wars? You had to have seen the German organisations, even right back in the smallest villages, to realise the force that was Germany, a force that no other people could equal. Certainly they are now giving in, but it's only really to a force many times superior in equipment and numbers to their own. Yes, it was tremendous and really went beyond anything one could imagine in France, this organisation, right down to the smallest details, of the Nazi force in the service of the war. It was formidable and unbelievable. You had to have seen it during the long months of captivity, where we saw every day unrolling in front of our eyes this gigantic coordination of war efforts. You ought to have seen how, without grumbling, without a word, without even a gesture of revolt, every order was executed without discussion of any kind. One couldn't have done such things back home. An order arrives, of requisition or else of service or a loan of horses, or vehicles for works or again, these last months, the order of general mobilisation, that's to say of all the handicapped that the preceding mobilisations had left at home because really they weren't soldiers. Well, we saw all these unhappy people or little boys of 14 years old, side by side with poor men completely lame of 65 years old, and even some older. There was even one with an artificial leg, whose only job was to inspect the slaughtering of pigs, and he had to follow the column of the people's grenadiers. Well, all these men were on manoeuvres all winter. On Sunday, in glacial cold, in the snow, they dug trenches, shelters, they practised shooting, two or three times a week, in the evening they attended courses, they learned how to lay mines, how to manoeuvre anti-tank weapons, at night they went on patrols, after having worked in their fields all day long. Well, all that they did without complaining. I know that the pitiless discipline meant that some of them paid dearly, the very few who, timidly, very gently, gave the impression of not wanting to obey. Immediately, on the same day, to the minute, all orders had to be executed. And you heard them discussing amongst themselves, there was never one who would have started off a false rumour as happened so often in France. It must be said that they distrusted each other and even their own kids. It was really fantastic to see how this unhappy painter had been able to make himself feared and respected and above all obeyed everywhere and by such a great people. For many the concentration camps and the penalties which rained thickly down like hail were naturally more than enough, for you had to see the rigour with which the police operated. For having secretly killed a weak pig, which was going to die anyway, one poor devil in the village, who had lost his three sons on the Russian front, was condemned to one year in prison, as well as a really heavy fine. And the police here are practical: they made him spend half of his prison sentence in the winter months, letting him return in a fairly poor state back to his own home at the end of March, to cultivate his land and work so as to resupply the great Reich. Then he returned at the end of October last to finish his time in prison. How very practical is the system in 'Greater Germany'. He has just come back again to his farm, not dead but very nearly, this man who is over 65 years old. With such methods, you can imagine how the others keep their noses clean. No more than the sight of a policeman on the road is enough to make them tremble. And I think that that was one of the greatest strengths of the National Socialist party. Now that they can't avoid smelling the stench of defeat, they tremble even more before the fear of reprisals, which they know they have rightly earned.

VI

GOING HOME

The Last Days

Tuesday, 1 May 1945. The week which has just drifted away has not changed our situation much. How long will we have to wait now before our return to France? For the moment we're not too bad but we're longing to return, to see France again, the Midi and the cherries which, in a few days, will be ripe down there, while here the vegetation is still shyly waking up from winter. Yet we will eat some grapes this year; it's so long since I've seen any. Since the grape harvest of 1938, that's a lot of months. I can't get myself used to the idea that in a little while I'm going to get back to my own country, my own village.

This week, even if nothing much important has happened, there have been constant incidents. The American army, that's to say the Ninth Army which was operating in our sector, has completely disappeared stretching down the banks of the Elbe, not far from us admittedly, since the Elbe is only 25 kilometres from the village, but it has completely evacuated the villages and small towns from hereabouts, not leaving even a soldier to act as policeman. It follows that there have been some constant incidents. Everyone's trying to run the place. The Germans, as we could foresee, are terrorised by this mass of foreigners that they have accumulated in their country and who now are taking their revenge. Above all the Poles, aided by the Russians, pursue the law of plunder pitilessly and the principle of 'what we see we take' is applied to the maximum. It's true that we French also have some serious accounts to settle with the Boche, but we, perhaps because we are older, or just that we don't have all the same customs and habits as the people of Eastern Europe, we also, it's true, do our bit of looting, but less obviously, in a completely different style from theirs, and that has produced some serious clashes amongst us, which nearly led to a fight recently.

Many Russians liberated from the camps, arriving maybe from around Hanover or Kassel, Bremen and even, some of them, from around Hamburg, are passing through and stop for several days with

257

us, lending a hand to the locals, and then the Germans really end up suffering.

Not a day goes by without incidents. Once it was the Poles who, having gone into a house and headed straight for the cellar, pretty poor it's true, but where they managed to find all the same some bottles of Schnapps, some dubious kinds of alcohol and some rather poor wine, drank them non-stop. Then it was also the Russians, who are going from house to house collecting all the bicycles. It's a little like everyone making his own law of requisition. The American army with its wonderful organisation, has gone through but hasn't left any orders or any discipline behind it. It's a general shambles, at least in the villages.

On another day there's looting of radio sets, but then when the chaos reaches its highest point it's at nightfall, when the whole mob is drunk. For it all starts to build up a little everywhere from the small distilleries which, during the length of the day, spread the poison – and what alcohol! In their eyes anything is good enough to be distilled: rye, corn, barley, dried pulp from sugar beet that the owners keep to feed to their calves, potatoes. And you have to see these people from the East drink a full mug of it as if it were simple plonk. I don't and will never touch such poisons, but I shudder to think what could happen if what I'm seeing here before my eyes, in regions which don't lend themselves at all to it, happened back home where there's no shortage of raw materials. In the evening, when everyone has been drinking, it's then that some fine things happen. There's crockery broken in many houses. The terrified Germans barricade themselves in their homes. Some people who went out onto the road were pretty roughly treated, and nearly every day a woman or a man comes to the French hut to ask for help. The Germans have the idea that it's us who ought to protect them. This is amazing, but it's like that. They come to tell us all their troubles and miseries. Nearly all of us have been there for around five years and they often take us for locals. Indeed sometimes we do go out to restore order, above all when it's a question of single women who are being badly treated. But now it's becoming more and more tough because, in every case there are disputes and the last very nearly cost me dearly; I barely avoided being stabbed by a Russian who was as drunk as a lord. It's terrible that it's come to this, and we can't wait to be rescued from the village where, one day or other, one of us is going to lose his life in these rows. The Poles and above all the Russians are conducting themselves very badly. It's true, I know that you have got to make the Germans understand what war is, but all the same you can do it without being cowardly, because they nearly always attack women on their own, taking their chickens, their eggs, their small provisions from them and leaving the house virtually empty. If we intervene to prevent it, immediately there's a dispute. The Poles and particularly the Russians call us Boche, helping the Germans, and I don't know exactly what they're telling us in the gibberish that they're yelling while brandishing the long pointed flick-knives that they bring out from the sheaths that hang permanently from their belts. Of course all the time we have about 15 rifles at our disposal and we could give them a sharp response, but then if we start killing each other it will be the Germans who'll be laughing. Anyway yesterday evening we decided to leave as quickly as possible, to get out of this village, whatever might happen after our departure.

As long as there were only the Poles, Ukrainians and Russians who worked here in the village, things could work. True enough, while they were drinking they weren't very easy to get along with, but at least I had a considerable hold on the Pole who was working with me and he was the foreman. But now their gangs have been swelled by about 15 Russians released recently from the camps near Hanover. They stop over with us before crossing the Elbe, while waiting for the road to be opened so as to go onto the other side of the Elbe to meet the Russian armies who now aren't far from us, but while waiting they're looting everything. On the other hand we are obliged to let things go a bit because the Germans must understand what war means, and if they hadn't brought so many foreigners here, it wouldn't rebound on them so much now.

Apart from that we wouldn't be too badly off. Now the bosses are looking after us pretty well, like they've never done. Virtually imploring our protection, and we're certainly not treating these Boche bastards very tenderly, but we do it more softly, respecting the rules more, than these hordes from the East. Instead of stealing a pig like they do, we go off to look for the Mayor or the Bürgermeister, and properly requisition what we need and pay for it, but they don't want any money from us. For in spite of the fact that we are eating with our bosses, every evening we make a big meal in the camp and we don't want for meat. Four or five hundred snares were put down and we went to beat all around, forcing the rabbits and hares into the traps. Furthermore five or six of our lads went off for the whole day, hunting enthusiasts who are taking their revenge. Two among them have issue rifles which they use to shoot deer, the others have some hunting rifles which managed to escape destruction, for the rabbits and hares and even some ducks are brought down. And in the evening, when we reckon things up, there are two or three deer, five or six hares and often ten rabbits stretched out on the floor. We eat a huge amount of meat, roast in gravy or in grills of all kinds! We have to break the habit or we could be ill. We requisition butter from the dairy and bread from the baker. Every room has its radio, and the nicest ones around, since the inhabitants implore us to take them from them, knowing that with us they are in safe hands, while in their homes they will be at the mercy of the first raid. Besides quite a lot have been destroyed and there are no longer many in the village. Well there you are, no more work, eating well, sleeping from time to time, a bit of hunting, all good for the digestion. We swap game with the French from Stendal and Bismark for tobacco, cigars and some decent bottles of wine. Here the only thing left to us is to listen four or five times a day for the information, for the news, that right now is very interesting.

There is heavy fighting around Berlin. Not far from us the American Ninth Army has just joined up with the Russians. As for the English they are pressing heavily on Bremen and Hamburg and now the German army has been driven back onto the Elbe, no longer knowing exactly on what side it has to fight, being restricted more and more into the narrow corridor which is all the time tightening around it. Many Frenchmen are turning up at Stendal, coming from Rathenow, and even quite a lot from Berlin or thereabouts. They arrive on foot, exhausted groups, no strength left in them, having marched flat out to escape the horrors of Berlin and to try to gain on the Russian columns which are advancing on the Elbe. Many have succeeded in crossing the Elbe and as a result find themselves in territory occupied by the Americans. Once arrived at Stendal, which is only five or six kilometres from the Elbe, they stop there knowing themselves safe, and they do not go on any further. But now the town is overrun with foreigners and above all with French. All the barracks, schools, colleges and churches which are still standing are full of people. The Americans are overwhelmed by all this invading flood-tide of another kind and cannot evacuate them for they have enough to do at the moment with the prisoners who surrender *en masse* to them, not wanting to be taken by the Russians.

Yesterday I went to Stendal. You only see French now. These rather young people who left France two years ago, being taken to work in Germany, are there in numbers. Civilians, women, many with young kids under their arms. It's pitiful this whole crowd of French. It's then that you realise what work Pétain and Laval did. Many are hungry, most are coming from factories, and therefore are pale and quite thin, war is pitiful to see! In town I meet a lieutenant that I knew in Bismark when we had taken those few prisoners. I chat with him since I know that he's responsible for our repatriation. He explains to me that what is happening hadn't been foreseen. The authorities of Stendal were not counting on more than 800 French prisoners and some 3,000 civilians. We ought to have been evacuated first as a priority, but now this invasion changes the whole programme and first of all it's the refugees who will leave, then it will be our turn, but it is necessary first of all to clear the town and we understand very well that these poor people who, for the most part, have suffered much more than us, deserve to be evacuated first. The town is in an appalling state, without counting the ruined houses, no longer with any doors or windows, shop fronts smashed in, pavements full of all kinds of unimaginable filth. We who had known Stendal so clean, so cheerful, we find a huge difference.

Goodbyes

Friday 4 May 1945. This day which will count in the history of my captivity as having been the best, the one I've been waiting for for so many long weeks, long months, long years I should say, this day which had kept us all going through all our miseries, our sufferings, this day which was the hope of so many down and outs, that thousands of men were waiting for and that unhappily, alas, not everyone will be able to see, has finally arrived for us. It was the last time that we would be leaving our straw mattress, the last time that we were seeing the sun rise on the Altmark plain, on the woods of Schorstedt. I asked myself if we weren't dreaming. Since 16 August 1940, nearly five years, a good chunk of our life, of our best years, since we were all about 30, had ebbed away in this hut we were about to leave. Was it possible? Was it really true, the last of the final days had arrived. Everything comes to pass, even the end of this long captivity.

On the evening of the day before, two mates from a neighbouring village, coming back from getting news in Stendal, where a team used to go every day to get information, had the job of informing the prisoners and the kommandos of the sector that all the kommandos answerable to Stendal had to turn up the next day with weapons and baggage at Stendal with the prospect of getting the next repatriation. Three cheers and a tremendous round of applause welcomed this last bit of news. No doubt the last but the best of all of the thousands of rumours more or less true which had been circulating during these five years and which had taxed the toughest, discouraging even those who'd never lost hope, and I was among them. In the end this was the last of them. Perhaps I go on a bit too much, but I should be excused, for anyone who will read these lines – if one day someone is called to read them – cannot imagine, cannot have an idea. You have to have lived it, to feel yourself watched over, menaced, spied on day and night for more than fifty months (not just one day!) and then suddenly you hear it said: 'It's finished, go home, you're free.' It must be a little like the kind of thing that happens to a madman who suddenly regains his senses.

Immediately the arrangements were made, we sent off three of us to find the Bürgermeister, to inform him of the last orders received, and really to make his arrangements so that tomorrow morning at eight o'clock two trailers with rubber tyres, each one drawn by two light mares with drivers, would be in front of the door of the kommando, waiting for our instructions. The cases were ready and the last meal eaten in the hut, where that evening a deer formed the main course, went on really late. Anyway nobody could sleep. All night long there was a hullabaloo that everyone took in good spirits. In the morning nearly everyone went to take their leave of the bosses. I went to see mine. My old Gandoule was in despair. She took me into her living room and straightaway broke down in sobs:

'You're going away, after so long being with us, we've got used to you. Now you're leaving us like this. The Polish girl has already disappeared, several days ago. The Polish chap is living it up and is menacing us with the worst kind of reprisals. The Russian woman doesn't want to work any longer, and you, you're going away. My two sons are soldiers, who knows where they are, I haven't had any news from them for such a long time. My God what's going to become of us?'

This old misery, who had been used to giving orders and seeing her least wishes obeyed, couldn't begin to understand that things had changed in such a short time. Finally she gave me a good dinner while still telling me all her woes. She couldn't get used to the idea, this ugly creature, that we also had a family, a village, parents, friends and that her village didn't mean much to us. I ate and didn't even take in what she was telling me. All my thoughts were down there, on the shores of the Mediterranean. She prepared me some rations for the journey, kissed me several times and finally I was able to escape after shaking hands with her husband who, white as a sheet, said not a word to me.

At the kommando there was the fever of the great departure, everyone telling the story of his last minutes with his bosses. Some had been cold, others had had touching farewells, while some of them had been bitter. Several flirtations and casual affairs came to an abrupt end. It was a terrible moment for a certain little widow whose husband had not come back from deepest Russia and who had found some consolations, but none amongst us let himself soften and we were a full complement, ready for departure.

At the head of the first trailer a pole had been nailed, at the end of which fluttered our flag. In the front one an orchestra was set up with a saxophone, a clarinet, an accordion and a jazz drum, then all the men from the first room. The second trailer was occupied by the second room and all the cases. A rendering of the Marseillaise rang out to say goodbye to the hut and off we go, while our little band banged out in double time 'you will never have Alsace and Lorraine'[1] At the sound of the music all the population went out onto the whole length of the main road that we had to go along, and our last goodbyes took place. Our friend Astier from la Grand-Combe who wasn't one to carry away in his heart any feelings of friendship, not for the Germans or for their women, banged on the big drum with all his strength to demonstrate his happiness. We turned the corner, it's over, goodbye Schorstedt forever, another page is going to turn for all of our lives.

The first stop is at Grassau. The neighbouring kommando hasn't yet left and we make a halt to celebrate the event with our neighbours while helping them to knock back a mountain of cakes that the Germans have made for them, and a barrel of beer is emptied. In exchange our music plays their goodbyes for them. And then it's forwards down the road of our return. Their vehicles join up with ours. In going through the little towns, the band plays a tune while on the trailer our two terrible devils from Paris contort themselves in most unexpected dances, which has the effect of irritating the Boche who find the joke rather bad and shut themselves up in their homes, grumbling under the jeers coming from the carts.

Midday. Stendal-sur-Elbe, everyone gets down. We are billeted in a girls high school, in a classroom on the third floor. Everyone looks for a place among the school benches and the dirty straw that others have used before us. There were plenty of nice barracks at Stendal but the Americans were occupying them, and many buildings have been ruined by the bombing. We stay several days and set up a canteen. Happily we'd brought quite a lot of game from the village so that does us pretty well here. From time to time, a convoy of lorries leaves towards Hanover for the train cannot go further because all communication is impossible. Nothing has yet been repaired between Hanover and Berlin, and besides there is still fighting going on there.

We walk around in the town from morning to night and spend hours and hours watching the ceaseless file-past of columns of German prisoners who are being taken to the airfield that's been transformed into a prison camp. How times change. These interminable columns of prisoners that I described during the French defeat, between Reims, Vitry, Saint-Dizier, the German débâcle is exactly the same, and even worse. But now it's us who are on the

pavement. It's our turn to cry to the prisoners: '*Warum gefangene?*'[2]
There is no end to this file-past. It's because the Germans are now
completely cornered on the Elbe where the Russians have arrived at
several points, and the Germans are surrendering *en masse* without any
resistance. The essential thing for them is not to be taken by the
Russians. They will do anything to cross the Elbe and to surrender to
the Americans. They would prefer to drown than to fall into the hands
of the Russians. All along the boulevards the civilians are downcast,
they lower their heads. It's a long way from the enthusiasm of the victory days, they have really been thrown back, in Gross Deutschland![3]

Today the Russian chief of staff is coming to pay a visit to the
American chief of staff who is billeted in one of the nicest hotels still
standing in the town, close to a barracks. Well before the time a guard
of honour of American soldiers in full uniform lines the boulevards
and we see the Russian chief of staff arrive followed by cavalry escort,
all of them very spick and span.

The Return

Finally we are lined up and embarked in the lorries which go to the rear to fill up with petrol. We are piled up on these lorries where there's no room to move, standing upright, and to crown it all a fine rain starts to fall, but nobody complains seeing that it's our great departure. On each lorry the French flags wave in the wind and we leave at a good speed. Goodbye Stendal, another one we'll never see again! The column of 40 to 50 big overloaded lorries goes along at a fair speed, at the beginning taking roads which are known to most of us. Some blown bridges and broken roads soon stop the rapid progress of the lorries. At several places the lorries leave the impassable road and the convoy crosses huge fields on the great plain to rejoin another road further on. In other places we drive through mud, some lorries having great difficulty in getting themselves out. Everywhere are the visions of war: burnt lorries, smashed up assault vehicles of all nationalities, ruined houses.

Finally, very tired, after some hours of more or less happy progress, the convoy stops and the order to get down is given. It's a relief for the journey wasn't one of the most comfortable. A big camp, three-quarters ruined, welcomes us. We are at Œbisfelde, not very far, a few kilometres, from Braunschweig, a very industrial town whose bombing had often woken us up. It's under American control: name, christian name, year of joining up, a de-lousing session where we are put in a bath of powdered DDT sprinkled by big motorised machines. We get a food parcel and a beer bottle full of water for each of us, which has to serve for the return journey. Divided up into groups of eight, we are immediately led onto the platforms of the station and every one is allocated a compartment: 'Embark straightaway!' . Our compartment with padded seats would be comfortable enough, but its roof must have been left behind in some bombing raid. We don't get angry – some people are higgledy-piggledy in the coal trucks. In the evening it moves, slowly, very slowly. We make a few kilometres then we stop for hours.

We start off again. In the morning we arrive at Hanover. Hanover, or what's left of it, is no more than a mass of ruins piled on ruins. We go round the town on a wide detour, slowly, very slowly, scarcely at walking pace on the makeshift lines put down there straight on the earth, across cultivated fields or vast prairies. Everything that one can see of the huge town is only a pile of ruins and rubble. It must have been pretty warm round here at certain points. The remains speak eloquently about what must have happened there.

Then we move away slowly, but in the right direction, making long, long detours, for so many railways including the most important are for now unusable. At one stage, and I think that it's when we're crossing the Weser, the viaduct which crosses the deep valley, high up, very high, is in ruins. They make us get down from the train which went down by a very rickety line to the bottom of the valley, then reclimb nearly vertically onto the opposite bank with eight or ten engines pulling or pushing the convoy on the makeshift lines. Thousands of German prisoners are working under the surveillance of American sentries, nearly all huge blacks who don't seem people to trifle with. We follow on foot and it's then that the German prisoners get it! Nearly all of us know a little German. We heard so much for over five years, and above all it's the abusive words which have stuck in our heads. Some speak German fluently and the Boche lower their heads, as they are not spared any abuse. In one place there is even a certain amount of beating with pickaxe handles, but the menacing sentries make us move on. We go through small towns and endless villages, putting to good use the frequent stops to look for something to eat in the nearby houses, but what can you find in these houses, which have been pillaged by our predecessors hundreds or even thousands of times? Some people pass the time shouting at and insulting the civilians within earshot. I think that those who live on the edge of the railway tracks will remember the return of the French prisoners for a long time. It seems ages since the children and sometimes even the adults threw stones at us and treated us as '*Schweine Französen*'.[4]

Towards midday we reach Herford. By the evening we are at Bielefeld. Everywhere towns and villages in ruins. Everywhere the same image of war. I wonder how there can still be people left after this hurricane, this cataclysm, this tidal wave that has passed through everywhere. Now we're crossing the huge industrialised regions of Germany and more and more as we approach the Rhine, the piles of ruins, impossible to describe, are ever more numerous. Now we're crossing the river. Everything's demolished, devastated as far as the eye can see. We halt for days, for entire nights, how long it is since we left I don't know exactly. You lose a sense of time. Finally we arrive at Aix-la-Chapelle. This is an awful sight: not a house, not a tree, nothing has escaped total destruction. Everything here has been engulfed, burnt, razed to the ground. We cross the Rhine on a temporary bridge, made by the American engineers, a wooden bridge of considerable height, without a guard rail, it's really quite a sight.

Immediately after going over the bridge there's a big camp of German prisoners billeted in open fields, over several hectares. Thousands and thousands of men are penned in there under the stars, with only a round path as a fence on which armoured cars and automatic machine-guns circle endlessly. We stop at the camp for a good while and many of the French recall how in June and July 1940 they were penned in in the same way in the fields of north-east France, under the rain, in all weathers. Now the Germans know the harshness of captivity in their turn. They are badly heckled. How times have changed! It's a long time from when they drank to our health and ate everything they had plundered from all round, shouting at us, showing us their bottles, and it had not been pleasant.

For a really long time now the small amount of provisions given to us on our departure had been used up. We have nothing to eat but what's it matter? We're used to it, we've been through it before and anyway we're going home, back to France.

One morning, finally, at daybreak, we are in Holland. We have a very long stop at Maastricht. There's nobody on the streets, nobody, nobody, it's too early. We start off again only to stop for a long time on the very banks of the Meuse. This Meuse where we slaved away so much in the Spring of 1940, here it is again to welcome us. The whole train has a wash, everyone spread out on the banks of the river. Then it's off again and it's not long before we get into Belgium. At midday we come into the station of Namur. The station is crammed full of people. There's music and we get ourselves into wild dancing on the boulevards of the town. Fanfares and tunes follow one after the other, the whole town is out on the streets. It's then that we learn that it's 8 May and that the Armistice has been signed that morning. That explains the enthusiasm, the crowd in the street. They take us to a hotel, there's a good and copious meal served to us with red and white wine. It's the first time for five years that I've drunk a glass of wine. It goes down really well. Immediately afterwards they press us to eat and drink again. The people, above all the women waiting for their men, cling to us to get some news. They're coming tomorrow, the next week, everyone's coming back. But alas many will not be there when the roll is called. It's with great difficulty that we find our train again and our wagon in the midst of this crowd waiting for the Belgian prisoners, and it's quite slowly to the sound of the music and dancing continuing for the new arrivals, that we leave Namur, and I will remember all my life the welcome given to the French prisoners by the Belgian people.

We cross through Belgium slowly. Everywhere, in the smallest villages or towns, there are flags, banners, music, and a handout of drinks and cakes. Despite our great fatigue joy has swept through the train's population and song follows song. Evening is falling when we enter France, at Jeumont. The whole town, a band to the fore, is on the platform. All the young people are there. The repatriated soldiers join in the party, and there's a huge conga, which goes from in front of the locomotive to the last wagon, across the lines and the halted train. For a very long time the station is paralysed and it's with great difficulty that we leave Jeumont and this tremendous reception on French soil. Maubeuge. The station is under military guard, there's a reception without any noise or din. Discipline reclaims its rights. I remain at Maubeuge with some friends, while other groups are distributed around the nearby town. We are taken in a column to the barracks, there's a decent enough meal, the regulation mug of wine and immediately an inspection where all our reports are noted down, then a shower, and delousing. They give me a shirt and a new jumper; my own are only held together by holes fastened by string. And now I see something I haven't seen for many years: a bed. Yes, a bed. A military bed, it's true, but with springs, a mattress, sheets, a cover, the whole thing very clean and around one o'clock in the morning I'm finally free and invited to take possession of this long forgotten toy.

It's 10 o'clock in the morning when my bed neighbour wakes me up. I've slept well. There are still some of us friends from the kommando at Schorstedt who lived for a long time together. Some are from the North, some of them even from round Maubeuge and it's as they leave us that we understand our ignorance of what could have happened in France during our long absence. To celebrate our separation we go into a small bar on a street in Maubeuge and we order five glasses of wine that they serve us virtually in liqueur glasses. I was the only one to have French money, a note of 50 francs which escaped all the numerous searches to which I was subjected. I handed over my 50 francs note and, to my great surprise the waiter said to me, 'That will be 200 francs'. All five of us, we were thunderstruck. 200 francs! But on our departure wine only fetched 120 francs for 100 litres! We explained our embarrassment to the bar owner and we offered to pay in the marks that camp prisoners get. Very kindly he wouldn't take anything and even gives us a second round on the house. As for us we were completely stupefied, dazed.

Midday. A good dinner served in the barracks and immediately all the Southerners are picked out and taken to the station in a column, a special train leaving for Lyon is full. We arrive at Reims via Laon during the night, we stay there a long time, and it's only at daybreak that the train starts off again and via Vitry-le-François we soon come to Saint-Dizier where a tremendous ovation comes from the train. There are many of us here, who five years earlier had left from there. Saint-Dizier! What memories that awakes. A train of coal trucks, stuffed full of German prisoners, is in the process of passing slowly under the powerful water crane to fill the tenders of the locomotives and some prisoners found nothing better to do than open them all completely. What a shower, my men! All the same they're going a little too far there.

Along the whole route they're giving us things to eat and drink. The greedy throw themselves gladly on it so that others are deprived. Dijon, and in the evening we arrive at Lyon. This is the terminus for the train. No welcome is provided. To go on from there, everyone must move himself by his own means. Only one train in the evening is leaving for Marseilles, already more than packed with civilians, corridors and links between the carriages included. There are several hundred of us who want to go down to the Midi. It's impossible to get on. There's grumbling, even shouting. Some people even lie down on the rails; the train will not go without us. A delegation goes to find the station-master to get him to add two or three wagons to accommodate us. He would really like to help, but explains that he has no equipment to put at our disposal. Two goods wagons are added to the train, and they are packed full even before being hooked up. The station employees help us, make a tour of the wagons, push and compress the travellers so that they're piled up and we then go down the Rhône valley very slowly packed in like sardines.

Avignon, it's better organised than Lyon where it really was a complete shambles. There's a welcoming committee, and we're very well received. A hundred of us get off to go on to Nîmes, Montpellier or further on, waiting for a problematic connection from Marseilles for, the bridge at Tarascon being blown, the journey has to be made via Avignon–Villeneuve. I remember, it's from Avignon that the 12th Zouaves left six years previously for a round trip that really turned out to be a bit too long. In the end a train turns up, also packed full of civilians and many prisoners arriving by sea from Russia, via the Black Sea and Marseille. It's impossible to get on, but the welcoming committee, which seems to know what's going on, has understood: it's necessary to get us on whatever it costs. Up front in the first two wagons all the lights have been put out so as to stay nice and quiet. Some gentlemen, a few superior officers, are there, barricaded in these wagons. We break in the windows and that's how we get into the wagons where these officer-gentlemen, receive us, complaining, although they then calm down when learning that, since most people are getting off at Nîmes, we will not put them out too much. They even offer us some cigarettes, questioning us on the regions from where we come and on our captivity.

Finally Nîmes. There are 150 or 200 of us getting off. Immediately, a row breaks out. A young woman complains loudly at seeing so many strangers arrive in the town, while everything is in such short supply. This young woman, treating us like strangers, is furiously jostled and owes her safety only to the arrival of some gendarmes and town officials who are on the platform. The organisation is good, there's a reception centre where we are immediately registered and recorded as returnees. They then take us to the Hotel Cheval Blanc where a meal is served to us. Some beds are put at our disposal, but the majority not being very far away now, including me, are looking to return home. Several of us are from Millau, Uchaud, Aubais and there are two from Sommières. Outside the hotel, a lorry prepares to depart for Sommières. The driver, not having very much fuel, doesn't want to make a detour by the main road and Aigues-Vives to drop us off. It's only after some palaver and the sight of cigars, cigarettes and packets of tobacco that he agreed to take us, after having stashed away about 20 packets of cigarettes. A golden opportunity given how things are going. And that's how it was that I came to get off outside the market at Aigues-Vives, the terminus of this really long round trip, on the night of the 11–12 May 1945 on the stroke of one o'clock in the morning.

Notes

Introduction

1 *Les carnets de guerre de Gustave Folcher, paysan languedocien 1939–1945*, edited by Rémy Cazals, (Paris, Actes et mémoires du peuple, Maspero, 1981).

2 For examples of the FAOL's work on 1914–18, see *Les Carnets de guerre de Louis Barthas tonnelier 1914–1918* (Paris, Maspero, 1978) and *Années Cruelles 1914–1918* (Villelongue d'Aude, Atelier du Gué, 1983), both edited by Rémy Cazals. To safeguard and study the many examples of notebooks and exercise books filled by ex-combatants, the FAOL set up a research group on 'La Mémoire de 1914–1918 en Languedoc'.

3 *Les Écoliers de Tournissan, 1939–1945* (Toulouse, Privat, 1978), introduced by Rémy Cazals.

4 This is a reference to a special pencil that produced an indelible script which turned violet under the impact of humidity.

5 The historian Jacques Godechot wrote to Rémy Cazals on 20 April 1986, saying that he had checked Folcher's account of the military campaign of 1939–40 against the detailed official history of regimental movements and found them to tally closely, apart from small errors of one day, or descriptions of Tunisians as Moroccans, which one would expect in such an amateur diary.

6 See Jean-Marie d'Hoop, 'Prisonniers français et la communauté rurale allemande', in *Guerres Mondiales et Conflits Contemporains*, No.147/July 1987, pp. 31–47, and Yves Durand, *Prisonniers de Guerre: dans les Stalags, les Oflags et les Kommandos, 1939–1945* (Paris, Hachette, 1987), p. 295.

7 Michael Howard, *The Franco-Prussian War* (London, Hart-Davis, 1961), Alistair Horne, *The Fall of Paris: the Siege and the Commune, 1870–1871* (London, Macmillan, 1965), and Richard Cobb, *French and Germans, Germans and French: A Personal Interpretation of France under Two Occupations, 1914–1918/1940–1944* (Hanover, New Hampshire, University Press of New England, 1983).

8 See J.E. Farquharson and S.C. Holt, *Europe from Below: An Assessment of Franco-German Popular Contacts* (London, George Allen and Unwin, 1975).

9 This was a word from the Great War not used until late in the diaries, presumably out of fear of discovery and reprisal.

273

10   *Nord Matin*, 2 October 1981.
11   George Coppard, *With a Machine-Gun to Cambrai* (London, Her Majesty's
     Stationery Office for the Imperial War Museum, 1969).
12   But Cobb, op. cit. p. 181 wrote 'I have drawn heavily on the diary of
     Barthas' (for the First World War). For Barthas, see footnote 2 above.
13   See, for example, James N. Rosenau, 'Citizenship in a Changing Global
     Order', in James N. Rosenau and Ernst-Otto Czempiel (Eds.), *Governance
     without Government: Order and Change in World Politics* (Cambridge,
     Cambridge University Press,1992), pp. 272–94. Rosenau considers
     (p. 283) that 'where people once complied habitually and automatically
     with the directives of authorities, today they are much more inclined to
     assess the performance of the authorities before attaching legitimacy to
     and complying with directives'. Such generalizations are stimulating;
     but they should always be read in conjunction with case-histories like that
     of Gustave Folcher, who like generations of the powerless before him
     understood very well that his own government was not necessarily on his
     side, and how even the Nazi regime could be defied in small ways so as
     to enlarge his sense of individual space.
14   The poem is 'Heureux qui comme Ulysse' (Happy the man who like
     Ulysses . . .) in *Les Regrets*, XXXI. du Bellay spent a homesick period in
     Rome as secretary to his cousin, a Cardinal.
15   Two of the places where the great battle of Verdun was fought in 1916,
     and where more than 300,000 Frenchmen are buried.
16   Indeed, a lengthy extract from this section of the diary has been
     included in France's equivalent of an A-Level history textbook, which
     given the centralised education system is used throughout France
     (*Manuel Scolaire d'Histoire, Classes Terminales*, Edition Bardas, 1983,
     p. 49).

The Phoney War

1   The Zouaves were a body of Algerian light infantrymen (1830–1962),
    composed of French soldiers in colourful dress uniform.
2   Unlike the other small towns or villages mentioned so far, Saint-Jean-du-
    Gard is not within the immediate vicinity of Aigues-Vives. It lies about 25
    miles to the north-west, in one of the gorges of the Cevennes.
3   *Belote* is a card game, rather like a lesser version of bridge, based on
    partners and trumps. Only 32 cards are used.
4   This episode seemed curious to Cazals, and he wrote to the Director of
    Archives in the Saône-et-Loire Département, asking him if there might
    be any details on it in the archives or in the press of the period. He
    kindly replied that he had found no trace of it either in the local press or
    in the many sources of information dealing with the first period of the
    war, the press probably not having been authorised to divulge the affair
    and the archival sources, caught up in the wreckage of June 1940, being

very patchy. The Director of Archives adds that being himself a Burgundian of that very period, he had got wind of the passage of the trains bearing the swastika and that current opinion was that the refugees had exhibited in all innocence what in their view were only trophies. If there had been found Nazis among them they would not have had the audacity or imprudence to display so publicly their beliefs.

For his part, Monsieur Folcher cannot give an explanation. He adds only this to his text from the period:

– it was the Alsatians that were being evacuated in front of the German invasion, the people who were closest to the frontier. In September 1939 no-one knew what was happening, one supposed that it would all move much quicker. Then there was a train of Alsatian refugees down to the Midi, and it was right next to my battalion's train, this train of refugees that was coming down. And the children had been peeing on the covers which then had to be put out of the windows to dry.

But how did it come about that they had had these clothes with swastikas? Do you believe they were sympathisers with the Nazi party?

– That I don't know anything about. We didn't ask them. Moreover we didn't understand them. They didn't speak French so it was difficult to know. We have to think yes. Why did they buy the bedclothes with swastikas? You know there were Alsatians who were Germans at heart! I'm going to tell you what happened in 1940 in the camp at Saint-Dizier where we were prisoners. Once we had been shut up in this factory, straightaway they separated all the Bretons, at first a little way off. Why? They wanted to make a separatist province of Brittany. And then they separated out even more the Alsatians. There were every evening, *every* evening, some Alsatians who made a tour round the yards of the factory with their swastika banners singing German hymns that we didn't understand.

M. Folcher does not then provide us with the answer over the affair of the refugees' bedclothes from September 1939. Were they trophies? Perhaps. But we also need to know how these refugees could have procured the trophies. And did they deliberately hoist them up? Perhaps, simply enough, they were trying to dry their bedclothes, carried away in a great rush in their flight, and then made wet by the children. But then we come back always to the same question, how was it that they came to have the covers in the first place? Perhaps they were flaunting their difference.

5 In the French Army the rank of Commandant was held by four men serving under the Colonel or Lieutenant-Colonel, but above the Captains and Lieutenants. They were in practice '*chefs de bataillon*' or '*chefs d'escadron*', the equivalent of Majors in the British Army.

6 One sou equals five centimes; ten sous therefore equals 50 centimes, though by 1939 this was familiar rather than official use.

7 The French word is *joyeux*, which was French military slang for soldiers from the 'African battalion', a punishment battalion (i.e. for criminals) stationed in Africa.

8 The phrase '*les cloches de tir*' in the original refers to the metal covers which could be raised and lowered over the gun emplacements along the Maginot line. I am grateful to Dr. Henrik Larsen for clarifying this issue for me.

9 In effect, 'jeeps', but the use of this American term would be anachronistic for the France of 1939.

10 The *vendanges* were an important marker of the seasons, and began on different dates according to latitude. By 9 October, they were already over in Folcher's Languedoc.

11 This is a type of grape that has disappeared today. They were black grapes, black as anything, no bigger than *petits pois*. They were original vines, which were not grafted. That has died out. Moreover, I only knew one vineyard here at Aigues-Vives. We harvested it, my wife and myself, one vineyard of 4,000 vines producing a black wine! Every year, on 11 November, the old soldiers of 1918 made a banquet. Now, you know that here it's the region of bullfighting – there are arenas here in the village – and every year they brought out a bull to amuse the public, and when they had finished amusing the people, they killed it and we ate it with a sauce that we called '*la gardianne*'. We made it with this *jacquez* wine, a wine that's very strong, it was 13 or 14 per cent, dark black like ink. At the time, we used it to blend with the *vin aramon**. The araman was colourless and we blended it with this *jacquez* wine which was really black and of a greater strength. Then the lesser *vin aramon* of 8 or 8.5 per cent like it was made here; we did it to pass on the *marc*** of these *jacquez* that made a wine of 10 per cent and that coloured it at the same time (Gustave Folcher, 1981).

     * *Aramon* was a simple, less strong *vin de table*, which would not travel without getting acidic.

     ** The *marc* is the residue of the pressed grapes.

12 In other words, they have been kept marching around in circles, but whether through indecision or the desire to instill toughness on the part of the commanding officer, is not clear.

13 The Départment of Gard, centred on Nîmes, was of course Folcher's own.

14 The stars (of David) mark the tombs of Jewish soldiers.

15 The Zouaves, with their billowing trousers and Arabic hats, made an exotic sight for those used to regular uniforms.

16 Cuppings refers to the bleeding of the patient, sometimes with a leech. At the time this was not unusual as a treatment for influenza in France. More common was the use of a hot cup on the loins (without leeches) to draw the blood to the surface.

17 – What was there in these leaflets?

– We gathered so many of them! If you had seen them, on the banks of the Meuse, loads of them came down! It was to disorganise us, to demoralise, so that we wouldn't fight . . . a political question, a question of our regime, that the German regime was better than ours. It was propaganda on Hitler's part. It was in French, in very good French. I had some of them, but I have lost them. We had been so much shaken from one side to the other . . . it was important to suspect them because they were also throwing down pencils, cigarette lighters, things like that. Then you gathered them up and they could explode in your face. It was before the attack, in the last days of April, in the first days of May. So in the end we stopped picking them up (Gustave Folcher, 1981).

A One-Sided Battle

1 *Suze* was a half sweet vermouth wine with a bitter plant inside.
2 CP = Command Post. Folcher uses the abbreviation P.C. throughout, for 'poste de commandement'.
3 No doubt to provide some of the meat for the non-pork-eating muslim soldiers of the Zouaves regiment.
4 It may also have been a question of the effect on empty stomachs of the alcohol in which the fruit was preserved.
5 The word M. Folcher uses is *roubine*, which refers to the ditches separating fields, and often planted with hedges or wild plum trees.
6 This was the Marne–Saône Canal. Since Le Buisson, the column had largely to follow a southerly route and reached this canal near Orconte.
7 Perhaps the village of Perthes, between Orconte and Saint Dizier.
8 A *prie-Dieu* is a kneeling-chair common in Catholic churches, often big enough to take two people.
9 Where we suffered most, that was at Saint-Dizier. In the factory there it was frightful, frightful! I wonder – and I say it not as a joke, this, I believe it – I ask myself if they didn't make us eat human flesh, I really wonder (Gustave Folcher, 1981).

France Left Behind

1 Ladies, Gents.
2 The vines had been attacked by mildew for lack of copper sulphate.
3 Sister Anne was the character in the childhood song about Blue Beard, always waiting for someone who never came.
4 This fuss about politics happened two or three times. We were put in a column. Then a German officer, who spoke very good French, said: 'All communists, step forward!' There weren't any. Obviously there weren't any. There were perhaps 150 of us . . . No one! Then the Germans said

amongst themselves: 'That's strange. No communists!' Imagine that! The lads would have been put straight into the concentration camps (Gustave Folcher, 1981).

Farming for the Reich

[1] The *garrigues* are the heath, or moorland in Languedoc with which Folcher was so familiar, and their dense scrub or undergrowth was comparable to, but much less hospitable than, the woods and mountains further North denoted by the term 'maquis', to which so many young men took in France in 1943 and which then gave its name to the resistance. See H.R. Kedward, *In Search of the Maquis: Rural resistance in Southern France 1942–4* (Oxford, the Clarendon Press), 1993, p. 29.

[2] *Pellkartoffeln*: jacket potatoes. Folcher often misspells the German. The errors have been left in place in this translation. The recipe he was referring to probably involved potatoes boiled in their skins and served up with a little butter and flour.

[3] The discrepancy between the figure given earlier in the chapter of seven for dinner and 18 in the kommando is explained by the fact that for eating and living purposes the *(Arbeits) kommando* – i.e. the work unit – was split into separate rooms, which doubled as dormitories and eating rooms. For the very varied conditions which existed in the numerous *Kommandos* where French prisoners worked, see Chapter 6 of Yves Durand, *La captivité, histoire des prisonniers français 1939–1945* (Paris, Fédération nationale des Combattants, Prisonniers de Guerre et Combattants d'Algerie, Tunisie, Maroc, 1980).

[4] Agen is in south central France, just south of the valley of the Dordogne – an area famous for paté de foie gras.

[5] Rillettes are potted mince meat and lard, often pork.

[6] I.e. paté, foie gras and sausage.

[7] When we received the parcels, all the children came round. When there were things, quince paste or thingummies like that, we handed them round to them. There were even some young Russians who came. There was one of them who spoke almost perfect French. (Gustave Folcher, 1981).

The Disintegration of Nazism

[1] The reference here is to the pronunciation of 'bunker'.

[2] '*Rentier*' does not have an exact translation. It refers to those whose income came from fixed unearned amounts, such as rents.

[3] Mus is the next village to Aigues-Vives, only two kilometres to the east.

[4] This a metric ton, i.e. 1,000 kilograms

[5] As indeed they were after the setback at Arnhem in the second half of September 1944.

⁶ Gilette Boudet was Gustave Folcher's fiancée. They married after the war and died in the same year, 1993.

⁷ The reference here is to the blackening effect of dirt and sunburn on the refugees, made worse by cold.

⁸ In fact known as Coubessac.

⁹ *Vor-Alarm*: early warning

¹⁰ This is M. Folcher's version of 'okay'.

¹¹ That is metric tonnes, which are 16 kilograms less than the British ton.

¹² A white dessert wine.

¹³ Once, with the boss, I went to take a cow to the town. When we had sold it, he said to me: *Komt!* He took me into a building. There was a convoy of deportees who had been sent from Russia, young girls of 17, 19 years old. He looked at them, he touched them, and he took two of them. We brought them back with us to the village. (G. Folcher, 1981)

¹⁴ If I had been free, I would also have enlarged on what I'd known of the troops who were going to Russia. They came home on leave and they didn't want to go back any more. Those who had tasted the Russian Front, they no longer wanted to go back. Police in the woods were always looking for deserters. Those who came from France, they returned singing, but those who came from the heart of Russia, they didn't go back singing, I assure you. There were some of them in the village, we knew . . . we knew of two of them who were hidden, who came back at night into the barns. Only we said nothing. Two who had originally gone away believing that they could conquer the world! But, when they had tasted a few months in Russia, they understood, they no longer wanted to go back. Young men, 18 or 19 years old. I knew one of them who was hiding behind straw in the barn, and then during the day he cleared off into the woods and the police were there looking for him . . . (Gustave Folcher, 1981)

¹⁵ 'Not good to be a prisoner! Oh yes! After all I've been five years a prisoner in this village myself.'

¹⁶ In fact M. Folcher uses the French in his text.

¹⁷ M. Folcher's version of *Geburtstag*, or birthday.

Going Home

¹ This song was a well-known nationalist ditty dating from the years before the First World War, an example of what the French call the 'songs of revenge' (for 1870).

² Why are you a prisoner?

³ German in the original, no doubt for extra irony.

⁴ 'French pigs'.